AAT

INTERMEDIATE
NVQ AND DIPLOMA PATHWAY
(ADVANCED CERTIFICATE)

REVISION **COMPANION**   Units 6 & 7

Costing & Reports and
Returns

LEARNING MEDIA

Seventh edition April 2007
First published 2001

ISBN 9780 7517 3230 6 (previous ISBN 07517 2611 7)

British Library Cataloguing-in-Publication Data
A catalogue record for this book is available from the British Library

Published by

BPP Learning Media Ltd
BPP House,
Aldine Place,
London W12 8AA

Printed in Great Britain by
Page Bros
Mile Cross Lane
Norwich
NR6 6SA

We are grateful to the AAT for permission to reproduce sample simulations
and simulations and examples from previous assessments. The answers to the
sample simulations for Units 6 and 7 and the specimen exam for Unit 6 have
been published by the AAT. All other answers have been prepared by BPP
Learning Media Ltd.

CONTENTS

INTRODUCTION

This is BPP Learning Media's AAT Revision Companion for Unit 6, Recording Cost Information and Unit 7 (of the NVQ), Preparing Reports and Returns. It is part of an integrated package of AAT materials.

It has been written in conjunction with the BPP Course Companion, and has been carefully designed to enable students to practise all aspects of the requirements of the Standards of Competence and performance criteria. It is fully up to date as at April 2007 and reflects the revised Standards of Competence.

This Revision Companion contains these key features:

- graded activities corresponding to each chapter of the Course Companion

- the AAT's sample simulations and answers for Units 6 and 7

- a further practice simulation and answers for Units 6 and 7

- five exam-based assessments set between December 2004 and December 2006, with full answers

The emphasis in all activities and questions is on the practical application of the skills acquired. All activities, practice assessments and simulations have full answers prepared by BPP Learning Media.

Tutors adopting our Companions (minimum of ten Course Companions and ten Revision Companions per Unit, or ten Combined Companions as appropriate) are entitled to free access to the Lecturers' Area resources, including the Tutor Companion. To obtain your log-in, e-mail lecturersvc@bpp.com.

Home Study students are also entitled to access to additional resources. You will have received your log-in details on registration.

If you have any comments about this book, please e-mail pippariley@bpp.com or write to Pippa Riley, Publishing Projects Director, BPP Learning Media Ltd, BPP House, Aldine Place, London W12 8AA.

Diploma pathway

Please note that under the Diploma Pathway students do not need to study Unit 7, as the content is included in Diploma Unit 31, Accounting Work Skills. Diploma pathway students, therefore, need only study chapters 1 to 9 of this book.

---

chapter 1:
COSTING INFORMATION

1 Explain the main differences between financial accounting and cost accounting.

2 Explain how cost information can be used to assist in the three main roles of management – decision making, planning and control.

3 Explain how costs are classified in the following ways:

a) Capital and revenue costs
b) According to function
c) Direct and indirect costs
d) According to behaviour

4 Show whether each of the following costs would be treated as capital or revenue costs:

	Capital	Revenue
Purchase of a car for resale by a car dealer		
Purchase of a car for use by a salesman		
Road tax payable on purchase of a car for use by a salesman		
Redecorating head office		
Installing new machinery		
Cleaning of new machinery after initial use		

5   Show how each of the following costs would be classified by function:

	Production cost	Selling and distribution cost	Administration cost
Depreciation of salesmen's cars			
Production manager's salary			
Depreciation of machinery			
Rent of office space			
Depreciation of delivery vans			
CDRoms for office computer			

6   Show how each of the following costs would be classified as either a direct cost or an indirect cost:

	Direct cost	Indirect cost
Wages of factory supervisor		
Hire of plant for construction of a building by a building firm		
Cleaning materials used in the factory		
Factory rent		
Wages of a trainee accountant in an accountancy firm		
Cement used for construction of a building by a building firm		

7   Classify each of the following costs according to their behaviour:

a)   Telephone bill for line rental and call charges
b)   Factory rent and rates
c)   Materials used in production
d)   Supervisor's salary
e)   Warehouse rental where additional space is rented when stock levels are high

8   Given below are the output levels and associated production costs for a factory for the last six months:

	Output in units	Cost £
February	125,000	375,000
March	142,000	418,000
April	110,000	340,000
May	120,000	362,000
June	145,000	424,000
July	130,000	394,000

Use the high(–)/low method to estimate the variable cost per unit and the overall fixed costs of the factory.

9   A factory produces a single product which has a raw materials input of £3.80 per unit, labour costs of £1.40 per unit and packaging costs of £0.30 per unit. The factory rent is currently £150,000 per annum but if production levels rise above 120,000 units then additional factory space must be rented at an additional cost of £40,000 per annum. The depreciation of the machinery is £30,000 per annum.

The factory production for the forthcoming year will depend upon the outcome of a promotion of this product and the management hope that production will be for 180,000 units. However if the promotion is not quite as successful as hoped then production will be only 130,000 units. If the promotion is not successful then production will only be for 80,000 units.

Produce a schedule showing the total production costs at each possible level of production.

10   Suggest the cost units which would be appropriate for management information systems in the following industries.

a)   A building contractor
b)   An airline

11   Wheely Wheels Ltd is a successful wheel making company which makes wheels for a variety of uses: wheelbarrows; carts; toys and so on.

The production operation consists of three departments: bending; cutting and assembly. The bending and cutting departments have general purpose machinery which is used to manufacture all the wheels produced.

Complete the table below by analysing the cost items for Wheely Wheels Ltd into the appropriate columns and agreeing the balances.

	Total	Prime cost	Production expense	Admin. expense	Selling and distribution expense
	£	£	£	£	£
Wages of assembly employees	6,750				
Wages of stores employees	3,250				
Tyres for toy wheels	1,420				
Safety goggles for operators	810				
Job advert for new employees	84				
Depreciation of delivery vehicles	125				
Depreciation of production machines	264				
Cost of trade exhibition	1,200				
Computer stationery	130				
Course fee for AAT training	295				
Royalty for the design of wheel 1477	240				
	14,568				

12   You are required to show a separate sketch graph of the cost behaviour patterns for each of the listed items of expense. The vertical axis of each graph should be total cost. You should label the horizontal axis of each graph clearly.

a)   Electricity bill: a standing charge is paid for each period plus a charge for each unit of electricity consumed.

b)   Supervisory labour.

c)   Production bonus, which is payable when output in a period exceeds 10,000 units. The bonus amounts in total to £20,000 plus £50 per unit for additional output above 10,000 units.

d)   Sales commission, which amounts to 2% of sales turnover.

e)   Machine rental costs of a single item of equipment; the rental agreement is that £10 should be paid for every machine hour worked each month, subject to a maximum monthly charge of £480.

13   Prepare a report for the managing director of your company explaining how costs may be classified by their behaviour, with particular reference to the effects of changes in activity both on total costs and on unit costs.

Your report should:

a)   explain why it is necessary to classify costs by their behaviour; and
b)   be illustrated by sketch graphs within the body of the report.

chapter 2:
MATERIALS COSTS

1 Complete the following sentences.

a) The three main categories of stock for a manufacturing business are ...., ... and ....

b) The internal document used to record the quantity of materials received from a supplier is known as a ....

c) The initial internal document that starts the purchasing process for materials is known as a ....

d) A .... is the document that is sent to a supplier to request the supply of materials

e) When materials are required from stores by the factory a .... is filled out

f) A .... is the document received from a supplier of materials requesting payment

2 Given below is a stock card for one of the materials used by a manufacturing business. During the month of June the following goods received notes and materials requisitions for this material were completed:

Goods received notes:

3 June	GRN 0326	340 units
12 June	GRN 0348	300 units
28 June	GRN 0363	320 units

Materials requisitions:

5 June	MR 0295	150 units
10 June	MR 0307	190 units
20 June	MR 0315	180 units
25 June	MR 0320	100 units

Write up the stock card for the month of June.

STOCK CARD

Description: 23 Electrical component   **Bin No:**   413
           EC23

Code No:

Receipts			Issues			Balance
Date	Reference	Quantity	Date	Reference	Quantity	Quantity
2007 1 June						50

3 Martin Ltd uses the weighted average cost method to value stock issues and closing stocks. Fill in the shaded boxes in the stores ledger account shown below for stock item LRM.

STORES LEDGER ACCOUNT

Stock item _____ LRM _____

Code _____ 8888 _____

	Receipts			Issues			Balance		
Date	Qty	Unit price £	£	Qty	Unit price £	£	Qty	Unit cost £	£
Op bal							100	2.00	
3 Sept	400	2.10					500		
4 Sept				200			300		
9 Sept	300	2.12					600		
11 Sept				400			200		
18 Sept	100	2.40					300		
20 Sept				100			200		

4 Given below are the purchases and issues to production of material XK2 for the month of July:

4 July	Issue	MR 416	320 kg
7 July	Purchase	GRN 668	500 kg @ £3.20 per kg
12 July	Issue	MR 422	180 kg
16 July	Issue	MR 428	300 kg
19 July	Purchase	GRN 674	500 kg @ £3.50 per kg
23 July	Issue	MR 433	230 kg
28 July	Issue	MR 440	300 kg

Opening stock at 1 July consists of 400 kg all purchased at a price of £3.00 per kg.

You are required to write up the stores ledger accounts given below for this material for the month of July on the following bases:

a) First in first out (FIFO)
b) Last in first out (LIFO)
c) Average cost (AVCO)

STORES LEDGER ACCOUNT

Stock item ___XK2___

Code ___O41861___

FIFO basis

Date	Receipts				Issues				Balance	
	GRN	Qty	Unit price £	£	Req No	Qty	Unit price £	£	Qty	£
1 July									400	1200.00

STORES LEDGER ACCOUNT

Stock item   __XK2__

Code   __O41861__

LIFO basis

Date	Receipts				Issues				Balance	
	GRN	Qty	Unit price £	£	Req No	Qty	Unit price £	£	Qty	£
1 July									400	1200.00

STORES LEDGER ACCOUNT

Stock item ___XK2___

Code ___O41861___

AVCO basis

| Date | Receipts | | | | Issues | | | | Balance | |
	GRN	Qty	Unit price £	£	Req No	Qty	Unit price £	£	Qty	£
1 July									400	1200.00

5 Given below are the stock movements for component JJ41 for the month of July:

1 July	Opening balance	220 units @ £5.60
3 July	Issue	160 units
7 July	Purchases	300 units @ £6.00
10 July	Issue	170 units
15 July	Issue	100 units
20 July	Purchases	250 units @ £6.30
24 July	Issue	200 units

You are required to calculate:

a)   the cost of issues
b)   the value of closing stock

in the month of July using FIFO, LIFO and AVCO methods of stock valuation.

6 Describe the FIFO and LIFO methods of stock valuation, and state the advantages and disadvantages of each method.

7 During the month of September a manufacturing business made purchases of materials on credit totalling £83,469. Stocks of raw materials at 1 September were valued at £12,523. During September issues of £79,247 were made to the factory for direct production and £6,248 of indirect materials were also issued to the factory.

Write up the cost ledger accounts to reflect these transactions.

8 Turner & Co sell 40,000 units of one of their stock lines each year. Each unit is purchased on credit at a price of £10 per unit with order costs of £100 per order. The cost of holding one unit of stock for a year is estimated to be 20% of purchase price.

The lead time and the usage per day both tend to vary as follows:

	Lead time (days)	Usage (units sold per day)
Minimum	2	130
Average	5	160
Maximum	8	200

a)   What is the re-order level?
b)   What is the economic order quantity
c)   What is the minimum stock level?
d)   What is the maximum stock level?

9   At a time of rapidly rising prices a manufacturing company decides to change from a FIFO system to a LIFO system of pricing material issues. What would be the effect on the following?

a)   Stock valuation

b)   Cost of materials charged to production

10   Protective gloves are used in the production departments of Flimsey Ltd and are drawn from stores at regular intervals. Records show the following for November.

1 November	Opening stock	100 pairs @ £2 each
7 November	Purchases	200 pairs @ £1.90 each
18 November	Issues	150 pairs

Calculate the value of the closing stock of gloves given that the FIFO system of valuing issues is used.

11   Wiggles plc, a printing company, specialises in producing accounting manuals for several accountancy training companies. The manuals are written by the training companies and passed to Wiggles plc for printing. The company uses three main stages in producing the manuals.

a)   The preparation of the text
b)   The printing of the text
c)   The assembly and binding of the manuals

Write up the following information on the stock card using the AVCO (average cost) method to value the issues.

Material: Paper – Code 1564A
Opening stock: 10,000 sheets – value £3,000

Purchases			Issues	
3 May	4,000 sheets	£1,600	6 May	7,000 sheets
12 May	10,000 sheets	£3,100	15 May	6,000 sheets
25 May	10,000 sheets	£3,200	22 May	7,200 sheets

Calculate the average cost to two decimal places of a £ and the value of the issues to the nearest £.

STOCK RECORD CARD

Material description: _Paper_

Code no: _1564A_

Date	Details	Receipts		Issues				Balance	
		Sheets	£	Sheets	Unit price £	£		Sheets	£

---

12 Roman Ltd sells and services cars.

Complete the following extract from the stock record card for May and calculate the quantity and value of stock on 24 May using the Last In, First Out (LIFO) method of stock valuation.

STOCK RECORD CARD

Product: Motor oil

Centre: Servicing

Date	Receipts			Issues			Balance	
	Quantity	Cost per litre	Total cost	Quantity	Cost per litre	Total cost	Quantity	Total cost
	litres	£	£	litres	£	£	litres	£
B/f May							2,100	2,100
4 May	2,400	1.20	2,880					
8 May				3,300				
10 May	3,000	1.10						
11 May				3,200				
17 May	5,000	1.00						
18 May				5,400				
23 May	6,400	0.95						
24 May				4,420				

13

chapter 3:
LABOUR COSTS AND EXPENSES

1   A business pays its employees on a time rate basis with time and half for any hours worked over 37 hours per week. George is paid a basic rate of £6.80 per hour and during the week ending 31 July he worked for 43 hours.

Calculate the following figures for the week:

a)   George's total gross pay;
b)   the overtime payment;
c)   the overtime premium.

2   An employee is paid on a differential piecework system on the following basis:

Up to 300 units produced a week – £1.00 per unit

Units over 300 and up to 400 – £1.15 per unit

Any units over 400 – £1.35 per unit

In the week ending 28 June the employee produced 430 units. What is his total gross pay for the week?

3   A business has a number of different types of employees who are remunerated by different methods. Harry is paid on a piecework basis as follows:

Per unit of product A produced   £10.40
Per unit of product B produced   £18.60

Stella is paid on a time rate basis at £8.40 per hour for 35 hours a week. For any hours over 35 each week she is paid overtime at the rate of time and a third.

Yvette is paid a salary of £20,000 per annum.

During the week ending 30 June Harry produced 22 units of product A and 7 units of product B and Stella worked for 43 hours. Yvette is paid her salary monthly and for the month of June a performance bonus of 5% of total salary is to be paid to all salaried employees.

Calculate the following figures:

a)   Harry's gross pay for the week;
b)   Stella's gross pay for the week;
c)   Yvette's gross pay for the month of June.

4   The payroll records for a business for the week ending 15 July show the following details:

	£
	£
Net pay	24,700
PAYE and NIC deductions	6,200
Company pension scheme deductions	2,400
Gross pay	33,300

The payroll analysis also shows that of this total £20,900 relates to direct labour costs and the remainder to indirect labour costs.

Write up the cost ledger accounts to reflect this.

5   A company owns three classes of fixed assets:

- A freehold building which was purchased for £450,000 including land which was valued at £50,000. Land is not depreciated but the building is depreciated on the basis that it has a remaining useful life of 40 years.

- Machinery with an original cost of £220,000. When the machinery was purchased it was estimated that it would have a life of 32,000 hours and would be sold for scrap at the end of this period for £20,000. During the current year the machinery was used for 4,200 hours.

- A fleet of cars for the sales team, which originally cost £120,000 and which have been depreciated by £52,500 at the start of the year. The cars are depreciated on the reducing balance basis at a rate of 25%.

What is the depreciation charge for each class of fixed assets for the current year?

6   During the month of October a manufacturing business incurred general production overheads of £39,256. It also paid £7,200 of hire costs in order to replace a machine that had broken down.

Write up the cost ledger accounts to reflect this.

7   The production manager of your organisation wishes to know the direct labour cost of jobs N172, N174 and M215 performed on 14 May. You have reviewed the time sheets of those direct employees who allocated their hours to those job numbers.

Using the information on the time sheets below, calculate the direct labour cost of jobs N172, N174 and M215.

Time Sheet No.	15					
Employee Name	N Davies	**Clock Code** 412		**Dept** 15		
Date	14/5/??	**Week No.** 7				

Job No.	Start time	Finsih time	Quantity	Checker	Hours	Rate	Extension
AB 64	0800	0830				6.60	
N172	0930	1145				6.60	
M215	1450	1650				6.60	

Time Sheet No.	19					
Employee Name	Y Chang	**Clock Code** 476		**Dept** 1		
Date	14/5/??	**Week No.** 7				

Job No.	Start time	Finsih time	Quantity	Checker	Hours	Rate	Extension
FJ15	0730	1030				6.50	
NI64	1045	1230				6.50	
AB64	1230	1630				6.50	
M215	1700	1830				6.50	

Time Sheet No.	20					
Employee Name	J Pitman	**Clock Code** 31		**Dept** 3		
Date	14/5/??	**Week No.** 7				

Job No.	Start time	Finsih time	Quantity	Checker	Hours	Rate	Extension
NI74	1200	1800				10.00	

Time Sheet No.	17							
Employee Name	R Khan			**Clock Code**	183		**Dept**	8
Date	14/5/??			**Week No.**	7			

Job No.	Start time	Finsih time	Quantity	Checker	Hours	Rate	Extension
NI68	0900	1200				6.80	
NI72	1200	1300				6.80	
M215	1430	1815				6.80	

8 a) Most expenses are direct costs. True/False?

b) Most expenses are not related to the production side of an organisation. True/False?

c) The cost of the power to run machines is always a direct expense. True/False?

d) Cleaners not on an organisation's payroll are an indirect expense. True/False?

chapter 4:
OVERHEADS

1   A manufacturing organisation has two production cost centres, the assembly department and the finishing department and two service cost centres, stores and the maintenance department.

The budgeted overheads for the following six month period was as follows:

	Total	Assembly	Finishing	Stores	Maintenance
	£	£	£	£	£
Indirect materials	18,700	16,500	2,200		
Indirect labour	22,800	7,500	6,200	4,500	4,600
Rent and rates	10,000				
Heat and light	7,400				
Supervisor's wages	9,880				
Depreciation of machinery	8,400				

You are also provided with the following information:

	Total	Assembly	Finishing	Stores	Maintenance
Floor area (sq m)	20,000	6,000	4,000	5,000	5,000
Net book value of machinery	£240,000	£150,000	£50,000	£15,000	£25,000
Supervisor's time in each department (hours)	38	22	16		
Materials requisitions	300	220	80		
Maintenance hours	1,200	700	500		

You are to:

a)   apportion the overheads to each of the production and service cost centres;

b)   reapportion the service cost centre costs to the production cost centres (the stores and maintenance cost centres do not provide any services to each other).

2 A manufacturing organisation has two production departments, A and B, and two service cost centres, stores and the canteen.

The budgeted overheads for the next period are as follows:

	Total £	A £	B £	Stores £	Canteen £
Indirect wages	75,700	7,800	4,700	21,200	42,000
Rent	24,000				
Buildings insurance	2,000				
Power	6,400				
Heat and light	4,000				
Supervisor's wages – Dept A	10,000				
Machinery depreciation	3,200				
Machinery insurance	2,200				

You are also provided with the following information:

	Total	A	B	Stores	Canteen
Net book value of machinery	£300,000	£140,000	£120,000	£15,000	£25,000
Power usage (%)	100%	45%	30%	5%	20%
Number of employees	126	70	40	10	6
Supervisor's hours	40	25	15		
Floor area (sq m)	30,000	12,000	8,000	4,000	6,000
Materials requisitions	500	300	200		

The stores staff use the canteen but the canteen makes no use of the stores services.

You are to:

a) allocate or apportion the overheads to each of the production and service cost centres on a fair basis;

b) reapportion the service cost centre costs to the production cost centres using the step down method.

3   The overheads for a business have already been apportioned to its two production and two service cost centres manufacturing as follows:

	Total £	Assembly £	Polishing £	Stores £	Maintenance £
	130,000	60,000	40,000	20,000	10,000

You are also given the following information:

	Total	Assembly	Polishing	Stores	Maintenance
Number of materials requisitions	400	200	160		40
Maintenance hours required	1,000	600	400		

You are required to reapportion the service cost centre costs using the step down method.

4   The budgeted overheads of a manufacturing business have been allocated and apportioned to the two production cost centres as follows:

Cutting   £58,600
Finishing   £42,400

The two production cost centres are budgeted to produce 10,000 units in the next period.

You are also provided with the following further information:

	Cutting	Finishing
Direct labour hours	4,000	24,000
Machine hours	12,000	2,000
Direct labour cost	£24,500	£168,000
Direct materials cost	£180,000	£25,000
Prime cost	£204,500	£193,000

You are required to calculate overhead absorption rates on each of the following bases and to state in what circumstances each absorption rate would be appropriate:

a)   rate per unit
b)   rate per direct labour hour
c)   rate per machine hour

5   The budgeted overheads apportioned to a business's two production cost centres, C and D, together with the budgeted labour hours and machine hours, are given below:

	C	D
Overheads	£125,000	£180,000
Direct labour hours	12,000	80,000
Machine hours	100,000	10,000

Production cost centre C is a highly mechanised department with only a few machine operatives whereas production cost centre D is a highly labour intensive department.

a)   You are to calculate separate departmental overhead absorption rates for each production cost centre using an appropriate basis and to justify the basis that you have used.

b)   Each unit of Product P spends the following hours in each production department:

	C	D
Direct labour hours	1	7
Machine hours	5	2

Determine how much overhead will be included in the cost of each unit of product P.

6   In each of the following situations calculate any under- or over-absorption of overheads and state how they would be dealt with in the profit and loss account:

a)   Budgeted production is 1,200 units and budgeted overheads were £5,400. Overheads are to be absorbed on a unit basis. The actual production was 1,000 units and the overheads incurred were £5,000.

b)   Budgeted production was 600 units to be produced in 1,800 labour hours. Budgeted overheads of £5,040 are to be absorbed on a direct labour hour basis. The actual production for the period was 700 units in 2,200 labour hours and the actual overheads were £5,100.

c)   Budgeted production was 40,000 units and the budgeted machine hours per unit was 2 hours per unit. Budgeted overheads were £320,000 and were to be absorbed on a machine hour basis. The actual overheads incurred were £320,000 and the production was 42,000 units. The total machine hours were 82,000.

7   Using the data from the previous activity write up the production overhead control account in each case clearly showing the transfer to the profit and loss account for under-/over-absorption of overheads.

8   Explain what is meant by under- and over-absorption of overheads, and how they occur.

9   The overhead absorption rate for the machining department at Jefferson Ltd is £5 per direct labour hour. During the year to 31 December 1,753 direct labour hours were worked and overheads incurred were £9,322.

You are are required to calculate the under- or over-absorption of overheads in the twelve-month period.

10 Happy Ltd manufactures and sells furnishing fabrics and its operations are organised by departments, as follows.

- Administration
- Manufacturing
- Sales
- Warehouse

The budgeted and actual fixed overheads of the company for November were as follows.

	£
Depreciation	14,600
Rent	48,000
Other property overheads	12,800
Administration overheads	28,800
Staff costs:	
Warehouse	4,800
Indirect manufacturing	14,340
Sales	12,250
Administration	8,410
Total actual fixed overheads	144,000

The following information is also relevant.

Department	% of floor space occupied	Net book value of fixed assets
	%	£'000
Warehouse	20	160
Manufacturing	65	560
Sales	5	40
Administration	10	40
	100	800

Overheads are allocated and apportioned between departments using the most appropriate basis.

You are required to complete the following table showing the allocation and apportionment of fixed overheads between the four departments.

Actual fixed overheads for November	Basis	Total £	Warehouse £	Manufacturing £	Sales £	Administration £
Depreciation		14,600				
Rent		48,000				
Other property overheads		12,800				
Administration overheads		28,800				
Staff costs		39,800				
		144,000				

chapter 5:
ABSORPTION COSTING AND MARGINAL COSTING

1 The following information relates to Trident Ltd for the month of March.

Note. There were no opening or closing stocks.

Sales revenue – March

4,000 units were sold at a selling price of £40 per unit.

Production costs – March

Direct material costs – £25,000
Direct labour costs – £50,000
Variable overhead costs – £15,000
Fixed costs – £30,000

You are required to, using the information given above, calculate the total contribution earned for the month of March.

2 A business produces a single product in its factory which has two production departments, cutting and finishing. In the following quarter it is anticipated that 120,000 units of the product will be produced. The expected costs are:

Direct materials		£12 per unit
Direct labour		2 hours cutting @ £7.40 per hour
		1 hour finishing @ £6.80 per hour
Variable overheads	cutting	£336,000
	finishing	£132,000
Fixed overheads	cutting	£144,000
	finishing	£96,000

Overheads are absorbed on the basis of direct labour hours.

What is the unit cost under:

a)   absorption costing
b)   marginal costing?

3 Given below are the budgeted production and sales figures for the single product that a business makes and sells for the months of July and August.

	July	August
Production	24,000 units	24,000 units
Sales	22,000 units	25,000 units

There were stocks of 1,500 units of the product at the start of July.

The expected production costs for each of the two months are as follows:

Direct materials	£6.80 per unit
Direct labour	£3.60 per unit
Variable production costs	£32,400
Fixed production costs	£44,400

Overheads are absorbed on the basis of the budgeted production level and the product is sold for £16 per unit.

a) Prepare the budgeted profit and loss account for the two months using:

　　i) absorption costing
　　ii) marginal costing

b) Prepare a reconciliation explaining any difference in the two profit figures in each of the two months.

4 You are given the budgeted data about the production of a business's single product for the following quarter:

Opening stock	840 units
Production	8,000 units
Sales	8,200 units
Direct materials	£23.60
Direct labour	4 hours @ £5.80 per hour
Variable overheads	£88,000
Fixed overheads	£51,200

Overheads are absorbed on the basis of units of production The product has a selling price of £70 per unit.

a) Prepare the budgeted profit and loss account for the quarter using:

　　i) absorption costing
　　ii) marginal costing

b) Prepare a reconciliation explaining any difference in the profit using absorption costing and profit using marginal costing.

5 Explain why marginal costing may be a more appropriate method than absorption costing for costing and reporting purposes.

chapter 6:
COSTING SYSTEMS

1 Fill in the missing words.

Batch costing is a form of costing that is similar to _____ costing except that costs are collected for _____. The cost unit is the _____. A cost per unit is calculated by _____.

2 Suggest appropriate costing methods for the following organisations.

a) A plumbing business
b) A clothing manufacturer
c) A caterer

3 Explain when the use of job costing is appropriate.

4 A manufacturer of custom-made bedroom furniture has been asked to supply bedroom fittings for a customer. The estimated costs are given below:

Materials for units – £2,800
Direct labour for fitting units – 27 hours @ £19.50 per hour
Overheads are absorbed on the basis of £8.70 per direct labour hour
Profit on each job is 20% of total costs
VAT is charged at 17.5%

You are to prepare a job costing schedule showing how much the bedroom fittings will cost the customer.

5   Given below is a job costing schedule based on the estimates made which is still to be completed.

JOB NUMBER 2856

	Budget £	Actual £	Variance £
Direct materials			
■ wood	1,650.00		
■ components	830.00		
■ plastic	320.00		
Direct labour			
■ Grade I – 30hours	414.00		
■ Grade III – 12 hours	132.00		
Direct expenses			
■ hire of equipment	300.00		
Overheads			
Total cost			
Profit			
VAT @ 17.5%			

Overheads are absorbed into the cost of jobs at a rate of £4.60 per direct labour hour. Profit on jobs is 25% of total cost.

On the completion of the job the cost of the wood was £1,830.00, the components £755.00 and the plastic £300. In total 33 hours of Grade I labour were charged to the job at a rate of £14.50 per hour and 7 hours of Grade III labour were charged at an hourly rate of £11.00. The equipment hired had to be kept for an additional two days increasing the hire cost to £380.

You are required to:

a)   complete the costing of the job to show the price to be charged to the customer;

b)   compare the actual costs to the budgeted costs showing the variances;

c)   complete the job costing schedule at the end of the job showing the final profit that was actually earned on the job.

6   Given below are the details for a process for the month of May:

Direct materials	100,000 kg	£287,000
Direct labour		£138,000
Overheads		£82,600
Normal loss		6%
Output		92,000 kg

Write up the ledger accounts to record the process results for the month.

7   Given below are the details for a process for the first week in March:

Direct materials   18,000 litres   £35,800
Direct labour   £ 7,200
Overheads   £11,720

The normal loss from the process is 5% and the output for the week was 17,500 litres.

Write up the ledger accounts to reflect the process costs for the week.

chapter 7:
COST BOOKKEEPING

1 A manufacturing business absorbs production overheads into work in progress at a rate of £3.20 per direct labour hour. In the month of August the overheads incurred totalled £4,720 and the direct labour hours worked were 1,400.

Write up the production overhead control account. Explain the accounting treatment of any balance on the account.

2 A manufacturing business absorbs production overheads at a rate of £6.45 per direct labour hour. In the month of July a total of 940 direct labour hours were worked and the production overhead incurred was £5,840.

Write up the production overhead control account and explain the accounting treatment of any balance on the account.

3 A manufacturing business has the following transactions for the week ending 7 September:

Materials purchased on credit	£14,365
Materials requisitions from the factory	£11,632
Total payroll costs – direct factory labour	£18,375
– indirect factory labour	£2,682
Production overheads incurred	£6,243
Production overheads to be absorbed	1,530 hours @ £5.20 per hour
Transfer of production to finished goods	£36,540

Write up the following ledger accounts in an integrated cost bookkeeping system to reflect these transactions:

- Materials control account
- Wages control account
- Production overhead control account
- Work in progress control account

4   Given below are extracts from the trial balance of a business at 1 August:

	Debit £	Credit £
Stock:		
Raw materials	1,290	
Work in Progress	1,540	
Finished goods	1,830	
Debtors	7,200	
Creditors		5,460
Cash at bank	3,070	

You are also given a summary of some of the transactions of the business for the month of August:

	£
Materials purchased on credit	7,640
Materials requisitions – factory	6,620
– administration	990
Wages cost – direct factory labour (490 hours)	5,430
– indirect factory labour	1,460
Sales invoices issued	14,700
Cheques received from debtors	6,800
Cheques paid to creditors	4,900
Production transferred to finished goods	12,200
Production overheads paid by cheque	4,290
Administration overheads paid by cheque	1,210
Closing stock of finished goods	1,650

Production overheads are absorbed at the budgeted overhead absorption rate of £11.10 per direct labour hour.

You are required to:

a) write up the ledger accounts given below to reflect these transactions;
b) balance each of the accounts at the end of the month;
c) prepare the profit and loss account for the month.

Materials control account

£	£

Wages control account

£	£

Production overhead control account

£		£

Work in progress control account

£		£

Finished goods control account

£		£

Debtors control account

£		£

Creditors control account

£		£

Cash at bank account

£		£

Administration overheads account

£		£

Sales account

	£		£

chapter 8:
SHORT-TERM DECISION MAKING

1   When making decisions about production and sales in the short term, explain why contribution per unit is a more useful figure than total production cost per unit.

2   A business sells a single product and has budgeted sales of 115,000 units for the next period. The selling price per unit is £28 and the variable costs of production are £17. The fixed costs of the business are £1,100,000.

    a)   What is the breakeven point in units?

    b)   Calculate the margin of safety:

        i)   in units
        ii)   as a percentage of budgeted sales

3   The following information relates to one period for Product D which is manufactured by Mild Ltd.

Expected sales revenue = £160,000
Selling price per unit = £16 per unit
Variable cost = £8 per unit
Fixed costs = £40,000

You are required to calculate the breakeven point both in terms of units and sales revenue.

4   The following information relates to one period for Product V which is manufactured by Hay-on-Wye Ltd.

Selling price per unit = £80
Variable cost per unit = £25
Budgeted fixed costs = £110,000
Budgeted sales = 2,500 units

You are required to calculate the margin of safety, in terms of both units and sales revenue.

5   A business sells a single product at a selling price of £83 and the variable costs of production and sales are £65 per unit. The fixed costs of the business are £540,000.

How many units of the product must the business sell in order to make a target profit of £300,000?

6   A business sells its single product for £40. The variable costs of this product total £28. The fixed costs of the business are £518,000.

What is the sales revenue required in order to make a target profit of £250,000?

7   A business produces three products. Production and sales details are given below:

	Product		
	R	S	T
Direct materials @ £5 per kg	£20	£25	£15
Direct labour @ £7 per hour	£14	£21	£21
Selling price	£45	£60	£55
Machine hours per unit	4	3	2
Maximum sales demand	20,000 units	25,000 units	8,000 units

During the next period the supply of materials is limited to 250,000 kgs, the labour hours available are 100,000 and the machine hours available are 180,000.

What is the production plan which will maximise contribution and what is the contribution that will be earned under that production plan?

8   Pure Delight Ltd is a company producing and selling three types of ice-cream sauce: fudge; butterscotch and chocolate. The expected monthly costs and sales information for each sauce is as follows.

Sauce	Fudge	Butterscotch	Chocolate
Sales and production (bottles)	500	700	600
Labour hours per month	60	50	40
Total sales revenue	£1,000	£1,400	£600
Total direct materials	£100	£175	£60
Total direct labour	£300	£350	£150
Total variable overheads	£25	£70	£30

The total expected monthly fixed costs relating to the production of all sauces is £300.

a)   You are required to complete the table below to show the profit volume ratio for each sauce.

Sauce	Fudge £	Butterscotch £	Chocolate £
Selling price per bottle			
Less: Unit variable costs			
Direct materials			
Direct labour			
Variable overheads			
Contribution per bottle			
Profit volume ratio (%)			

b)   If the company only manufactures chocolate sauce, calculate the sales revenue that it would need to earn each month to cover the monthly fixed costs of £300.

chapter 9:
LONG-TERM DECISION MAKING

1 Explain what is meant by the time value of money.

2 Given below are the anticipated cash flows from investment in new plant and machinery that a business is considering.

		£
1 Jan 2008	Outflow	95,000
31 Dec 2008	Inflow	15,000
31 Dec 2009	Inflow	25,000
31 Dec 2010	Inflow	35,000
31 Dec 2011	Inflow	30,000
31 Dec 2012	Inflow	30,000

a) The business policy is only to accept projects with a payback period of 3 years or less. On this basis would you advise the managers of the business to invest in this project?

b) The business has a cost of capital of 10%. Calculate the net present value of the project. Would you now change your advice to the managers of the business?

c) State any assumptions that you have made in parts a) and b).

d) What might this situation indicate about the payback period method of investment appraisal?

3 Today's date is 1 April 2007. What is the present value of each of the following independent cash flows?

a) Payment of £24,000 on 31 March 2009 – interest rate 7%
b) Receipt of £1,500 on 31 March 2008, 2009 and 2010 – interest rate 12%
c) Receipt of £2,000 every 31 March from 2008 onwards – interest rate 6%
d) Payment of £30,000 on 1 April 2007 – interest rate 8%

4   A company is considering the purchase of a small sole trader's business for a cost of £84,000 on 30 June 2007. The estimated cash inflows from the purchased business are:

	£
30 June 2008	26,000
30 June 2009	30,000
30 June 2010	21,000
30 June 2011	14,000

Thereafter the purchased business will be closed down and its operations merged with the other operations of the company.

The company has a cost of capital of 7% and analyses potential investments using the net present value method.

What would your advice be to the directors of the company concerning the purchase of the sole trader's business? Justify that advice.

5   The managers of a business are considering investing in a new factory. It has been estimated that the cost now would total £355,000. The anticipated profit for the factory for each of the next five years are as follows:

	Profit
	£
Year 1	47,000
Year 2	55,000
Year 3	68,000
Year 4	53,000
Year 5	22,000

The profit figures given are after charging depreciation of £60,000 in each year. The business has a cost of capital of 12%.

a)   What is the net present value of the potential investment?
b)   State any assumptions that you have made in your calculations.
c)   What would be your advice to the managers about this potential investment?

6 The managers of a business are considering investment in a new production line which would cost £180,000 on 1 October 2007. The estimated cash cost savings from the new production line are:

	£
30 Sept 2008	42,000
30 Sept 2009	50,000
30 Sept 2010	75,000
30 Sept 2011	80,000

By the end of September 2011 the production line will require replacing.

a) Calculate the NPV of the project at the company's cost of capital of 15%, and state whether the company should accept the project. Justify your conclusion.

b) The company may be able to obtain finance for the project with an interest rate of 10%. Re-evaluate whether the project is worthwhile at this new cost of capital.

c) The internal rate of return (IRR) of the project is 12.5%. Explain the meaning of the IRR and why this can be useful in project evaluation.

7 Confectioners Unlimited is a cake and ice-cream manufacturer. The company requires an annual rate of return of 15% on any new project. The Managing Director has asked you to appraise the financial effects of setting up a new ice-cream parlour. You are given the following information relating to this project.

	Year 1 £'000	Year 2 £'000	Year 3 £'000	Year 4 £'000	Year 5 £'000
Set-up costs	(160)				
Sales revenues		60	100	320	100
Variable costs		(30)	(50)	(160)	(50)
15% present value factor	0.8696	0.7561	0.6525	0.5718	0.4972

a) Calculate the following for the new project.

   i) The payback period, where cashflows are received at the end of each year.
   ii) The net present value.

b) Use the data from a) above to prepare a report for the Managing Director on the new ice-cream parlour. Your report should:

   i) recommend whether to accept or reject the project based on its net present value

   ii) recommend whether to accept or reject the project based on its Internal Rate of Return which you are told is approximately 26%.

REPORT

To:

From:

Date:

---

chapter 10:
INTERNAL INFORMATION

1 Knight Industrial makes a range of electronic components in its factory. The factory employees clock in and out using clock cards and work a standard 35 hour week. Any hours that are worked in excess of the 35 hours are paid at time and a half if on a week day and double time at weekends.

What type of information about the labour force would be likely to be required by the following personnel in the organisation?

a) The factory Supervisor
b) The Manufacturing Director
c) The Managing Director

2 Outline what are the general requirements of useful information.

3 Give four examples of internal sources of business information.

4 Cost and management accounting is concerned entirely with providing information in the form of periodic performance reports or special 'one-off' reports. Give six examples of cost and management accounting information.

5 What would be the typical type of information that might be required by the partners in a firm of solicitors in order to appraise the performance of the firm for the last month?

6 Kenzo Stores has three shops in Abberville, Bacup and Calver. Given below are the summarised profit and loss accounts for the three stores for the month of July.

	Abberville £	Bacup £	Calver £
Sales	137,489	195,374	104,328
Cost of sales	53,621	72,288	41,731
Gross profit	83,868	123,086	62,597
Expenses	33,373	37,121	22,952
Net profit	50,495	85,965	39,645

You are required to produce the consolidated profit and loss account figures for the three stores for the month of July.

chapter 11:
PERFORMANCE MEASURES

1 Distinguish between the terms production and productivity.

2 A manufacturing business has produced 330,000 of its product in the quarter ending 30 June 2007 at a total manufacturing cost of £567,900. The budgeted production for the quarter had been 350,000 units and the actual hours worked in the quarter were 12,600.

In the quarter ending 31 March 2007 the budgeted production was 320,000 units and actual production was 332,000 units. This production level was achieved in 12,300 hours and the total cost of production in that quarter was £580,400.

Calculate the following performance measures for the quarter ending 30 June 2007 and compare them to the same performance measures for the previous quarter:

- cost per unit
- labour productivity
- productivity index

3 A mail order manufacturing business employs 280 factory employees and 27 telephone sales staff. For the month of July the following performance figures were available:

Units produced	128,700
Budgeted units	120,000
Manufacturing cost of units produced	£557,800
Factory labour hours	39,400
Telephone orders processed	9,180
Telephone sales department costs	£14,560

From the information given produce a schedule that summarises the performance of the factory and the telephone sales department for the month.

4 Explain the difference between avoidable and unavoidable idle time.

5 The number of labour hours worked and the number of idle time hours for a factory for the last six months was as follows:

	Jan	Feb	Mar	Apr	May	June
Hours worked	2,100	2,050	2,220	2,200	2,310	2,250
Idle time hours	90	80	20	100	120	100

The hours worked plus the idle time hours total to the number of hours available for work in the month.

Calculate the labour utilisation percentage for each of the six months to one decimal place.

6 You are given the following information about a business for the last three months:

	May	June	July
Sales	£360,000	£402,000	£398,000
Capital	£300,000	£310,000	£320,000
NBV of fixed assets	£210,000	£190,000	£200,000
Machine hours worked	28,000	32,000	31,000

For each of the three months calculate measures to indicate the fixed asset utilisation, machinery utilisation and capital utilisation or asset turnover.

7 What do you understand by the term return on capital employed?

8 Given below are the summarised profit and loss accounts for a business for the last three months:

	May £'000	June £'000	July £'000
Sales	1,320	1,420	1,500
Cost of sales	790	850	970
	530	570	530
Expenses	290	330	290
Net profit	240	240	240

The capital of the business was as follows for the three months:

	May £'000	June £'000	July £'000
Capital	2,600	2,840	3,080

Prepare a schedule showing the gross profit margin, net profit margin and return on capital employed for each of the three months, calculated to one decimal place, making brief comment as to what the performance measures indicate about the business.

9   Given below is a variety of information about a manufacturing business for the last three months:

	May	June	July
Sales	£595,000	£600,000	£610,000
Manufacturing cost	£416,000	£402,000	£403,000
Expenses	£131,000	£144,000	£149,000
Number of units produced	220,000	215,000	216,000
Budgeted number of units	220,000	220,000	220,000
Hours worked	1,400	1,360	1,430
Budgeted hours	1,400	1,400	1,400
Net book value of fixed assets	£320,000	£300,000	£340,000
Capital	£460,000	£508,000	£562,000

You are required to calculate the following performance measures and to comment on the results that you find:

a)   Cost per unit
b)   Productivity per labour hour
c)   Productivity index
d)   Labour utilisation percentage
e)   Fixed asset utilisation
f)   Asset turnover (capital utilisation)
g)   Gross profit margin
h)   Net profit margin
i)   Return on capital employed

10   S plc compares its 2007 results with 2006 results as follows.

	2007 £	2006 £
Sales	800,000	600,000
Cost of sales		
Direct materials	200,000	100,000
Direct labour	200,000	150,000
Production overhead	110,000	100,000
Marketing overhead	210,000	175,000
	720,000	525,000
Profit	80,000	75,000

Calculate the net profit margins for S plc for 2006 and 2007.

chapter 12:
WRITING A REPORT

1 What are the major elements of a report?

2 Given below are the summarised profit and loss account figures for the last six months for one shop that is part of a chain of retail stores.

	Jan £'000	Feb £'000	Mar £'000	Apr £'000	May £'000	June £'000
Sales	420	450	500	550	580	630
Cost of sales	248	261	285	310	325	345
Gross profit	172	189	215	240	255	285
Expenses	110	119	145	160	165	190
Net profit	62	70	70	80	90	95
Capital	660	720	780	810	840	900

Write a report on the profitability of the shop for the last six months for the Sales Director showing any performance indicators that can be calculated in an appendix.

Today's date is 19 August 2007.

3 Given below are productivity details of the three manufacturing divisions of an organisation, which each produce the same product, for the last quarter.

	Division A	Division B	Division C
Number of units produced	400,000	240,000	300,000
Cost of manufacture	£1,248,000	£739,200	£915,000
Hours worked	14,000	8,000	10,400
Budgeted production – units	450,000	250,000	330,000
Budgeted hours	15,000	8,333	11,000

You are required to write a report commenting to the Manufacturing Director upon the productivity of the three divisions.

Today's date is 20 July 2007.

chapter 13:
TABLES AND DIAGRAMS

1   Significant digits

State 2,197.283 correct to:

a)   Six significant digits
b)   Five significant digits
c)   Four significant digits

2   Decimal places

State 38.1784 correct to:

a)   Three decimal places
b)   Two decimal places
c)   One decimal place

3   Independent variable

What is an independent variable and which axis on a graph represents it?

4   Scattergraph

What is a scattergraph?

5 You are given the following information about a company for the last four months.

	June £	July £	Aug £	Sept £
Sales	48,700	50,200	45,600	46,800
Cost of sales	30,200	31,600	29,200	30,000
Expenses	12,200	12,500	11,400	11,700
Capital	52,500	52,500	55,000	55,000

a) Prepare a computer spreadsheet which will calculate the following performance measures by inserting appropriate formulae for:

   i)   gross profit percentage
   ii) net profit percentage
   iii) return on capital employed
   iv) asset turnover

	A	B	C	D	E
1		June	July	August	September
2	Sales				
3	Cost of sales				
4	Gross profit				
5	Expenses				
6	Net profit				
7	Capital				
8	Gross profit %				
9	Net profit %				
10	ROCE				
11	Asset turnover				

b) Show the amount for these performance measures that appear once the spreadsheet is completed.

	A	B	C	D	E
1	Sales	June	July	August	September
2	Cost of sales				
3	Gross profit				
4	Expenses				
5	Net profit				
6	Capital				
7	Gross profit %				
8	Net profit %				
9	ROCE				
10	Asset turnover				
11					

6 A manufacturing business has produced 330,000 of its product in the quarter ending 30 June 2007 at a total manufacturing cost of £567,900. The budgeted production for the quarter had been 350,000 units and the actual hours worked in the quarter were 12,600.

In the quarter ending 31 March 2007 the budgeted production was 320,000 units and actual product was 332,000 units. This production level was achieved in 12,300 hours and the total cost of production in the quarter was £580,400.

Tabulate this information on a computer spreadsheet and insert appropriate formulae in order that the following performance indicators can be calculated for each quarter:

a) Cost per unit
b) Labour productivity
c) Productivity index

	A	B	C	D	E
1					
2					
3					
4					
5					
6					
7					
8					
9					
10					
11					

7 Given below are the sales figures for a business for each of the last six months.

	Feb £'000	Mar £'000	Apr £'000	May £'000	June £'000	July £'000
Sales	320	300	360	400	350	310

You are to show these sales figures in a simple bar chart.

8   Given below are the summarised profit and loss figures for a business for the last three years:

	30 June 2005 £'000	30 June 2006 £'000	30 June 2007 £'000
Sales	280	350	400
Cost of sales	175	200	220
Gross profit	105	150	180
Expenses	60	70	80
Net profit	45	80	100

Show the sales, gross profit and net profit for each of the three years in a compound bar chart.

9   Given below are the sales figures for each of the three divisions of a company for four quarters.

	To 30 Sept 2006 £'000	To 31 Dec 2006 £'000	To 31 Mar 2007 £'000	To 30 June 2007 £'000
Division A	160	180	220	250
Division B	150	120	100	100
Division C	120	140	150	170
	430	440	470	520

You are to show the sales for each division for each quarter in a component bar chart.

10 Given below are the profit figures for three hotels owned by a business for the last three years:

	2005 £'000	2006 £'000	2007 £'000
Royal Hotel	320	350	300
Mermaid Hotel	110	70	50
Crown Hotel	290	340	320

You are to illustrate these figures in the following ways:

a)   Show the total profit for the three years in a simple bar chart
b)   Show the breakdown of profit between the hotels in a compound bar chart
c)   Show the breakdown of the profit between the hotels in a component bar chart

11   Given below is a breakdown of the costs of a manufacturing business for the last three months:

	May £'000	June £'000	July £'000
Production costs	400	500	460
Selling and distribution costs	120	250	160
Administration costs	100	140	180
Finance costs	50	50	150
	670	940	950

You are to illustrate the breakdown of these costs in a pie chart for each of the three months.

12   Present the following information in the form of a table, including in your table the percentage changes in the volume of UK car sales of different origins of manufacture and overall between the first quarter of 2006 and the first quarter of 2007.

453,000 cars were sold in the United Kingdom during the first three months of 2007: this is an increase of 46,000 on the same period one year earlier. Of these 453,000 vehicles, 205,000 were made in Britain, with 188,000 coming from the rest of the European Union (EU). Cars built in Japan made up 41,000 of the 453,000 total. Imports from countries other than EU members and Japan comprised 19,000 cars in the first quarter of 2007. This compares with a figure of 18,000 cars originating in these other countries for the same period one year earlier. In the first quarter of 2005, 184,000 of cars built in Britain were sold in the UK. In this period, UK car sales included 166,000 vehicles imported from the rest of the EU and 39,000 vehicles imported from Japan.

13 M, N, O, P, Q and R are operatives employed in the sheet metal work department of A\
Engineering Ltd, whose records for the week ended 12 June show their attendance, in hours, as\
follows.

	Mon	Tue	Wed	Thu	Fri	Sat
M	8	8	9	9	8	4
N	9	8	10	8	4	
O	8	8	8	8	8	
P	9	10	9	10	9	4
Q	10	9	10	9	10	4
R	8	4	6	8	8	

Hours worked in excess of eight on Mondays to Fridays are paid at basic hourly rate plus one third\
and all hours worked on Saturdays are paid at double the basic rate.

The basic hourly rates for each operative are as follows.

M, O and R   £7.20
N and P   £7.50
Q   £8.40

a)   Prepare a statement showing the wages of each of the six operatives and the total wages fc\
     the week ended 12 June.

b)   Using the total wages of all six operatives, calculate the weighted average wages cost, to the\
     nearest penny, per operative hour.

Averages

Write brief notes explaining the following terms to a colleague.

a)   The mean
b)   The median
c)   Time series

Given below are the number of customers served in a restaurant each day for the last seven days:

Sunday	159
Monday	62
Tuesday	55
Wednesday	86
Thursday	104
Friday	168
Saturday	192

What is the average number of customers each day?

Given below are the monthly sales figures for a business for the last year:

	£
July 2006	337,600
August 2006	415,300
September 2006	289,500
October 2006	266,400
November 2006	198,700
December 2006	258,600
January 2007	177,200
February 2007	199,300
March 2007	222,900
April 2007	256,100
May 2007	265,800
June 2007	365,700

Calculate a three-month moving average for these sales figures.

4 Given below are the weekly production costs for the first 16 weeks of the year for a manufacturing business:

Week	Costs £
1	128,500
2	195,400
3	148,600
4	177,800
5	137,500
6	165,700
7	148,200
8	183,400
9	177,300
10	164,700
11	155,400
12	193,600
13	158,100
14	174,500
15	162,900
16	159,400

Calculate a four-week moving average for these production figures.

5   Using the figures from the previous activity, prepare a computer spreadsheet to calculate the four-week moving average.

	A	B	C	D
1				
2				
3				
4				
5				
6				
7				
8				
9				
10				
11				
12				
13				
14				
15				
16				
17				
18				
19				
20				
21				
22				
23				
24				
25				
26				
27				
28				
29				
30				
31				

6 Given below are the monthly production cost figures for a small manufacturing business:

2006	£
January	55,600
February	52,700
March	56,100
April	56,800
May	58,300
June	60,500
July	58,900
August	59,200
September	61,300
October	62,100
November	63,400
December	62,700
2007	
January	61,300
February	62,500
March	64,100
April	65,200
May	64,900
June	66,700

You are required to:

a) calculate a three-month moving average in order to show the trend of these figures

b) plot the monthly figures and the trend line on a graph.

7 Explain the difference between interpolation and extrapolation.

8 What is a price index?

9   Given below are the sales figures for a business for the last year:

2006	£
August	527,500
September	513,400
October	556,700
November	523,400
December	582,300
2007	
January	561,300
February	532,600
March	524,300
April	515,700
May	529,600
June	538,200

Using August 2006 as the base month with an index of 100, show the index for each of the subsequent month's sales.

10   Sales for V plc over the last five years were as follows.

Year	Sales £'000
2003	35
2004	42
2005	40
2006	45
2007	50

V plc's Managing Director decides that he wants to set up a sales index (ie an index which measures how sales have done from year to year), using 2003 as the base year. The £35,000 of sales in 2003 is given the index 100%. What are the indices for the other years?

11 Given below are the sales for a business for the first eight months of the year together with the Retail Price Index for that month:

	£	RPI
January	162,400	171.1
February	163,800	172.0
March	165,900	172.2
April	167,200	173.0
May	166,200	172.1
June	164,100	171.3
July	162,300	171.0
August	160,500	170.3

a) Calculate the RPI adjusted sales figures for the eight months with prices being reflected in terms of January prices.

b) Using the RPI adjusted sales figures produce an index for the sales for each month with January as the base period.

c) Prepare a computer spreadsheet which will calculate the RPI adjusted index by inserting appropriate formulae.

	A	B	C	D	E
1					
2					
3					
4					
5					
6					
7					
8					

12 The following data relates to an express passenger coach service operator over the last three years 2005 to 2007. The operation faced new competition on its main routes from another coach company in 2007.

	2005	2006	2007
Total passenger kilometres	54,748,148	61,273,617	64,788,492
Total loaded coach kilometres	1,921,261	1,964,325	1,981,380
Total receipts (fares) (£)	3,119,842	3,799,421	4,145,014
Total operating expenses (£)	2,327,452	2,458,123	2,531,770

Notes. Loaded coach kilometres represent distance travelled when coaches are in service. Coaches have a full capacity of either 46 or 48 passengers.

You are required from the information above, calculate the following performance indicators for each of the three years.

a)   Receipts per loaded coach kilometre (in pounds, to two decimal places)

b)   Receipts per passenger kilometre (in pence, to one decimal place)

c)   Passenger kilometres per loaded coach kilometre (average coach load) (in number of passengers, to one decimal place)

d)   Total operating expenses per loaded coach kilometre (in pounds, to two decimal places)

13   a)   Adjust the indicators you have calculated in Activity 12 to real terms, where it is appropriate to do so, using the following price index.

	Index
2005	93.2
2006	96.1
2007	100.0

b)   Comment briefly on trends in the performance indicators you have calculated.

chapter 15:
EXTERNAL REPORTING

1 Name as many of the thirteen 'themes' included in the government's National Statistics as you can remember.

2 Given below is a grant application form for a grant from the local authority:

BARDEN LOCAL DISTRICT COUNCIL
GRANT APPLICATION

PART 1 BUSINESS DETAILS

Business name . . . .

. . . .

Business address . . . .

. . . .

. . . .

Business telephone . . . .

Business fax . . . .

Owner's name . . . .

. . . .

E-mail address . . . .

Type of business . . . .

. . . .

. . . .

. . . .

PART 2 FINANCIAL DETAILS

2A TURNOVER AND PROFIT

Figures are to be provided for annual turnover and reported net profit for the last three complete financial years

Financial year ended:	UK turnover £	Export turnover £	Net profit £
Month Year			

2B WORKING CAPITAL

Figures are to be provided for working capital at the end of the most recent financial year.

Year ending:

£

Current assets . . . .

Minus: current liabilities . . . .

Working capital . . . .

2C FIXED ASSETS

Figures are to be provided for fixed asset totals at the end of the most recent financial year.

Year ending:

£

Land and buildings . . . .

Plant and machinery . . . .

Other . . . .

Total fixed assets . . . .

PART 3 NON FINANCIAL DETAILS

3A EMPLOYMENT DETAILS

Figures are to be provided for the number of employees for the last three financial years.

Financial year ended:	Number of full time employees	Number of part time employees
Month Year		

3B BUSINESS DETAILS

Date business started: . . . .

Business type -	Sole trader	☐
	Partnership	☐
	Company	☐

PART 4 GRANT APPLICATION

Indicate in the space provided the reasons for the grant application. If the grant application is processed further more detail will be requested at a later date.

. . . .

. . . .

. . . .

. . . .

. . . .

. . . .

. . . .

You work for a partnership called D & G Harper which was set up in 1998 by David and Gareth Harper to manufacture curtains and blinds, largely for businesses. The business is run on a day-to-day basis by David Harper and in the year ended 30 June 2007 employed 14 full-time employees and three part-time employees. The business expanded in the year ended 30 June 2006 and in that year 5 more full-time employees were taken on and two part-time employees.

The grant application is for £15,000 to help fund additional factory space and the potential employment of potentially six additional full-time employees.

The business is run from Harper House, East Park Road, Barden, BD4 6GK and the telephone number and fax number are 02185 3743 and 02185 3264 respectively. The e-mail address used by David and Gareth is dgh@dandgharper.co.uk.

You have been asked to complete the grant application form prior to it being signed and checked by David Harper. From the accounting records you have been able to find summaries of the profit and loss accounts for the last three years and a summarised balance sheet as at 30 June 2007.

Summarised profit and loss accounts

	Y/e 30 June 2005 £	Y/e 30 June 2006 £	Y/e 30 June 2007 £
UK sales	378,690	735,400	882,400
Export sales	10,580	38,600	48,340
	389,270	774,000	930,740
Cost of sales	210,580	387,400	446,750
	178,690	386,600	483,990
Expenses	104,580	224,060	279,220
Net profit	74,110	162,540	204,770

Summarised balance sheet as at 30 June 2007

	£	£	£
Fixed assets:			
Land and buildings			184,500
Machinery			190,400
Cars			84,500
Office equipment			13,200
			472,600
Current assets:			
Stock of fabrics		28,400	
Debtors		65,400	
Cash at bank		3,670	
		97,470	
Current liabilities:			
Trade creditors	38,600		
PAYE/NIC	3,570		
		42,170	
			55,300
			527,900

You are required to complete the grant application form ready for checking and signature.

3 You work as an Accounting Technician for a medium-sized building firm with a turnover for the year ended 30 June 2007 of £367,400 and for the previous year of £283,400. The net profit made in the year ended 30 June 2007 was £48,414 compared to £39,382 for the previous year. The owner of the business is confident that turnover and profits will continue to increase in the foreseeable future. All of the business takes place in the UK.

You are required to complete the Chamber of Commerce Annual Economic Review that has been sent to your business in order to aid in the collection of National Statistics.

CHAMBER OF COMMERCE
ANNUAL ECONOMIC REVIEW

Please tick the appropriate box in answer to each question – all answers will be treated in the strictest confidence. All answers should be based upon the business performance for the last full financial year.

1   BUSINESS DETAILS

End of last full financial year:

Turnover range:

Upto £50,000 ☐

£50,000 - £100,000 ☐

£100,000 - £250,000 ☐

£250,000 - £500,000 ☐

£500,000 - £1,000,000 ☐

Over £1,000,000 ☐

Main business activity:

Engineering ☐		Health ☐
Construction ☐		Art and design ☐
Agriculture ☐		Transport ☐
Energy ☐		Tourism ☐
Retail ☐		Other (please state) . . . .
Education ☐		. . . .

---

2 TURNOVER

Percentage of total turnover accounted for by export sales:

0%	☐	30% to 50%	☐
up to 10%	☐	50% to 75%	☐
10% to 20%	☐	75% to 100%	☐
20% to 30%	☐		

Percentage increase/decrease in turnover compared to previous financial year:

Decrease upto 20%	☐	Increase upto 20%	☐
Decrease of 20% to 50%	☐	Increase of 20% to 50%	☐
Decrease of more than 50%	☐	Increase of more than 50%	☐

Percentage increase/decrease in net profit compared to previous financial year:

Decrease upto 20%	☐	Increase upto 20%	☐
Decrease of 20% to 50%	☐	Increase of 20% to 50%	☐
Decrease of more than 50%	☐	Increase of more than 50%	☐

3 BUSINESS CONFIDENCE

Do you consider that over the following 12 months:

Turnover	will increase	☐	Profitability	will increase	☐
	remain the same	☐		remain the same	☐
	decrease	☐		decrease	☐

chapter 16:
VALUE ADDED TAX

1 Complete the following sentences:

a) From 1 April 2007 the VAT registration threshold is £ ....

b) From 1 April 2007 the VAT deregistration limit is £ .... for taxable supplies

c) VAT on purchases is known as .... tax

d) VAT on sales is known as .... tax

e) A VAT return is normally completed every .... months

2 What are the three rates of VAT in the UK currently?

....

....

....

3 A business has made purchases during a month of £13,500 plus VAT. What is the total cost of these purchases for each of the following businesses and why?

a) A business that makes exempt supplies

b) A business that makes zero-rated supplies

....

....

4 Why might a business register for VAT even if its turnover has not reached the VAT registration limit?

....

....

....

5   A VAT registered business has made the following purchases:

   a)   A car for use by the Sales Manager for £14,200 plus VAT
   b)   A business lunch for clients costing £120 plus VAT.

What is the cost to the business of each of these expenses and why?

....

....

6   What is the tax point in each of the following situations and is it a basic tax point or an actual tax point?

   a)   An invoice is dispatched to a customer on 13 August 2007 and the goods are delivered the following day.

   b)   Goods are delivered on 15 August 2007 and the invoice is sent to the customer on 31 August 2007.

   c)   Services are provided to a customer on 8 August 2007 and an invoice is sent out on 12 August 2007.

   d)   A customer pays for goods on 20 August 2007 and the goods are delivered two days later.

....

....

....

....

7   Calculate the amount of VAT that should be charged in each of the following situations:

   a)   Goods sold for £146.80 plus VAT

   b)   Goods sold for £220.00 plus VAT less a trade discount of 10%

   c)   Goods sold for £200.00 plus VAT with a settlement discount of 3% offered

   d)   Goods sold for £320.00 plus VAT less a trade discount of 20% and a settlement discount of 2%

....

....

....

....

8   Calculate the VAT and the net of VAT amount in each of the following.

   a)   £432.16 including VAT
   b)   £262.77 including VAT
   c)   £216.90 including VAT
   d)   £310.18 including VAT

   ....

   ....

   ....

   ....

9   Explain what details would appear on a less detailed VAT invoice for a retail sale of less than £100.00.

   ....

   ....

   ....

   ....

10   Clipper Ltd holds the following invoices from suppliers.

   a)

VAT reg no 446 9989 57		Jupiter plc
Date: 4 January 2007		1 London Road
Tax point: 4 January 2007		Reading
Invoice no.		RL3 7CM

Clippers Ltd
13 Gale Road
Chester-le-Street
NE1 1LB

Sales of goods

Type	Quantity	VAT rate %	Net £
Earrings @ £0.5 per unit	2,700	17.5	1,350.00
Earring studs @ £0.5 per unit	2,800	17.5	1,400.00
			2,750.00
VAT at 17.5%			457.19
Payable within 60 days			3,207.19
Less 5% discount if paid within 14 days			137.50
			3,069.69

b)

HILLSIDE LTD
'The Glasgow Based Suppler of Quality Jewellery Items'

VAT reg no 337 4849 26

Clipper Ltd
13 Gale Road
Chester-le-Street
NE1 1LB

Invoice no. 0010
Date: 10 August 2007
Tax point: 10 August 2007

	£
Sale of 4,000 Jewellery boxes @ £2 per unit	8,000
VAT at 17.5%	1,450
Total	9,450

Terms: strictly net 30 days

c)

GENEROUS PLC

11 Low Fell
Leeds
LS1 XY2

Clipper Ltd
13 Gale Road
Chester-le-Street
NE1 1LB

Invoice no: 2221
Date: 12 December 2007
Tax point: 12 December 2007

	Net £	VAT £	Total £
4,000 Earrings @ £0.5 per unit	2,000.00	350.00	2,350.00
8,000 Brooches @ £0.3125 per unit	2,500.00	437.50	2,937.50
2,500 'How to make Jewellery' books @ £2 per book	5,000.00	0.00	5,000.00
	9,500.00	787.50	10,287.50

d)

> ## JEWELS & CO
>
> 101 High Street, Gateshead NE2 22P
>
> VAT reg no 499 3493 27
>
> Date: 2 January 2007
>
> 30 necklaces sold for £4 each totalling £120.00 including VAT at 17.5%.

For each of the above invoices, state whether it is a valid VAT invoice. Give your reasons.

chapter 17:
VAT RECORDS

1   Peter Perfect runs a retail business supplying both tradespeople and the general public, and is registered for VAT. He does not use the cash accounting scheme or any retail scheme.

Peter had the following transactions in the quarter ended 31 March 2007.

Date	Type	Net amount £	VAT rate %
2 January	Sale	6,237	17.5
4 January	Purchase	9,950	17.5
4 January	Sale	14,850	0.0
7 January	Purchase	5,792	17.5
10 January	Sale	19,008	17.5
21 January	Sale	2,079	0.0
2 February	Sale	29,700	0.0
14 February	Purchases returned	743	17.5
14 February	Sale	3,416	0.0
16 February	Purchase	8,168	17.5
27 February	Sales returned	1,188	0.0
1 March	Sale	1,084	17.5
13 March	Purchases returned	178	17.5
17 March	Sale	2,525	0.0
31 March	Sales returned	505	17.5

All returns of goods are evidenced by credit notes for both the net price and (where applicable) the VAT. All returns related to current period transactions, except for the return on 14 February.

On the previous period's VAT return, output VAT was overstated by £700 and input VAT was understated by £800. These errors are to be corrected through the VAT account for this quarter.

You are required to prepare Peter's VAT account for the quarter.

2 In the quarter ended 31 March 2007, Control plc made sales as follows. All amounts given exclude any VAT.

	£
Standard rated sales	6,000,000
Zero rated sales	1,500,000
Exempt sales	2,800,000

The VAT on purchases attributable to standard rated and zero rated sales was £600,000. The VAT on purchases attributable to exempt sales was £258,000. In addition, VAT on purchases not attributable to any particular type of sale was £96,000.

Included in standard rated sales was £20,000 for the sale of plant no longer required by the business.

You are required to compute the amount payable to or recoverable from HM Revenue & Customs in respect of the quarter.

3 Given below is information about the VAT of a business that has been taken from the books of prime entry:

VAT figures

	£
From the sales day book	3,474.89
From the sales returns day book	441.46
From the purchases day book	2,485.61
From the purchases returns day book	210.68
From the cash receipts book	993.57
From the cash payments book	624.78
EU acquisitions	925.47

Write up the VAT control account.

VAT account

£		£

4   Given below is information about the VAT of a business taken from the books of prime entry:

	£
From the sales day book	6,275.78
From the sales returns day book	726.58
From the purchases day book	4,668.14
From the purchases returns day book	510.36
From the cash receipts book	1,447.30
From the cash payments book	936.47
EU acquisitions	772.46
Bad debt relief	284.67
VAT underpaid in a previous period	126.57
VAT overpaid in a previous period	221.68

You are to write up the VAT control account.

VAT account

£		£

5   Given below are extracts from the books of prime entry for a business Waltzer Enterprises, Adam Industrial Park, Yarden, LR3 9GS. The business's VAT registration number is 234 4576 12 and the tax period is April 2007 to June 2007.

Sales day book summary

	Zero-rated sales £	Standard rated sales £	VAT £	Total £
Total	3,628.47	57,615.80	10,082.76	71,327.03

Purchases day book summary

	Zero-rated purchases £	Standard rated purchases £	VAT £	Total £
EU acquisitions		1,572.45	275.17	1,847.62
UK purchases	2,636.47	33,672.57	5,892.69	42,201.73

Sales returns day book summary

	Zero-rated sales £	Standard rated sales £	VAT £	Total £
Total	236.34	4,782.57	836.94	5,855.85

Purchases returns day book summary

	Zero-rated purchases £	Standard rated purchases £	VAT £	Total £
Total	125.34	3,184.57	557.29	3,867.20

Cash receipts book summary

	Net £	VAT £	Total £
Cash sales	5,325.65	931.98	6,257.63

Cash payments book summary

	Net £	VAT £	Total £
Cash purchases	3,157.46	552.55	3,710.01

You are required to complete the VAT return given.

Value Added Tax Return
For the period
01 04 07 to 30 06 07

For Official Use

Registration number | Period

You could be liable to a financial penalty if your completed return and all the VAT payable are not received by the due date.

Due date:

For Official Use

If you have a general enquiry or need advice please call our National Advice Service on 0845 010 9000

ATTENTION

If this return and any tax due are not received by the due date you may be liable to a surcharge.

If you make supplies of goods to another EC Member State you are required to complete an EC Sales List (VAT 101).

Before you fill in this form please read the notes on the back and the VAT Leaflet "*Filling in your VAT return*" and "*Flat rate schemes for small businesses*", if you use the scheme. Fill in all boxes clearly in ink, and write 'none' where necessary. Don't put a dash or leave any box blank. If there are no pence write "00" in the pence column. Do not enter more than one amount in any box.

For official use		£	p
	VAT due in this period on sales and other outputs **1**		
	VAT due in this period on acquisitions from other EC Member States **2**		
	Total VAT due (the sum of boxes 1 and 2) **3**		
	VAT reclaimed in this period on purchases and other inputs (including acquisitions from the EC) **4**		
	Net VAT to be paid to Customs or reclaimed by you (Difference between boxes 3 and 4) **5**		
	Total value of sales and all other outputs excluding any VAT. Include your box 8 figure **6**		00
	Total value of purchases and all other inputs excluding any VAT. Include your box 9 figure **7**		00
	Total value of all supplies of goods and related services, excluding any VAT, to other EC Member States **8**		00
	Total value of all acquisitions of goods and related services, excluding any VAT, from other EC Member States **9**		00

If you are enclosing a payment please tick this box.

DECLARATION: You, or someone on your behalf, must sign below.

I, _____ declare that the
(Full name of signatory in BLOCK LETTERS)
information given above is true and complete.

Signature_____ Date _____ 20 ____

A false declaration can result in prosecution.

6 What would you do if you discovered that your business had made an error on an earlier VAT return which was more than £2,000?

....

....

....

....

....

....

7 Explain how the annual accounting scheme for VAT works.

....

....

....

....

....

....

....

....

....

....

....

....

....

....

....

....

....

8   Zag plc had the following sales and purchases in the three months ended 30 June 2007. All amounts exclude any VAT, and all transactions were with United Kingdom traders.

	£
Sales	
Standard-rated	877,500
Zero-rated	462,150
Exempt	327,600
Purchases	
Standard-rated	
Attributable to taxable supplies	585,000
Attributable to exempt supplies	146,250
Unattributable	468,000
Zero-rated	8,190
Exempt	15,405

You are required to compute the figures which would be entered in boxes 1 to 5 of Zag plc's VAT return given for the period.

Value Added Tax Return

For the period
01 04 07 to 30 06 07

For Official Use

Registration number

Period

You could be liable to a financial penalty if your completed return and all the VAT payable are not received by the due date.

Due date:

For Official Use

ATTENTION

If you have a general enquiry or need advice please call our National Advice Service on 0845 010 9000

If this return and any tax due are not received by the due date you may be liable to a surcharge.

If you make supplies of goods to another EC Member State you are required to complete an EC Sales List (VAT 101).

Before you fill in this form please read the notes on the back and the VAT Leaflet "*Filling in your VAT return*" and "*Flat rate schemes for small businesses*", if you use the scheme. Fill in all boxes clearly in ink, and write 'none' where necessary. Don't put a dash or leave any box blank. If there are no pence write "00" in the pence column. Do not enter more than one amount in any box.

For official use		£	p
	VAT due in this period on sales and other outputs **1**		
	VAT due in this period on acquisitions from other EC Member States **2**		
	Total VAT due (the sum of boxes 1 and 2) **3**		
	VAT reclaimed in this period on purchases and other inputs (including acquisitions from the EC) **4**		
	Net VAT to be paid to Customs or reclaimed by you (Difference between boxes 3 and 4) **5**		
	Total value of sales and all other outputs excluding any VAT. Include your box 8 figure **6**		00
	Total value of purchases and all other inputs excluding any VAT. Include your box 9 figure **7**		00
	Total value of all supplies of goods and related services, excluding any VAT, to other EC Member States **8**		00
	Total value of all acquisitions of goods and related services, excluding any VAT, from other EC Member States **9**		00

If you are enclosing a payment please tick this box.

DECLARATION: You, or someone on your behalf, must sign below.

I, _____ declare that the
(Full name of signatory in BLOCK LETTERS)
information given above is true and complete.

Signature_____ Date _____ 20 ____

A false declaration can result in prosecution.

PRACTICE EXAM 1
UNIT 6

BRECKVILLE DAIRIES LTD
These tasks were set by the AAT in December 2006.

Time allowed: 3 hours plus 15 minutes' reading time

This examination paper is in TWO sections.

You have to show competence in BOTH sections.

You should therefore attempt and aim to complete EVERY task in EACH sections.

Section 1 contains 6 tasks and Section 2 contains 5 tasks.

All essential workings should be included within your answers, where appropriate.

You should spend about 85 minutes on Section 1 and about 95 minutes on Section 2.

Both sections are based on Breckville Dairies Ltd.

SECTION 1 (Suggested time allowance: 85 minutes)

DATA

You work as an Accounting Technician at Breckville Dairies Ltd, a large processing company. The business buys milk and other farm produce from farmers and then converts these into dairy products such as cheese, butter and yoghurt. It then sells these on to high street retail chains.

The company operates a process costing system.

The Chief Accountant has given you the following tasks.

DATA FOR TASK 1.1

The stock record card shown below refers to entries for bio-protein additive for the month of November 2007. This commodity has been rapidly increasing in price over the past few weeks. The card has been partially written up using the First In First out (FIFO) method of stock issue and valuation, rather than the Weighted Average Cost (AVCO) method which should have been used.

STOCK RECORD CARD								
	Receipts			Issues			Balance	
Date	Quantity (litres)	Cost per litre (£)	Total cost (£)	Quantity (litres)	Cost per litre (£)	Total cost (£)	Quantity (litres)	Total cost £
Balance as at 1 Nov							2,000	4,000
6 Nov	1,000	2.60	2,600				3,000	6,600
14 Nov				1,000	2.00	2,000	2,000	4,600
22 Nov	1,000	3.40	3,400					
27 Nov				2,000				

Task 1.1

a) Redraft the stock record card on the previous page for the entries up to and including that on 14 November 2007.

b) Complete the entries for the rest of the month.

	Receipts			Issues			Balance	
STOCK RECORD CARD								
Date	Quantity (litres)	Cost per litre (£)	Total cost (£)	Quantity (litres)	Cost per litre (£)	Total cost (£)	Quantity (litres)	Total cost £
Balance as at 1 Nov								
6 Nov								
14 Nov								
22 Nov								
27 Nov								

c) Identify ONE other method (that is, other than FIFO and AVCO) of stock issue and valuation based on historical cost (excluding standard costing).

d) State whether this method would lead to a lower or higher valuation of the stock balance at 27 November (as compared to AVCO).

ADDITIONAL DATA

The issue of bio-protein additive on 14 November was for use in the production of product X, whilst that on 27 November was for the production of product Y.

The following cost accounting codes are used:

Code	Description
2004	Stocks of bio-protein additive
7012	Work in progress – Product X
7039	Work in progress – Product Y
5030	Creditors Control

Task 1.2

Complete the Journal below to record separately the FOUR cost accounting entries for the two receipts and two issues during the month of November.

Date	Code	Dr £	Cr £
6 November			
6 November			
14 November			
14 November			
22 November			
22 November			
27 November			
27 November			

ADDITIONAL DATA

The following information relates to direct labour costs incurred in producing product Z during November 2007.

Normal time hours worked	350 hours
Overtime at time and a half worked	60 hours
Overtime at double time worked	40 hours
Total hours worked	450 hours
Normal time hourly rate	£8 per hour

Task 1.3

Overtime premiums paid are included as part of direct labour cost.

Calculate the total cost of direct labour for product Z for the month of November 2007.

ADDITIONAL DATA

Breckville Dairies Ltd. has the following departments involved in one of the stages of production:

- Materials Mixing
- Product Packing
- Maintenance

The budgeted fixed overheads relating to the departments for the next quarter are:

	£	£
Insurance of machinery		33,600
Rent and rates		91,200
Indirect labour costs:		
Materials Mixing	35,750	
Product Packing	87,450	
Maintenance	12,250	
Total		135,450
Total fixed overheads		260,250

The following information is also available:

Department	Net book value of fixed assets £000	Square metres occupied	Number of employees
Materials mixing	360	550	7
Product packing	180	400	24
Maintenance	60	50	3
Total	600	1,000	34

Fixed overheads are allocated or apportioned to the departments on the most appropriate basis. The total maintenance overheads are then reapportioned to the two production departments. 60% of the Maintenance department's time is spent maintaining equipment in the Materials mixing department.

Task 1.4

Use the following table to allocate or apportion the fixed overheads between the production departments, using the most appropriate basis.

Fixed overhead	Basis of allocation or apportionment	Total cost £	Materials Mixing £	Product Packing £	Maintenance £
Insurance of machinery		33,600			
Rent and rates		91,200			
Indirect labour costs		135,450			
Maintenance					
		260,250			

ADDITIONAL DATA

The Materials Mixing department is highly automated, and operates with expensive machinery. The Product Packing department, on the other hand, is highly labour intensive.

The following budgeted information relates to next quarter:

	Materials Mixing	**Product Packing**
Number of machine hours	3,940	2,840
Number of labour hours	3,200	10.920

Task 1.5

Using your calculations in Task 1.4 and the information above, calculate the budgeted fixed overhead absorption rates (recovery rates) for the next quarter using the most appropriate bases of absorption for:

a)   the Materials Mixing department
b)   the Product Packing department

Note. You should round your answers to whole pounds.

_____

_____

_____

_____

_____

_____

_____

_____

_____

_____

_____

_____

ADDITIONAL DATA

The following information relates to product R during the month of October 2007.

	£	Units
Direct materials cost per unit	12.20	
Direct labour cost per unit	27.80	
Total variable overheads cost	20,000	
Total fixed overheads cost	50,000	
Number of units sold		800
Number of units produced		1,000

Note. There were no opening stocks.

Task 1.6

a)   Calculate the cost per unit of product R under:

   i)   variable (marginal) costing

_____

_____

_____

_____

_____

_____

_____

   ii)   full absorption costing

_____

_____

_____

_____

_____

_____

_____

b) State how much the difference in the closing stock valuation and the reported profit for October would be under the two costing principles.

_____

_____

_____

_____

_____

_____

SECTION 2 (Suggested time allowance: 95 minutes)

ADDITIONAL DATA

The company has produced three forecasts of activity levels for the next quarter for product S. The original budget was to produce only 1,000 units, but production levels of 1,200 units and 1,500 units are also feasible.

Task 2.1

a) Complete the table below, in order to estimate the production cost per unit of S at the three different activity levels.

Units made	1,000	1,200	1,500
Costs	£	£	£
Variable costs:			
■ direct materials	3,000		
■ direct labour	7,000		
■ overheads	6,000		
Fixed costs:			
■ indirect labour	9,800		
■ overheads	19,000		
Total cost	44,800		
Cost per unit	44.80		

b) Identify THREE factors that are relevant to predicting how the cost per unit of S would change if sales and production could be increased to 10,000 units per quarter.

i) _____

_____

_____

ii) _____

_____

_____

iii) _____

_____

_____

ADDITIONAL DATA

Product S will be sold for £40.00/unit at all three feasible activity levels of 1,000; 1,200; and 1,500 units.

Task 2.2

a) Calculate the budgeted break-even sales, in units, for product S.

_____

_____

_____

_____

_____

_____

b) Complete the table below to calculate:

i) the margin of safety (in units) at each of the three feasible activity levels, by comparing the level of sales forecast with the break-even level

ii) the margin of safety as a percentage for each of the three activity levels.

Forecast sales (units)	1,000	1,200	1,500
Break-even sales (units)			
Margin of safety (units)			
Margin of safety (%)			

c)   Explain the significance of your calculation of the percentage margin of safety for each of the three
      feasible activity levels.

    i)   1,000 units

    ii)   1,200 units

    iii)   1,500 units

ADDITIONAL DATA

The company produces product T within a single production process. During the month of October 2007 the input into the process was 1,200 litres at a cost of £12,000. There were no opening or closing stocks and all output was fully completed.

The table below shows the actual process results for the month:

Input (litres)	Output (litres)	Normal loss (litres)	Abnormal loss (litres)	Abnormal gains (litres)	Scrap value of all losses (£ per litre)
1,200	1,000	200	0	0	£5

Task 2.3

a) Calculate the cost per litre of output.

_____

_____

_____

_____

_____

b) Complete the entries in the product T process account below.

Description	Litres	Unit cost (£)	Total cost (£)		Description	Litres	Unit cost (£)	Total cost (£)
Input to process					Normal loss			
					Output from process			

ADDITIONAL DATA

The company has two products, V and W, that need the same machine mixing process. The number of available machine hours, however, for this particular mixing machine is limited to only 3,000 during the next quarter.

The following information is available:

Product	V	W
Selling price/unit (£)	30	40
Marginal cost/unit (£)	20	25
Machine hours required/unit	2	5
Demand (forecast sales next quarter)	1,000	1,500
Total fixed costs for both products	£9,000	

Task 2.4

Using the above information, complete the table below to recommend how many units of products V and W should be made in order to maximise profits, taking account of the machine hours available.

Product	V	W	Total
Contribution/unit (£)			
Machine hours/unit			
Contribution/machine hour (£)			
Product ranking			
Machine hours available			
Machine hours allocated to: Product....... Product.......			
Units made			
Total contribution earned (£)			
Less: Fixed costs (£)			
Profit/loss made (£)			

ADDITIONAL DATA

The company is considering investing in a new mixing machine that will cost £1.5million and which will reduce operating costs. The following information is relevant to this decision.

- The payback period would be 3.6 years. The company's policy is for projects to pay back within 4 years.

- The net present value is £200,000 negative.

- The internal rate of return is 12%. The company's cost of capital is 15%

Task 2.5

Based on the information given above, write a BRIEF report to the Chief Accountant in which you advise on the basis of EACH of the three criteria above whether the proposed investment should be made. Make an overall accept/reject recommendation.

REPORT	
To:	**Subject:**
From:	**Date:**

This page is for the continuation of your report. You may not need all of it.

PRACTICE EXAM 2
UNIT 6

CASTON FINE FOODS LTD

These tasks were set by the AAT in June 2006.

Time allowed: 3 hours plus 15 minutes' reading time

This examination paper is in TWO sections.

You have to show competence in BOTH sections.

You should therefore attempt and aim to complete EVERY task in BOTH sections.

All essential workings should be included within your answers, where appropriate.

You should spend about 80 minutes on Section 1 and about 100 minutes on Section 2.

Both sections are based on Caston Fine Foods Ltd.

SECTION 1 (Suggested time allowance: 80 minutes)

DATA

You are employed as an accounting technician with Caston Fine Foods Ltd, a company that manufactures a wide range of ready-made foods. Its customers are mainly the large High Street supermarkets, but the company also sells to a large number of small independent retailers.

The company operates a batch costing system.

It has five cost centres that relate to the manufacture of its products:

Production centres

Ingredients Mixing where batches of raw ingredients are mixed together to make the ready-made foods

Containerisation where the batches of ready-made foods are put into individual containers

Packing and Despatch where the containers are wrapped, and placed into final display packaging. The finished products are then put into large cardboard boxes and loaded onto pallets ready for delivery to customers.

Service centres

Maintenance

Stores

The company's year end is 31 May.

The data and tasks given in the paper cover activities during May and June 2007.

You report to the Management Accountant, who has set you the following tasks.

Task 1.1

The stock record card shown below for food ingredient RM 1546 for the month of May 2007 has only been filled out for the first half of the month.

a) Complete ALL entries in the stock record card for the following TWO transactions:

    20 May: Received 8,000 kg at a total cost of £12,800
    25 May: Issued 5,000 kg with a total cost of £7,600

b) Identify the stock issue method being used for valuing issues of this ingredient to production.

c) Complete ALL entries in the stock record card for the remaining two transactions in the month, and for the closing balance at 31 May.

STOCK RECORD CARD FOR FOOD INGREDIENT RM 1546								
	Receipts			Issues			Balance	
Balance as at	Quantity kg	Cost per kg (£)	Total cost (£)	Quantity kg	Cost per kg (£)	Total cost (£)	Quantity kg	Total cost (£)
16 May							4,000	6,000
20 May								
25 May								
28 May	8,000	1.70						
31 May				6,000				

105

ADDITIONAL DATA

Ingredient RM 1546 was issued on 25 May to produce a batch of lasagna, and issued on 31 May to produce a batch of vegetable pies.

The following cost accounting codes are used:

Code	Description
4320	Stocks of ingredient RM 1546
5052	Work in progress – lasagna
5038	Work in progress – vegetable pies
1100	Creditors Control

Task 1.2

Complete the Journal below to record separately the FOUR cost accounting entries in respect of the two receipts and two issues.

Date	Code	Dr £	Cr £
20 May			
20 May			
25 May			
25 May			
28 May			
28 May			
31 May			
31 May			

ADDITIONAL DATA

The weekly timesheet for one of the production employees appears below. The basic working week is eight hours per day from Monday to Friday, with any overtime during this period paid at time and a half (basic pay plus an overtime premium equal to half of basic pay). Any hours worked on Saturday or Sunday are paid at double time (basic pay plus an overtime premium equal to basic pay).

Note. Only pay at more than the basic rate per hour should be included in the Overtime Premium column.

Task 1.3

Complete:

a)   the columns headed Basic pay, Overtime premium and Total pay

   Note. The employee's total pay for the week was £549.

WEEKLY TIMESHEET FOR WEEK ENDING 31 MAY 2007						
Employee: J Stone			**Cost Centre:** Packing			
Employee number: P12			**Basic pay per hour:** £9.00			
	Hours worked on direct work	**Hours worked on indirect work**	**Notes**	**Basic pay £**	**Overtime premium £**	**Total pay £**
Monday	8	–				
Tuesday	6	2	9–11 am Staff training course			
Wednesday	12					
Thursday	10					
Friday	5	3	1–4 pm Departmental stock taking			
Saturday	4					
Sunday	2					
Total	47	5				549

b)   the analysis of total pay for the week, as shown in the table below.

   Note. Overtime premium is classed as an indirect labour cost.

Analysis of total pay for the week	£
Direct labour cost	
Indirect labour cost	
Total pay	

ADDITIONAL DATA

The budgeted overheads relating to the company's five cost centres for Quarter 1 of the next financial year are:

	£	£
Depreciation of machinery		1,200,400
Rent and rates		600,800
Light and heat		200,000
Power (for Ingredients Mixing and Containerisation)		500,000
Indirect labour costs:		
Ingredients mixing	501,644	
Containerisation	316,896	
Packing and despatch	558,460	
Maintenance	75,800	
Stores	141,000	
Total indirect labour cost		1,593,800

The following information is also available:

Department	Net book value of machinery (£000)	Square metres occupied	Number of machine hours	Number of direct labour hours
Ingredients Mixing	5,200	1,800	3,000	–
Containerisation	3,900	1,500	2,000	–
Packing and Despatch	2,600	1,800	–	5,000
Maintenance	650	300	–	–
Stores	650	600	–	–
Total	13,000	6,000	5,000	5,000

Overheads are allocated or apportioned on the most appropriate basis. The service cost centres' total overheads are then reapportioned to the three production departments using the direct method:

- 60% of the Maintenance department's time is spent maintaining machinery in the Ingredients Mixing cost centre and the remainder in the Containerisation cost centre.

- The Stores department makes 40% of its issues to the Ingredients Mixing cost centre, 40% to the Containerisation cost centre and the rest to the Packing and Despatch cost centre.

There is no reciprocal servicing between the two service cost centres.

Task 1.4

Use the following table to allocate or apportion the overheads between the cost centres, using the most appropriate basis.

Department	Basis of allocation or apportionment	Ingredients mixing £	Containerisation £	Packing and despatch £	Maintenance £	Stores £	Totals £
Depreciation of machinery							
Rent and rates							
Light and heat							
Power							
Indirect labour							
Totals							
Re-apportion maintenance							
Re-apportion stores							
Total production cost centres							

Task 1.5

Ingredients Mixing and Containerisation recover their overheads on a machine hour basis, and Packing and Despatch on a direct labour hour basis.

Using the Data and your calculations from Task 1.4, calculate the overhead absorption rates for each of the three production cost centres.

ADDITIONAL DATA

The following information relates to the manufacture of batches of cheese pies during the month of May 2007:

Direct materials per batch	£316.80
Direct labour per batch	£412.50
Total variable overheads	£197,800
Total fixed overheads	£278,300
Number of batches produced	230

Task 1.6

Calculate the cost per batch under:

a)   variable (marginal) costing

_____

_____

_____

_____

_____

_____

_____

b)   full absorption costing

_____

_____

_____

_____

_____

_____

_____

SECTION 2 (Suggested time allowance: 100 minutes)

ADDITIONAL DATA

The company has produced three forecasts of activity levels for the next three months for its TV dinners range. The original budget involved producing 5,000 batches but, due to an increase in demand, production levels of between 6,000 and 7,000 batches now seem likely.

Task 2.1

Complete the table below to estimate the profit per batch (to three decimal places) of the TV dinners range at the different activity levels.

Batches made and sold	5,000	6,000	7,000
	£	£	£
Sales revenue	30,000		
Variable costs:			
■ direct materials	1,250		
■ direct labour	3,000		
■ overheads	7,500		
Fixed costs:			
■ indirect labour	2,750		
■ overheads	8,800		
Total cost	23,300		
Total profit	6,700		
Profit per batch	1,340		

Task 2.2

a) Using the data and your own calculations from Task 2.1, calculate:

i) the budgeted break-even volume, in number of batches (rounded up to the nearest whole batch) and sales revenue, for the TV dinners range

ii) the margin of safety, in number of batches and sales revenue, for the TWO forecast activity levels shown below

iii) the margin of safety, as a percentage (to two decimal places), for the TWO forecast activity levels shown below.

Batches made and sold	5,000	6,000
	£	£
Sales revenue		
Fixed costs		
Contribution per batch		
Break-even number of batches		
Break-even sales revenue		
Margin of safety in number of batches		
Margin of safety in sales revenue		
Margin of safety %		

b) Explain the terms 'budgeted break-even volume' and 'margin of safety'. Use your calculations in part a) to illustrate your answer.

_____

_____

_____

_____

_____

_____

_____

_____

_____

ADDITIONAL DATA

The company is considering replacing its existing batch costing system with a new process costing system.

The Production Director has been to a recent seminar on process costing systems and has asked you to give him a brief explanation of some of the terms used.

Task 2.3

Explain briefly the following terms, using examples to illustrate your answer.

Normal loss:

_____

_____

_____

_____

_____

_____

_____

_____

_____

Abnormal loss:

_____

_____

_____

_____

_____

_____

_____

_____

_____

_____

Abnormal gain:

_____

_____

_____

_____

_____

_____

_____

_____

_____

_____

_____

ADDITIONAL DATA

Caston Fine Foods Ltd is considering introducing a new type of oven-ready meal, and has produced the following estimates of capital expenditure, sales and costs. This new product is expected to have a three-year economic life.

	Year 0 £'000	Year 1 £'000	Year 2 £'000	Year 3 £'000
Capital expenditure	600			
Other cash flows:				
Sales income		760	920	1,060
Operating costs		456	542	612

The company's cost of capital is 14%.

Present value (PV) factors for a 14% discount rate are:

	Year 0 £'000	Year 1 £'000	Year 2 £'000	Year 3 £'000
PV factor	1.00000	0.87719	0.76947	0.67497

The company's policy is that all capital investment projects must recover their costs within a period equal to half of the specific project's expected economic life.

Task 2.4

Calculate for the proposed new oven-ready meal range:

a)   the net present value

	Year 0 £'000	Year 1 £'000	Year 2 £'000	Year 3 £'000
Capital expenditure				
Other income				
Operating costs				
Net cash flows				
PV factors				
Discounted cash flows				
Net present value				

b)   the payback period

_____

_____

_____

_____

_____

_____

_____

Task 2.5

Based on the Data and your own calculations from Task 2.4, write a report to the Management Accountant in which you:

a) recommend, with reasons, whether the proposed new oven-ready meal range should be introduced

b) identify and explain ONE other technique that could have been used to appraise this investment.

REPORT	
To:	**Subject:**
From:	**Date:**

_____

_____

_____

_____

_____

_____

_____

_____

_____

_____

_____

_____

_____

This page is for the continuation of your report. You may not need all of it.

PRACTICE EXAM 3
UNIT 6

WRAPWELL LTD

These tasks were set by the AAT in December 2005.

Time allowed: 3 hours plus 15 minutes' reading time

This examination paper is in TWO sections.

You have to show competence in BOTH sections.

You should therefore attempt and aim to complete EVERY task in EACH section.

You should spend about 80 minutes on Section 1 and about 100 minutes on Section 2.

All essential workings should be included within your answers where appropriate.

Both sections are based on Wrapwell Ltd.

SECTION 1 (Suggested time allowance: 80 minutes)

DATA

You work as an Accounting Technician at Wrapwell Ltd., a company that manufactures and sells a wide range of specialist packaging materials. Its customers are mainly manufacturers of ready-made foods, soft drinks and pharmaceuticals.

The Management Accountant has given you the following tasks.

Task 1.1

The stock record card shown below for plastic component Z for the month of November 2007 has only been partially completed.

STOCK RECORD CARD PLASTICS COMPONENT 2								
	Receipts			Issues			Balance	
Date 2007	Quantity kg	Cost per kg (£)	Total cost (£)	Quantity kg	Cost per kg (£)	Total cost (£)	Quantity kg	Total cost £
Balance as of 1 Nov							4,000	8,800
11 Nov	12,000	2.00	24,000				16,000	32,800
15 Nov				8,000	2.05	16,400		
22 Nov	8,000	2.20						
29 Nov				4,000				

a) Identify the stock issue method being used for valuing issues to production and stocks.

_____

_____

b) Complete the remaining entries in the stock record card using this method.

ADDITIONAL DATA

The issue of component Z on 15 November 2007 was for the production of plastic bottles, and that on 29 November 2007 was for the production of plastic food containers.

The following cost accounting codes are used:

Code number	Description
203	Stocks of component Z
305	Work in progress – plastic bottles
306	Work in progress – plastic food containers
600	Creditors control

Task 1.2

Complete the journal below to record separately the FOUR cost accounting entries in respect of the two receipts and two issues during the month of November.

JOURNAL

Date	Code	Dr £	Cr £
11 November			
11 November			
15 November			
15 November			
22 November			
22 November			
29 November			
29 November			

ADDITIONAL DATA

The following information relates to direct labour costs incurred in producing 18,000 type Y pharmaceutical bottles during November 2007.

Normal time hours worked	600 hours
Overtime at time and a half worked	120 hours
Overtime at double time worked	90 hours
Total hours worked	810 hours
Normal time hourly rate	£6 per hour

Overtime premiums paid are included as part of direct labour cost.

The Production Supervisor has produced the following INCORRECT calculation of the total cost of direct labour used to produce type Y pharmaceutical bottles during November.

	£
Cost at normal rate 810 hours at £6	4,860
Cost at time and a half 90 hours at £9	810
Cost at double time 120 hours at £12	1,440
Total direct labour cost	7,110

Task 1.3

a) Calculate the correct total cost of direct labour used to produce type Y pharmaceutical bottles during the month of November.

_____

_____

_____

_____

_____

_____

_____

_____

b) Calculate the direct labour cost per bottle.

_____

_____

_____

_____

_____

_____

ADDITIONAL DATA

Wrapwell Ltd has the following departments involved in the first stage of production:

- Plastics Moulding
- Plastics Extrusion
- Maintenance

The budgeted fixed overheads relating to the departments for Quarter 1, 2008 are:

	£	£
Insurance of machinery		22,400
Rent and rates		60,800
Indirect labour costs:		
Plastics Moulding	90,500	
Plastics Extrusion	78,300	
Maintenance	22,800	
Total		191,600
Total fixed overheads		274,800

The following information is also available.

Department	Net book value of fixed assets £000	Square metres occupied	Number of employees
Plastics Moulding	720	1,100	14
Plastics Extrusion	360	800	12
Maintenance	120	100	4
Total	1,200	2,000	30

Fixed overheads are allocated or apportioned to the departments on the most appropriate basis. The total maintenance overheads are then reapportioned to the two production departments. 70% of the Maintenance department's time is spent maintaining equipment in the Plastics Moulding department.

Task 1.4

Use the following table to allocate or apportion the fixed overheads between the production departments, using the most appropriate basis.

Fixed overhead	Basis of allocation or apportionment	Total cost £	Plastics Moulding £	Plastics Extrusion £	Maintenance £
Insurance of machinery		22,400			
Rent and rates		60,800			
Indirect labour costs		191,600			
Maintenance					
Totals		274,800			

ADDITIONAL DATA

The Plastics Moulding department recovers its fixed overheads on the basis of the budgeted machine hours. The Plastics Extrusion department, however, recovers its fixed overheads on the basis of the budgeted direct labour hours.

The following information relates to these two departments for October 2007.

	Plastics Moulding department	Plastics Extrusion department
Budgeted fixed overhead absorption rate	£60/hour	£25/hour
Actual machine hours worked	850	
Actual direct labour hours worked		1,520
Actual fixed overheads	£55,000	£36,000

Task 1.5

a)   Calculate the fixed overhead absorbed during October in:

   i)   the Plastics Moulding department

   _____

   _____

   _____

   _____

   _____

   ii)   the Plastics Extrusion department

   _____

   _____

   _____

   _____

b)   Calculate the over- or under-absorption of fixed overheads during October, stating clearly whether overheads have been over- or under-absorbed, for:

   i)   the Plastics Moulding department

   _____

   _____

   _____

   _____

   _____

   ii)   the Plastics Extrusion department

   _____

   _____

   _____

   _____

ADDITIONAL DATA

The following information relates to the manufacture of batches of microwave containers during the month of September 2007.

Direct materials per batch	£220.80
Direct labour per batch	£386.40
Total variable overheads	£89,900
Total fixed overheads	£130,200
Number of batches produced	620

Task 1.6

Calculate the cost per batch of microwave containers under:

a) variable (marginal) costing

_____

_____

_____

_____

_____

_____

_____

b) full absorption costing

_____

_____

_____

_____

_____

_____

_____

SECTION 2 (Suggested time allowance: 100 minutes)

Wrapwell Ltd has produced three forecasts of activity levels for the next three months for its type M chilled food container. The original budget involved producing 10,000 units, but sales are increasing, and it looks as if production levels of between 12,000 and 14,000 units are now more likely.

Task 2.1

a) Complete the table below in order to estimate the production cost per unit of the type M chilled food container at the different activity levels.

Units made	10,000	12,000	14,000
Costs	£	£	£
Variable costs:			
■ direct materials	2,200		
■ direct labour	3,300		
■ overheads	4,200		
Fixed costs:			
■ indirect labour	1,800		
■ overheads	5,600		
Total cost	17,100		
Cost per unit	1.71		

b) If the production volume for this product were to increase to 50,000 units per three-month period, explain what the likely effect would be on the fixed costs and cost per unit.

_____

_____

_____

_____

_____

_____

_____

_____

_____

_____

_____

_____

_____

_____

_____

_____

_____

_____

_____

_____

_____

_____

_____

ADDITIONAL DATA

The following budgeted annual sales and cost information relates to chilled food containers types N and P.

Product	N	P
Units made and sold	150,000	250,000
Machine hours required	300	2,000
Sales revenue (£)	135,000	200,000
Direct materials (£)	30,000	62,500
Direct labour (£)	18,000	35,000
Variable overheads (£)	22,500	47,500

Total fixed costs attributable to N and P are budgeted to be £95,600.

Task 2.2

Complete the table below (to two decimal places) to show the budgeted contribution per unit of N and P sold, and the company's budgeted profit or loss for the year from these two products.

	N	P	Total (£)
Units selling price (£)			
Less unit variable cost per unit			
■ direct materials (£)			
■ direct labour (£)			
■ varriable overheads (£)			
Contribution per unit (£)			
Sales volume (units)			
Total contribution (£)			
Less: fixed costs			
Budgeted profit or loss			

ADDITIONAL DATA

The £95,600 of fixed costs for products N and P has now been split between the two products as follows: £51,600 to N and £44,000 to P.

The latest sales forecast is for 160,000 units of product N and 240,000 units of product P to be sold during the year.

Task 2.3

Complete the table below so as to calculate:

- the budgeted breakeven sales, in units, for each of the two products
- the margin of safety (in units) for each of the two products
- the margin of safety as a percentage (to two decimal places)

Product	N	P
Fixed costs (£)		
Unit contribution (£)		
Break-even sales (units)		
Forecast sales (units)		
Margin of safety (units)		
Margin of safety (%)		

ADDITIONAL DATA

As a result of extra maintenance in the factory, the number of available machine hours has now been reduced to only 2,100 during the year.

Task 2.4

Given this limitation and your calculations from Task 2.2, complete the table below to recommend how many units of products N and P should now be made in order to maximise the profits or minimise the loss for the year.

Product	B	C	Total
Contribution/unit (£)			
Machine hours/unit			
Contribution/machine hr. (£)			
Product ranking			
Machine hours available			
Machine hours allocated to: Product Product			
Total contribution earned (£)			
Less: fixed costs (£)			95,600
Profit/loss made (£)			

ADDITIONAL DATA

Wrapwell Ltd. is considering introducing a new type of plastic drink bottle. The following estimates of capital expenditure, sales and costs have been produced. The new product is expected to have a three-year economic life:

	Year 0 £'000	Year 1 £'000	Year 2 £'000	Year 3 £'000
Capital expenditure	800			
Other cash flows				
Sales income		1,200	1,400	1,400
Operating costs		840	910	860

The company's cost of capital is 11%.

Present value (PV) factors for an 11% discount rate are:

	Year 0	Year 1	Year 2	Year 3
PV factor	1.0000	0.9009	0.8116	0.7312

Task 2.5

For the proposed new plastic drink bottle, calculate:

a)   the net present value

	Year 0 £'000	Year 1 £'000	Year 2 £'000	Year 3 £'000
Capital expenditure				
Sales income				
Operating costs				
Net cash flows				
PV factors				
Discounted cash flows				
Net present value				

b)   the payback period

_____

_____

_____

_____

_____

_____

_____

_____

_____

_____

_____

_____

_____

_____

_____

_____

_____

Task 2.6

Using the information and your own calculations from Task 2.5, write a report to the Management Accountant in which you:

a)   recommend whether the proposed new plastic drinks bottle should be introduced

   Note. This should be based on your calculations of the net present value and the payback period

b)   identify TWO commercial factors that are also relevant to this decision

c)   explain the meaning of the term 'internal rate of return'

REPORT	
To: The Management Accountant	**Subject:**
From:	**Date:**

This page is for the continuation of your report. You may not need all of it.

PRACTICE EXAM 4
UNIT 6

DELCOM LTD

These tasks were set by the AAT in June 2005.

Time allowed: 3 hours plus 15 minutes' reading time

This examination paper is in TWO sections.

You are required to demonstrate competence in BOTH sections.

You should, therefore, attempt and aim to complete EVERY task in BOTH sections. All tasks should be completed in numerical order.

You should spend about 90 minutes on each section.

Essential workings should be included within your answers, where appropriate.

Both sections are based on Delcom Ltd.

DATA

You are employed as an accounting technician with Delcom Ltd, a company that manufactures and sells a small range of precision engineering parts. Its customers base is the European car market.

You report to the Management Accountant, who has asked you to carry out the following tasks.

SECTION 1 (Suggested time allowance: 90 minutes)

Task 1.1

Complete the stock record card shown below for steel component M, for the month of May.

The company uses the First In, First Out (FIFO) method of stock valuation.

	Receipts			Issues			Balance	
Date	Quantity kg	Cost per kg (£)	Total cost (£)	Quantity kg	Cost per kg (£)	Total cost (£)	Quantity kg	Total cost £
Balance as of 1 May							25,000	50,000
9 May	30,000	2.30	69,000					
12 May				40,000				
18 May	20,000	2.50	50,000					
27 May				10,000				

STOCK RECORD CARD FOR STEEL COMPONENT M

ADDITIONAL DATA

The issue of component M on 12 May was for the production of product A, whilst that on the 27 May was for the production of product B.

The following cost accounting codes are used:

Code	Description
306	Stocks of component M
401	Work in progress – Product A
402	Work in progress – Product B
500	Creditors Control

Task 1.2

Complete the journal below to record separately the FOUR cost accounting entries in respect of the two receipts and two issues during the month of May.

JOURNAL

Date	Code	Dr (£)	Cr (£)
9 May			
9 May			
12 May			
12 May			
18 May			
18 May			
27 May			
27 May			

ADDITIONAL DATA

The following information relates to direct labour costs incurred in producing product C during May:

Normal time hours worked	8,000 hours
Overtime at time and a half worked	1,500 hours
Overtime at double time worked	1,000 hours
Total hours worked	10,500 hours
Normal time hourly rate	£7 per hour

Task 1.3

Overtime premiums paid are included as part of direct labour costs.

Calculate the total cost of direct labour for product C for the month of May.

ADDITIONAL DATA

Delcom has the following four production departments:

- Machining 1
- Machining 2
- Assembly
- Packaging

The budgeted fixed overheads relating to the four production departments for Quarter 3 are:

	£	£
Depreciation		80,000
Rent and rates		120,000
Indirect labour costs:		
Machining 1	40,500	
Machining 2	18,300	
Assembly	12,400	
Packaging	26,700	
Total		97,900
Direct assembly cost		15,600
Total fixed overheads		313,500

Fixed overheads are allocated or apportioned to the production departments on the most appropriate basis.

The following information is also available:

Department	Net book value of fixed assets (£000)	Square metres occupied	Number of employees
Machining 1	1,280	625	8
Machining 2	320	250	4
Assembly	960	500	3
Packaging	640	1,125	7
Total	3,200	2,500	22

Task 1.4

Use the table below to allocate or apportion the fixed overheads between the four production departments, using the most appropriate.

Fixed overhead	Basis of allocation or apportionment	Total cost (£)	Machining 1 (£)	Machining 2 (£)	Assembly (£)	Packaging (£)
Depreciation		80,000				
Rent and rates		120,000				
Indirect labour costs		97,900				
Direct assembly costs		15,600				
Totals		313,500				

ADDITIONAL INFORMATION

You have consulted the manager of a separate production division, who tells you that this division is highly automated, and operates with expensive machinery which is run whenever possible on a 24 hour a day, seven days a week basis.

The following information relates to this division for July:

Total departmental overheads	£400,000
Total budgeted direct labour hours	3,000
Total budgeted machine hours	10,000
Total actual direct labour hours	2,500
Total actual machine hours	9,000

Task 1.5

Calculate the budgeted fixed overhead absorption rate for the division for July, using the most appropriate basis of absorption.

_____

_____

_____

_____

_____

_____

_____

ADDITIONAL INFORMATION

The following information relates to the manufacture of product D during the month of April.

Direct materials per unit	£10.60
Direct labour per unit	£16.40
Total variable overheads	£60,000
Total fixed overheads	£80,000
Number of units produced	10,000

Task 1.6

Calculate the cost per unit of product D under:

a) i) variable (marginal) costing

_____

_____

_____

_____

_____

ii) full absorption costing

_____

_____

_____

_____

_____

b) Explain how it is possible to UNDER-recover fixed overheads

Explanation of fixed overhead under-recovery:

_____

_____

_____

_____

_____

_____

_____

_____

_____

SECTION 2 (Suggested time allowance: 90 minutes)

Task 2.1

Delcom Ltd has produced three forecasts of activity levels for the next year for product A. The original budget was to produce only 1,000,000 units, but production levels of 1,500,000 units and 2,000,000 units are also feasible.

a) Complete the table below, in order to estimate the production cost per unit of A at the different activity levels.

Units made	1,000,000	1,500,000	2,000,000
Costs:	£	£	£
Variable costs:			
■ direct materials	5,000,000		
■ direct labour	4,600,000		
■ overheads	3,200,000		
Fixed costs:			
■ indirect labour	2,500,000		
■ overheads	6,300,000		
Total cost	21,600,000		
Cost per unit	21.60		

b) Briefly explain how and why the cost per unit of product A change as the level of activity increases.

_____

_____

_____

_____

_____

_____

:) The cost schedule above assumes that all production costs are either variable or fixed.

Briefly explain whether this is realistic. Give ONE example of another way that costs can behave, and provide an example of a type of cost that may behave in this way.

_____

_____

_____

_____

_____

_____

_____

_____

_____

_____

Task 2.2

Products B and C have the following budgeted annual sales and cost information:

Product	B	C
Units made and sold	500,000	750,000
Machine hours required	1,000,000	3,750,000
Sales revenue (£)	5,000,000	9,000,000
Direct materials (£)	1,000,000	2,250,000
Direct labour (£)	1,250,000	2,625,000
Variable overheads (£)	1,500,000	1,500,000

Complete the table below to show the budgeted contribution per unit of B and C sold, and the company's budgeted profit or loss for the year from these two products. Total fixed costs attributable to B and C are budgeted to be £3,450,000.

Product	B	C	Total (£)
Units selling price (£)			
Less unit variable cost			
■ direct materials (£)			
■ direct labour (£)			
■ variable overheads (£)			
Contribution per unit (£)			
Sales volume (units)			
Total contribution (£)			
Less: fixed costs			
Budgeted profit or loss			

Task 2.3

A special exercise has now been carried out to split the £3,450,000 of attributable fixed costs between products B and C. £1,000,000 was found to relate to B and £2,450,000 to C.

The latest sales forecast is that 480,000 units of product B and 910,000 units of product C will be sold during the year.

a) On the basis of this new information you are required to complete the table below to:

    i) calculate the budgeted breakeven sales, in units, for each of the two products;

    ii) calculate the margin of safety (in units) for each of the two products, by comparing the level of sales currently forecast with the breakeven level;

    iii) calculate the margin of safety as a percentage (to two decimal places).

Product	B	C
Fixed costs (£)		
Unit contribution (£)		
Breakeven sales (units)		
Forecast sales (units)		
Margin of safety (units)		
Margin of safety (%)		

b) Explain the meaning of the term 'percentage margin of safety', using your calculations of this figure for products B and C to illustrate your answer.

_____

_____

_____

_____

_____

_____

Task 2.4

Due to unforeseen circumstances the number of available machine hours is now found to be limited to 3,500,000 during the year.

Using the information, and your calculations from Task 2.2, complete the table below to recommend how many units of products B and C should be made in order to maximise the profits or minimise the loss, taking account of the machine hours available.

Product	B	C	Total
Contribution/unit (£)			
Machine hours/unit			
Contribution/machine hr. (£)			
Product ranking			
Machine hours available			
Machine hours allocated to: Product.......... Product..........			
Total contribution earned (£)			
Less: fixed costs (£)			3,450,000
Profit/loss made (£)			

Task 2.5

Delcom is considering introducing a new product, E, for which the following capital expenditure, sales and cost estimates have been produced for its planned three year product life:

	Year 0 £'000	Year 1 £'000	Year 2 £'000	Year 3 £'000
Capital expenditure	1,500			
Other cash flows				
Sales income		700	800	1,000
Operating costs		200	250	300

The company's cost of capital is 12%/

Present value (PV) factors for 12% discount rate are:

	Year 0	Year 1	Year 2	Year 3
PV factor	1.0000	0.8929	0.7972	0.7118

You are required to calculate both the net present value and the payback period for the proposed new product E.

a)   The net present value

	Year 0 £'000	Year 1 £'000	Year 2 £'000	Year 3 £'000
Capital expenditure				
Sales income				
Operating costs				
Net cash flows				
PV factors				
Discounted cash flows				
Net present value				

150

b)   The payback period

_____

_____

_____

_____

_____

_____

_____

Task 2.6

Based on the information given in Task 2.5 and your calculations for this task, write a report to the Management Accountant in which you:

a)   recommend, on the basis of both the net present value and the payback period, whether the proposed new product E should be introduced.

b)   identify ONE other method of investment appraisal which might also have been used to assess this proposal.

c)   identify TWO commercial factors which are also relevant to this decision.

Use the report stationery on the next two pages if necessary.

REPORT

To: **The Management Accountant**   **Subject:**

From: **Date:**

This page is provided for the continuation of your report. It will not be needed by everyone.

PRACTICE EXAM 5
UNIT 6

CHINA LTD

These tasks were set by the AAT in December 2004 (amended).

Time allowed: 3 hours plus 15 minutes' reading time

This examination paper is in TWO sections.

You have to show competence in BOTH sections.

You should therefore attempt and aim to complete EVERY task in EACH section.

You should spend about 90 minutes on each section.

All essential workings should be included within your answers where appropriate.

Both sections are based on China Ltd.

SECTION 1 (Suggested time allowance: 90 minutes)

DATA

China Ltd manufactures and sells pottery made from clay. You work as an Accounting Technician at China Ltd, reporting to the Finance Director.

The company operates an integrated absorption costing system. Stocks are valued on a first in first out (FIFO) basis.

The Finance Director has given you the following tasks.

Task 1.1

The following stock card has been prepared for clay for the month of November.

STOCK CARD

Product: Clay

Date	Receipts Quantity kgs	Receipts Cost per kg £	Receipts Total cost £	Issues Quantity kgs	Issues Cost per kg £	Issues Total cost £	Balance Quantity kgs	Balance Cost per kg £	Balance Total cost £
B/f at 1 Nov							15,000	0.50	7,500
8 Nov	60,000	0.45	27,000				15,000 60,000	0.50 0.45	7,500 27,000 34,500
9 Nov				45,000		21,000	30,000	0.45	13,500
16 Nov	40,000	0.55	22,000				30,000 40,000	0.45 0.55	13,500 22,000 35,500
17 Nov				50,000		24,500	20,000	0.55	11,000

a) Identify the method of valuing issues to production and stocks of materials that has been used to prepare the stock card shown above.

b) How have the following stock valuations for issues to production been calculated?

   i)   9 November – 45,000 kgs valued at £21,000

   ....

   ....

   ....

   ....

   ii) 17 November – 50,000 kgs valued at £24,500

   ....

   ....

   ....

   ....

ADDITIONAL DATA

The company's production budget requires 25,000 kgs of clay to be used each week. The company plans to maintain a buffer stock of clay equivalent to one week's budgeted production. It takes between one and two weeks for delivery of clay from the date the order is placed with the supplier.

Task 1.2

Calculate the reorder level for clay.

....

....

....

ADDITIONAL DATA

During November, gross direct labour costs of £33,000 were incurred as follows:

	£
Net wages	20,500
Income tax deductions	7,400
Employees' national insurance contributions	2,100
Employer's national insurance contributions	3,000

The accounting codes used to record direct labour costs are as follows:

Code number	Description
1000	Work in progress
7000	Income tax payable
7001	National insurance contributions payable
9001	Net wages control account

Task 1.3

Complete the table below to record the direct labour costs for November.

Code	Dr	Cr
	£	£
1000		
7000		
7001		
9001		

ADDITIONAL DATA

The manufacturing department has two production centres and two service centres as follows:

Production centres

- Moulding
- Glazing

Service centres

- Maintenance
- Canteen

The budgeted fixed production overheads for the manufacturing department for November were as follows:

	£
Indirect glazing materials	1,140
Rent and other property overheads	15,000
Power costs	5,040
Indirect staff costs	8,910
Machine depreciation	8,310
Total budgeted fixed overheads	38,400

The following information is also relevant:

	Moulding	Glazing	Maintenance	Canteen
		Centres		
Floor space (sq m)	3,000	1,000	500	500
Power costs	£1,200	£3,290	£250	£300
Indirect staff costs	£1,100	£2,010	£3,800	£2,000
Machine depreciation	£1,710	£6,600		
Number of employees	26	8	4	

Overheads are allocated and apportioned between centres on the most appropriate basis. The total canteen overheads are reapportioned to the other three centres based on the number of employees. Maintenance centre overheads are then reapportioned to the moulding and glazing centres. The maintenance records show that 20% of time is spent in the moulding centre and 80% in the glazing centre.

Task 1.4

Complete the following table showing the allocation and apportionment of fixed overheads between the four centres.

Fixed overheads for November	Total £	Moulding £	Glazing £	Maintenance £	Canteen £
Indirect glazing materials	1,140				
Rent and other property overheads	15,000				
Power costs	5,040				
Indirect staff costs	8,910				
Machine depreciation	8,310				
	38,400				
Canteen					( )
Maintenance				( )	
	38,400				

ADDITIONAL DATA

Moulding centre fixed overheads are absorbed on the basis of direct labour hours. Glazing department fixed overheads are absorbed on the basis of machine hours. The following information relates to the moulding and glazing centres for November:

	Moulding centre	Glazing centre
Budgeted labour hours	4,000	
Budgeted machine hours		6,000
Actual labour hours worked	4,200	
Actual machine hours worked		5,600
Actual fixed overheads	£17,200	£20,850

Task 1.5

a) Calculate the budgeted overhead absorption rate for November for:

i) the moulding centre

....

....

....

....

ii) the glazing centre

....

....

....

....

b) Calculate the under- or over-absorbed production overheads for November, showing clearly whether the overheads are under- or over-absorbed for:

i) the moulding centre

....

....

....

....

ii)   the glazing centre

....

....

....

....

Task 1.6

Explain how an increase in budgeted activity in the moulding and glazing centres would affect the overhead cost to be charged to an individual product.

....

....

....

....

SECTION 2 (Suggested time allowance: 90 minutes)

DATA

China Ltd manufactures and sells three ranges of pottery, Alpha, Beta and Gamma. The following information has been provided by the Finance Director.

Estimates of revenues and costs for January

	Alpha	Beta	Gamma
Sales and production in units	1,000	200	500
Selling price per unit	£50	£120	£80
Direct materials per unit	£10	£24	£16
Direct labour hours per unit – moulding center	2	4	3
Direct labour hours per unit – glazing center	0.5	4	1
Direct labour rate per hour – moulding center	£5	£5	£5
Direct labour rate per hour – glazing center	£6	£6	£6

Direct material and direct labour costs are considered wholly variable. The total expected monthly fixed overheads are £52,000.

Task 2.1

Complete the table below to calculate the total forecast contribution and profit for January.

Product	Alpha £	Beta £	Gamma £	Total £
Sales revenue				
Less: Variable costs				
Direct materials				
Direct labour – moulding				
Direct labour – glazing				
Total contribution				
Fixed overheads				
Profit				

Task 2.2

Calculate the forecast contribution per unit for the Alpha, Beta and Gamma ranges.

....

....

....

....

....

....

ADDITIONAL DATA

The Production Director believes there will be a shortage of direct labour hours in the glazing centre in January. He estimates there will be a maximum availability of 1,400 direct labour hours which includes any overtime working. The maximum unit sales for January of Alpha are 1,000 units, Beta 200 units and Gamma 500 units.

Task 2.3

Calculate the number of units of each product range the company should make and sell to maximise its profits for January.

....

....

....

....

....

....

....

....

....

....

....

....

ADDITIONAL DATA

The Sales Manager believes the company should adopt a policy to only sell the high value Beta range.

Task 2.4

a) If the company only manufactures the Beta range, calculate the number of units it would need to sell each month to break even.

....

....

....

....

....

....

b) Give TWO reasons for NOT recommending this policy.

....

....

....

....

....

....

....

....

....

....

....

....

....

ADDITIONAL DATA

The Board of Directors is considering an investment of £50,000 to buy new machinery for the glazing centre. The Board has been given the following data relating to this purchase:

Payback period	3 years
Internal rate of return	12%
Net present value	£4,800

Task 2.5

Write a memo to the Board of Directors to:

a)   explain the meaning of the terms 'payback', 'internal rate of return' and 'net present value'
b)   explain how these methods are used to assess investment proposals
c)   give a recommendation, together with reasons, on whether to proceed with the investment.

Use the memo on the next page.

MEMO

To: Board of Directors   **Subject:**

From: **Date:**

....
....
....
....
....
....
....
....
....
....
....
....
....
....
....
....
....
....
....
....
....
....
....
....

AAT

SAMPLE SIMULATION
UNIT 6

QUALITY CANDLES LTD

This is the AAT's Sample Simulation for Unit 6. Its purpose is to give you an idea of what an AAT simulation looks like. It is not intended as a definitive guide to the tasks you may be required to perform.

The suggested time allowance for this Assessment is four hours. Up to 30 minutes' extra time may be permitted in an AAT simulation. Breaks in assessment may be allowed in the AAT simulation, but it must normally be completed in one day.

Calculators may be used but no reference material is permitted.

COVERAGE OF PERFORMANCE CRITERIA AND RANGE STATEMENTS

All performance criteria are covered in this simulation.

Element	PC Coverage
6.1	**Record and analyse information relating to direct costs and revenues**
A	Identify direct costs in accordance with the organisation's costing procedures.
B	Record and analyse information relating to direct costs.
C	Calculate direct costs in accordance with the organisation's policies and procedures.
D	Check cost information for stock against usage and stock control practices.
E	Resolve or refer queries to the appropriate person.
6.2	**Record and analyse information relating to the allocation, apportionment and absorption of overhead costs**
A	Identify overhead costs in accordance with the organisation's procedures.
B	Attribute overhead costs to production and service cost centres in accordance with agreed bases of allocation and apportionment.
C	Calculate overhead absorption rates in accordance with agreed bases of absorption.
D	Record and analyse information relating to overhead costs in accordance with the organisation's procedures.
E	Make adjustments for under and over recovered overhead costs in accordance with established procedures.
F	Review methods of allocation, apportionment and absorption at regular intervals in discussions with senior staff, and ensure agreed changes to methods are implemented.
G	Consult staff working in operational departments to resolve any queries in overhead cost data.
6.3	**Prepare and evaluate estimates of costs and revenues**
A	Identify information relevant to estimating current and future revenues and costs.
B	Prepare estimates of future income and costs.
C	Calculate the effects of variations in capacity on product costs.
D	Analyse critical factors affecting costs and revenues using appropriate accounting techniques and draw clear conclusions from the analysis.
E	State any assumptions used when evaluating future costs and revenues.
F	Identify and evaluate options and solutions for their contribution to organisational goals.
G	Present recommendations to appropriate people in a clear and concise way and supported by a clear rationale.

Any missing range statements should be assessed separately.

PART ONE

INSTRUCTIONS

This simulation is designed to let you show your ability to record and evaluate costs and revenues.

The simulation is designed to be attempted in two parts. You are allowed four hours in total to complete your work. You should spend:

- two hours on the tasks in Part 1, covering Elements 6.1 and 6.2;
- two hours on the tasks in Part 2, covering Element 6.3.

The simulation contains a large volume of data which you will need in order to complete the tasks. The information you require is provided in the sequence in which you will need to deal with it. However you are advised to look quickly through all of the material before you begin. This will help you to familiarise yourself with the situation and the information available.

Write your answers in the Answer Booklet provided on pages 187 to 206. If you need more paper for your answers, ask the person in charge.

You should write your answers in blue or black ink, not pencil. You may use correcting fluid, but in moderation. You should cross out your errors neatly and clearly.

Your work must be accurate, so check your work carefully before handing it in.

Coverage of performance criteria and range statements

It is not always possible to cover all performance criteria and range statements in a single simulation. Any performance criteria and range statements not covered must be assessed by other means by the assessor before a candidate can be considered competent.

Performance criteria and range statement coverage for this simulation is shown on page 170.

THE SITUATION

Your name is Bobby Forster and you work as the Accounts Assistant for Quality Candles Limited. The company manufactures candles of all kinds, including hand made candles. The candles are sold to wholesalers, to retailers, and direct to the public through the company's mail order division.

The manufacturing operations

The manufacturing operations involve three production cost centres and two service cost centres.

Production cost centres	Service cost centres
Manufacturing	Stores
Painting and finishing	Maintenance
Packing	

The time period covered by this simulation

The company's year end is 31 December. This simulation is concerned with activities during the quarter ending 31 December 2007, and with planning activities for the year ending 31 December 2008.

THE TASKS TO BE COMPLETED (PART ONE)

Element 6.1 (one hour)

1. Refer to the stores record card on page 189 of the Answer Booklet.

   - Complete this stores record card using the information from the materials documentation on pages 189 and 190 of the Answer Booklet and page 175 of this book. You will need to identify and apply the stock valuation method in use and you are advised that VAT is not entered in the cost accounting records.

   - Show the volume and value of the stock at the close of the week ending 10 October 2007. Any returns from production cost centres to stores are valued at the price of the most recent batch issued from stores.

2. Refer to the materials requisition note and materials returned note on page 190 of the Answer Booklet.

   - Complete the column headed 'Cost office use only' on each of the two documents.

3. Refer to your completed stores record card on page 189 of the Answer Booklet.

   - Prepare a memo for the general manager, drawing attention to any unusual issues concerning the stock levels for this item during the week. Your memo should highlight the issues, point out any possible consequences, and suggest any action that might be taken to prevent the unusual situations occurring. Use the blank memo form on page 191 of the Answer Booklet.

4. Refer to the internal policy document on page 176 of this book and the piecework operation card on page 192 of the Answer Booklet.

   - Complete the piecework operation card using the information provided. You will need to do the following:
     - Calculate the piecework payment for each day.
     - Calculate any bonus payable for the day.
     - Calculate the total wages payable for the day.
     - Complete the analysis of total wages payable for the week.

5. Refer to the piecework operation card on page 192 of the Answer Booklet.

   - Identify any possible discrepancy in the activity data and write a memo to the supervisor, Roy Hart, explaining clearly what you think the discrepancy might be. Use the blank memo form on page 193 of the Answer Booklet.

Element 6.2 (one hour)

6. Refer to the memo on page 177 of this book.

    ■   Perform the production overhead allocation and apportionment exercise using the analysis sheet on page 194 of the Answer Booklet. You will see that the task has already been started in respect of indirect labour. The data that you have gathered is on pages 177 and 178 of this booklet.

7. Refer to the first memo on page 179 of this book.

    ■   Calculate the production overhead absorption rates for 2008. You will need to make use of the following:

    –   The blank working paper on page 195 of the Answer Booklet;

    –   The data on pages 177 and 178 of this booklet;

    –   Your results for the total production department overhead for 2007 on page 194 of the Answer Booklet.

    All absorption rates should be calculated to the nearest penny.

8. Refer to the second memo on page 179 of this book.

    ■   Re-calculate the total production overhead for each production department, reversing the order of apportionment of the service department overheads. Use the working paper on page 196 of the Answer Booklet. You will need to do the following:

    –   Transfer your figures for total department overhead for all five departments from your overhead analysis sheet on page 194 of the Answer Booklet.

    –   Re-apportion the service department overheads, apportioning the stores costs first to the other four departments on the basis of the number of material requisitions. Then re-apportion the total overhead of the maintenance department to the three production departments, on the basis of maintenance hours.

    Perform all calculations to the nearest £000.

9   ■   Review your results from Task 8 and write a memo to the General Manager. In your memo you should:

    –   comment on the effect of the change in method;

    –   explain whether you think it is necessary to instigate a change in the method of re-apportionment of service department costs.

    Use the blank memo form on page 197 of the Answer Booklet.

10. Refer to the memo and the production overhead data on page 180 of this book.

    ■   Complete the journal entry form on page 198 of the Answer Booklet.

    ■   Write a memo to the production manager detailing any queries concerning the data and suggesting possible causes of any discrepancies you have identified. Use the blank memo form on page 199 of the Answer Booklet.

SALES INVOICE
Threadshop Limited
25 Lyme Street, Taunton TA2 4RP

Invoice to:
Quality Candles Limited
2 Norman Lane
Winterbury
RT5 8UT

VAT Registration:	254 1781 26
Date/tax point:	9 October 2007
Invoice numvber:	T543
Your order:	47346

Description of goods/services	Total (£)
Candlewick thread, 200 metre rolls 80 rolls @ £2.38	190.40
Goods total VAT @ 17.5%	190.40 33.32
Total due	223.72

Checked against GRN number:	427
Date received:	9 October 2007
Signed:	J Jones

Terms: net 30 days

INTERNAL POLICY DOCUMENT

Document no: 18
Subject: Wages
Issued: August 2007

Piecework scheme

A piecework scheme is to be introduced into the manufacturing department in order to reward efficient and productive operatives.

A piecework rate per batch of £0.50 will be paid for each batch of accepted output produced during a day.

In addition a bonus will be paid of 4 per cent of the piecework payment for any day on which the number of batches rejected by Quality Control is less than 5 per cent of the total number of batches produced.

A guaranteed daily wage of £50 is payable if the piecework payment + bonus amounts to less than £50 in any day.

Analysis of wages

Piecework payments and guaranteed daily wages paid will be treated as direct wages costs.

Bonus payments will be treated as indirect wages costs.

Discrepancies on piecework operation cards

The company wishes to pay wages and report labour rates promptly. Therefore employees will initially be paid for the total wages calculated according to the data contained on the weekly piecework operation card.

Any discrepancies on operation cards will be referred to the supervisor. Any alterations to wages will be agreed with the employee before adjustment is made to the next wage payment.

INTERNAL MEMO

To: Bobby Forster, Accounts Assistant
From: General Manager
Subject: Budgeted production costs for 2008
Date: 28 October 2007

As you know we have begun our budgetary planning exercise for 2008.

I understand that you have been working on the analysis of budgeted production costs. Could you please pull together all the information you have gathered and carry out the allocation and apportionment exercise for production overhead costs for 2008.

Thanks. Then we will have the necessary information that we need to calculate the pre-determined overhead absorption rates for 2008.

Data for production overhead analysis for 2008

1.   Summary of budgeted production costs for 2008

	£000
Direct materials	200
Indirect materials	40
Direct labour	420
Indirect labour:	
Manufacturing department	22
Painting and finishing department	14
Packing department	11
Stores	35
Maintenance	16
Rent and rates	105
Protective clothing	31
Power	40
Insurance	24
Heat and light	35
Depreciation	48
Other production overheads	15
Total budgeted production costs	1,056

2.   **Other data**

	Manufact-uring	Painting/finishing	Packing	Stores	Mainten-ance
Direct materials cost (£000)	150	25	25	–	–
Floor area (000 sq metres)	30	10	16	8	6
Power usage (%)	50	10	30	5	5
Net book value of equipment (£000)	220	80	120	40	20
Maintenance hours (000)	7	4	3	1	–
Materials requisitions (000)	18	10	9	–	11
Direct labour hours (000)	20	28	10	–	–
Machine hours (000)	200	14	90	–	–

3.   **Company procedures for the allocation and apportionment of production overheads**

- 30 per cent of the total indirect materials cost is apportioned to stores and 30 per cent to maintenance. The remaining 40 per cent is apportioned to the production departments according to the direct materials cost.

- Rent and rates and heating and lighting costs are apportioned according to the floor area occupied by each department.

- The cost of protective clothing is allocated to the manufacturing department.

- Power costs are apportioned according to the power usage in each department.

- Insurance and depreciation costs are apportioned according to the net book value of equipment in each department.

- Other production overheads are apportioned equally to the production departments.

- The total cost of the maintenance department is apportioned to the other four departments according to the number of maintenance hours.

- After a charge has been received from the maintenance department, the total cost of the stores department is apportioned to the three production departments according to the number of material requisitions.

- All calculations are rounded to the nearest £000.

INTERNAL MEMO

To: Bobby Forster, Accounts Assistant
From: General Manager
Subject: Pre-determined overhead absorption rates
Date: 28 October 2007

Many thanks for all your hard work on the overhead analysis.

Could you please now use the results of your analysis to calculate overhead absorption rates for the three production departments for 2008. We have decided that the most appropriate bases of absorption will be as follows:

- Manufacturing department: machine hour rate;

- Painting and finishing department: labour hour rate;

- Packing department: machine hour rate.

Thanks for your help.

INTERNAL MEMO

To: Bobby Forster, Accounts Assistant
From: General Manager
Subject: Re-apportionment of service department costs
Date: 4 November 2007

I have been giving some thought to the method that we use to re-apportion the service department costs to the production departments.

As you know, at present it is our policy to apportion the maintenance costs to all cost centres before we re-apportion the total stores costs to the production cost centres.

I would like to see the effect of altering the order of re-apportionment of service department costs. Could you please rework the figures so that we can review the results?

Let me have the results and your views as soon as possible, please.

INTERNAL MEMO

To: Bobby Forster, Accounts Assistant
From: General Manager
Subject: Overhead absorption for October 2007
Date: 8 November 2007

___

As you know it is company policy to accumulate the under or over-absorbed production overhead each month in an account maintained for this purpose.

The production overhead data for October 2007 has now been finalised.

Could you please complete the journal entry for the absorption of production overhead into the work in progress accounts and transfer any under or over absorption for the month. Complete the entries using the data provided, but please let the production manager know if you have any queries concerning the data.

Summary of production overhead data for October 2007

	£
Actual production overhead incurred	15,800
Production overhead to be absorbed into work in progress	
Manufacturing department	18,500
Painting and finishing department	7,400
Packing department	8,300

PART TWO

INSTRUCTIONS

This simulation is designed to let you show your ability to record and evaluate costs and revenues.

The simulation is designed to be attempted in two parts. You should already have completed the tasks in Part 1 and you should ensure that you have your answers to those tasks with you.

You are allowed four hours in total to complete your work.

- Two hours for the tasks in Part 1, covering Elements 6.1 and 6.2;

- Two hours for the tasks in Part 2, covering Element 6.3.

The simulation contains a large volume of data which you will need in order to complete the tasks. The information you require is provided in the sequence in which you will need to deal with it. However you are advised to look quickly through all of the material before you begin. This will help you to familiarise yourself with the situation and the information available.

Write your answers in the Answer Booklet provided on pages 187 to 206. If you need more paper for your answers, ask the person in charge.

You should write your answers in blue or black ink, not pencil.

You may use correcting fluid, but in moderation. You should cross out your errors neatly and clearly.

Your work must be accurate, so check your work carefully before handing it in.

THE SITUATION

Your name is Bobby Forster and you work as the Accounts Assistant for Quality Candles Limited. The company manufactures candles of all kinds, including hand made candles. The candles are sold to wholesalers, to retailers, and direct to the public through the company's mail order division.

The manufacturing operations

The manufacturing operations involve three production cost centres and two service cost centres.

Production cost centres	Service cost centres
Manufacturing	Stores
Painting and finishing	Maintenance
Packing	

The time period covered by this simulation

The company's year end is 31 December. This simulation is concerned with activities during the quarter ending 31 December 2007, and with planning activities for the year ending 31 December 2008.

THE TASKS TO BE COMPLETED (PART TWO)

Element 6.3 (two hours)

1. Refer to the memo on page 184 of this book and prepare the necessary information in response to the general manager's query. You will need to do the following.

- Use the data on page 184 of this book and the working paper on page 200 of the Answer Booklet to identify the cost and revenue behaviour patterns to be used in your projections.

- Use your identified cost and revenue behaviour patterns to complete the planned profit projection on page 201 of the Answer Booklet. There is space for your workings at the bottom of that page.

2. Refer to the first memo on page 185 of this book and answer the General Manager's queries. You will need to do the following.

(i) Use your identified cost and revenue behaviour patterns, adjusted for the change in materials cost, to prepare a revised planned profit statement for December. Complete the profit statement on page 202 of the Answer Booklet. There is space for your workings at the bottom of that page.

(ii) Calculate the breakeven point in terms of the number of cases to be sold in December if the bulk discount is accepted. Use the blank working paper on page 203 of the Answer Booklet and round your answer up to the nearest number of whole cases. Also use the same working paper to calculate the margin of safety. Express your answer as a percentage of the increased planned activity for December.

(iii) Prepare a memo to the general manager evaluating the results of your calculations. Your memo should contain the following:

- Your comments on the resulting profit, breakeven point and margin of safety;
- A statement of any assumptions you have used in evaluating the proposal.

Use the blank memo form on page 204 of the Answer Booklet.

3. Refer to the second memo on page 185 of this book and do the following:

(i) Use the working paper on page 205 of the Answer Booklet to calculate the payback period and the net present value of the proposed investment. Ignore inflation and perform all monetary calculations to the nearest £.

(ii) Write a memo to the General Manager evaluating the proposal from a financial viewpoint and stating any assumptions you have made in your analysis. Use the blank memo form on page 206 of the Answer Booklet.

```
┌──────────────────────────────────────────────────────────────────────────┐
│                            INTERNAL MEMO                                   │
│                                                                            │
│   To:        Bobby Forster, Accounts Assistant                             │
│   From:      General Manager                                               │
│   Subject:   Mail order division: revised plan for December 2007           │
│   Date:      9 November 2007                                               │
│  ──────────────────────────────────────────────────────────────────────   │
│                                                                            │
│   Could you please prepare the revised cost and revenue plan for the mail  │
│   order division for December.                                             │
│                                                                            │
│   The plan is to sell 6,800 cases of candles and we will base our          │
│   projections on the cost and revenue behaviour patterns experienced       │
│   during August to October.                                                │
│                                                                            │
│   Thanks for your help.                                                    │
│                                                                            │
└──────────────────────────────────────────────────────────────────────────┘
```

Quality Candles Limited: mail order division

Actual results for August to October 2007

	August	September	October
Number of cases sold	7,000	6,200	5,900
	£	£	£
Candles cost	9,100	8,060	7,670
Packing materials cost	5,250	4,650	4,425
Packing labour cost	2,100	1,860	1,770
Packing overhead cost	5,400	5,240	5,180
Other overhead cost	2,500	*3,000	2,500
Total costs	24,350	22,810	21,545
Sales revenue	28,000	24,800	23,600
Profit	3,650	1,990	2,055

* Other overhead cost was £500 higher than usual during September owing to an unexpected machine breakdown which necessitated the hire of a packing machine to maintain production. This event will not recur in the future.

INTERNAL MEMO

To: Bobby Forster, Accounts Assistant
From: General Manager
Subject: Mail order division: bulk discounts for December 2007
Date: 10 November 2007

Many thanks for your splendid work on the cost and revenue projections for December.

We are looking for opportunities to increase profit and we have just heard that we can obtain a bulk discount for packing materials in December if we increase our activity level to 7,600 cases for the month. This will mean that packing material unit costs will reduce by 20 per cent.

Could you please recalculate the profit projection for December if we decide to increase activity to take advantage of the discount.

Also, please calculate the breakeven point in terms of the number of cases to be sold in December if we make this change. I would also like to have a note of the margin of safety we will have.

Please let me have the results of your calculations and your comments on the outcome as soon as you can.

INTERNAL MEMO

To: Bobby Forster, Accounts Assistant
From: General Manager
Subject: Purchase of delivery vehicles for mail order division
Date: 12 November 2007

We are considering the purchase and operation of our own fleet of delivery vehicles at the end of this year.

The distribution manager informs me that we will be able to cancel our current delivery contract and as a result we will enjoy cash savings of £34,800 each year from 2007 onwards, after taking account of the vehicle operating costs.

The vehicles will cost us £90,000 and will have a resale value of £5,000 when they are sold at the end of 2010.

Can you please appraise this proposal from a financial viewpoint? I need to know the payback period and the net present value at our usual discount rate of 12 per cent. As you know our minimum required payback period for all capital projects is three years.

Please let me have the results as soon as possible.

AAT SAMPLE SIMULATION
UNIT 6

QUALITY CANDLES LTD

ANSWER BOOKLET

ANSWER BOOKLET

PART 1

STORES RECORD CARD

Materials description: Candlewick thread, 200 metre rolls
Code no: CW728

Maximum quantity: 400
Minimum quantity: 140
Reorder level: 230
Reorder Quantity: 80

Date	Receipts Document number	Qty	Price per roll (£)	Total (£)	Issues Document number	Qty	Price per (£)	Total (£)	Stock balance Qty	Price per roll (£)	Total (£)
1 Oct									28	2.20	61.60
									26	2.30	59.80
									54		121.40
3 Oct					249	26	2.30	59.50			
						4	2.20	8.80			
						30		68.80	24	2.20	52.80
6 Oct	419	80	235	188.00					24	2.20	52.80
									80	2.35	188.00
									104		240.80

Tasks 1 and 2

MATERIALS REQUISITION

Department: Manufacturing

Document no: 252

Date: 08/10/2007

Code no	Description	Quantity	Cost office use only Value of issue (£)
CW728	Candlewick thread 200m rolls	40	

Received by: .... **Signature:** ....

MATERIALS RETURNED

Department: Manufacturing

Document no: 75

Date: 10/10/2007

Code no	Description	Quantity	Cost office use only Value of issue (£)
CW728	Candlewick thread 200m rolls	3	

Received by: .... **Signature:** ....

Task 3

MEMO

To:
From:
Subject:
Date:

Task 4

QUALITY CANDLES LIMITED
PIECEWORK OPERATION CARD

Operative name   Mary Roberts   Department: Manufacturing

Clock number   R27

Week beginning   6 October 2007

Activity	Monday	Tuesday	Wednesday	Thursday	Friday
Batches produced	120	102	34	202	115
Batches rejected	5	7	4	11	5
Batches accepted					
Rate per batch	£ 0.50	£ 0.50	£ 0.50	£ 0.50	£ 0.50
Piecework payment	£	£	£	£	£
Bonus payable	£	£	£	£	£
Total payable for day*	£	£	£	£	£

Total wages payable for week:
     £

Direct wages

Indirect wages

Total wages

* Guaranteed daily wage of £50 is payable if piecework payment plus bonus amounts less than £50

Supervisor's signature: *A Peters*

Task 5

INTERNAL MEMO

To:
From:
Subject:
Date:

Task 6

Production overhead analysis sheet for 2008

Production overhead item	Total £000	Manufacturing £000	Painting/ finishing £000	Packing £000	Stores £000	Maintenance £000
Indirect labour	98	22	14	11	35	16
Total department overheads						
Apportion maintenance total	–					( )
Apportion stores total	–				( )	
Total production dept overheads						

Task 7

Working paper

Calculation of production overhead absorption rates for 2008

Manufacturing department

Painting and finishing department

Packing department

Task 8

Sample calculations: working paper
Reversing the order of service department re-apportionments

Production overhead item	Total £000	Manufacturing £000	Painting/ finishing £000	Packing £000	Stores £000	Maintenance £000
Total department overheads (from task 6)						
Apportion stores total	–				( )	
Apportion maintenance total	–				–	( )
Total production dept overheads						

Task 9

INTERNAL MEMO

To:
From:
Subject:
Date:

_____

_____

_____

_____

_____

_____

_____

_____

_____

_____

_____

_____

_____

_____

_____

_____

_____

_____

_____

_____

_____

_____

_____

_____

_____

_____

_____

_____

_____

_____

Task 10

Journal entry for production overheads

October 2007

Entries for overhead absorbed during the month

	Debit (£)	Credit(£)
Work in progress: manufacturing dept		
Work in progress: painting and finishing dept		
Work in progress: packing dept		
Production overhead control		

Entries for overhead under-/over-absorbed during the month

	Debit (£)	Credit(£)
Overhead over-/under-absorbed (P+L)		
Production overhead control		

Task 10 (continued)

INTERNAL MEMO

To:
From:
Subject:
Date:

PART 2

Task 11

Workings for determination of revenue and cost behaviour patterns

---

Sales revenue

Candles cost

Packing materials cost

Packing labour cost

Packing overhead cost

Other overhead cost

Task 11 (continued)

Quality Candles Limited: mail order division

Planned results for December 2007

December

Number of cases to be sold

£

Candles cost

Packing materials cost

Packing labour cost

Packing overhead cost

Other overhead cost

Total costs

Sales revenue

Profit

Space for workings

Task 12 (i)

Quality Candles Limited: mail order division

Planned results for December 2007: increased activity

	December
Number of cases to be sold	7,600
	£
Candles cost	
Packing materials cost	
Packing labour cost	
Packing overhead cost	
Other overhead cost	
Total costs	
Sales revenue	
Profit	

Space for workings

Task 12 (ii)

Quality Candles Limited: mail order division

Planned results for December 2007: increased activity

Calculation of breakeven point and margin of safety: working paper

_____

_____

_____

_____

_____

_____

_____

_____

_____

_____

_____

_____

_____

_____

_____

_____

_____

_____

_____

_____

_____

_____

_____

_____

_____

_____

_____

Task 12 (iii)

INTERNAL MEMO

To:
From:
Subject:
Date:

Task 13 (i)

Working paper for the financial appraisal of purchase of delivery vehicles

Year	Cashflow £	Discount factor @ 12%	Present value £
2007	_____	1.000	_____
2008	_____	0.8929	_____
2009	_____	0.7972	_____
2010	_____	0.7118	_____
2011	_____	0.6355	_____

Net present value   _____

Working space for calculation of payback period

Task 13 (ii)

INTERNAL MEMO

To:
From:
Subject:
Date:

AAT

PRACTICE SIMULATION
UNIT 6

HIGH HEAT LTD

COVERAGE OF PERFORMANCE CRITERIA AND RANGE STATEMENTS

All performance criteria are covered in this simulation.

Element	PC Coverage

6.1   **Record and analyse information relating to direct costs and revenues**

A   Identify direct costs in accordance with the organisation's costing procedures.

B   Record and analyse information relating to direct costs.

C   Calculate direct costs in accordance with the organisation's policies and procedures.

D   Check cost information for stock against usage and stock control practices.

E   Resolve or refer queries to the appropriate person.

6.2   **Record and analyse information relating to the allocation, apportionment and absorption of overhead costs**

A   Identify overhead costs in accordance with the organisation's procedures.

B   Attribute overhead costs to production and service cost centres in accordance with agreed bases of allocation and apportionment.

C   Calculate overhead absorption rates in accordance with agreed bases of absorption.

D   Record and analyse information relating to overhead costs in accordance with the organisation's procedures.

E   Make adjustments for under and over recovered overhead costs in accordance with established procedures.

F   Review methods of allocation, apportionment and absorption at regular intervals in discussions with senior staff, and ensure agreed changes to methods are implemented.

G   Consult staff working in operational departments to resolve any queries in overhead cost data.

6.3   **Prepare and evaluate estimates of costs and revenues**

A   Identify information relevant to estimating current and future revenues and costs.

B   Prepare estimates of future income and costs.

C   Calculate the effects of variations in capacity on product costs.

D   Analyse critical factors affecting costs and revenues using appropriate accounting techniques and draw clear conclusions from the analysis.

E   State any assumptions used when evaluating future costs and revenues.

F   Identify and evaluate options and solutions for their contribution to organisational goals.

G   Present recommendations to appropriate people in a clear and concise way and supported by a clear rationale.

Any missing range statements should be assessed separately.

DATA AND TASKS

This simulation is designed to let you show your ability to record and evaluate costs and revenues.

This simulation is divided into 13 tasks. You are advised to look through the whole simulation first to gain a general appreciation of your tasks.

The situation is provided below. The tasks to be completed are set out on pages 210 to 213.

Your answers should be set out in the Answer Booklet using the documents and working papers provided. You may require additional pages.

You are allowed a total of **four hours** to complete your work.

A high level of accuracy is required. Check your work carefully.

Correcting fluid may be used, but it should be used in moderation. Errors should be crossed out neatly and clearly. You should write in blue or black ink, not pencil.

THE SITUATION

You work as the Management Accounts Assistant for High Heat Limited. The company manufactures oven ranges for use in restaurants and other mass catering establishments. It employs about 75 people at its factory in Andover.

Cost centres

The production cost centres in High Heat Limited are a Machine Shop (incorporating raw materials stores) and an Assembly Shop.

The company also operates two service cost centres: a Testing Centre and a Staff Amenity Centre (including a canteen and a small gym).

The people involved in this simulation

Yourself	Management Accounts Assistant
Malcolm Harrison	Machine Shop Manager
Lynn Tilling	Assembly Shop Manager
Pamela Robinson	Purchasing Clerk
Karim Huq	Purchasing Manager
Ismay Ratliff	Production Director

The time period covered by this simulation

In this simulation you will be dealing with transactions and activities that occur in October and November 2007. You will also be preparing budget and forecast data for 2008 and evaluating information that relates to a four year planning horizon. At the end of this period of time the company plans to be operating from three sites, providing other types of kitchen appliance and consultancy services in addition to its current products. You perform the first task on 2 November 2007.

THE TASKS TO BE COMPLETED

PART ONE – Record and analyse information relating to direct costs and revenues

Task 1

Refer to the extract of accounting information on page 214 of this booklet in relation to the production and sale of the Oven 900 model.

You are required to calculate the contribution to fixed costs made by the Oven 900 line in October on page 229 of the Answer Booklet.

Task 2

Refer to the stock record (stock card) for hi-grade filters on page 230 of the Answer Booklet and the documentation relating to receipts and issues of this part to the Assembly Shop on pages 214 to 216 of this booklet.

You are required to complete the stock record as far as the information available will allow, showing clearly the month end balance in units and value. Note that all issues are currently priced using the FIFO stock valuation method.

Task 3

You are required to:

a)   check whether the company's stock control practices have been followed correctly for hi-grade filters during October

b)   draft a memo to the Production Director, Ismay Ratliff, setting out your conclusions about stock control and purchasing practice, and suggesting actions which may address any problems. Use the memo form on page 231 of the Answer Booklet.

Task 4

You are required to:

a)   refer to the memo about stock valuation from the Production Director, Ismay Ratliff, on page 217 of this booklet

b)   complete the stock records on page 233 of the Answer Booklet using the AVCO method

c)   draft a memo in reply to her queries on page 232 of the Answer Booklet

Task 5

Refer to the Time Sheets for Sanjeev Patel and Jacob Ellis on page 234 and 235 of the Answer Booklet and the extract from the Payroll Guide on page 218 of this booklet.

You are required to:

a)   complete the total columns on the time sheets
b)   complete the analysis of hours sections of the time sheets
c)   complete the analysis of gross pay sections of the time sheets.

Task 6

Draft a memo to Malcolm Harrison, the Machine Shop Manager, setting out any discrepancies in Jacob Ellis's time sheet and asking for help in identifying the reason for it. Use the blank memo form on page 236 of the Answer Booklet.

PART TWO – Record and analyse information relating to the allocation, apportionment and absorption of overhead costs

Task 7

Refer to the memo about production overhead absorption rates for 2008 from Ismay Ratliff, the Production Director, dated 5 November on page 217 of this booklet.

On page 237 of the Answer Booklet complete the calculation of under-/over-absorption of production overheads, and indicate clearly whether the under-/over-absorbed amount is to be debited or credited in the profit and loss account.

Task 8

Refer to the memo about production overhead absorption rates for 2008 from Ismay Ratliff, the Production Director dated 12 November on page 219 of this booklet and the data on page 220 of this booklet.

You are required to:

a) at the top of the memo on page 238 of the Answer Booklet, calculate a single factory-wide production overhead absorption rate per direct labour hour for 2008

b) complete the memo to the Production Director, explaining why the change in absorption methods would be a good idea

Task 9

Refer to the memo about production overhead absorption rates for 2008 from Ismay Ratliff, the Production Director, dated 19 November on page 221 of this booklet.

You are required to using the overhead analysis sheets on pages 239 and 240 of the Answer Booklet, calculate the production overhead absorption rates (to two decimal places) as requested, using first the step down method and then the direct method for apportioning primary allocations to the production areas.

PART THREE – Prepare and evaluate estimates of costs and revenues

Task 10

Refer to the memo about new sites and products from Ismay Ratliff, the Production Director, dated 25 November on page 222 of this booklet.

You are required to:

a) on page 241 of the Answer Booklet, calculate the payback period and the net present value of the project

b) on page 242 of the Answer Booklet, prepare a memo to the Production Director by detailing your results and commenting on the proposal. State any assumptions that you have made in your calculations.

Task 11

Refer to the memo about producing large size dishwashers from Ismay Ratliff, the Production Director, dated 27 November on page 223 of this booklet. Refer also to the data on page 223 of this booklet concerning the proposal.

You are required to:

a)   on page 243 of the Answer Booklet, use the information concerning selling prices to determine the projected sales volume for the large-size dishwashers

b)   on page 243 of the Answer Booklet, use the unit cost estimates to analyse the dishwashers's cost behaviour patterns and to determine the projected costs for your calculated sales volume

c)   complete the projected costs and revenues statement on page 244 of the Answer Booklet

Task 12

Refer to the memo about further analysis of the dishwasher product from Ismay Ratliff, the Production Director, dated 29 November on page 224 of this booklet.

You are required to:

a)   on page 245 of the Answer Booklet, carry out the calculations requested by the Production Director in relation to further analysis of the dishwasher. Calculate all figures to the nearest whole number

b)   prepare a memo to the Production Director detailing your results and commenting on the proposal. You should also explain any assumptions that you have made in your calculations concerning the proposals. Use the blank memo form on page 246 of the Answer Booklet.

Task 13

Refer to the memo about new products at the new sites from Ismay Ratliff, the Production Director, dated 30 November on page 225 of this booklet.

You are required to on page 247 of the Answer Booklet, carry out the calculations requested by the Production Director in relation to the two new products. Calculate all figures to the nearest whole number.

Oven 900 – extract of accounting information

Ledger account balances as at 31 October 2007

Ledger code	Account name	£	Debit or credit
S900	Sales Oven 900	78,530	Credit
M901	Material 1 issued to Oven 900 production	10,540	Debit
M902	Material 2 issued to Oven 900 production	5,960	Debit
M903	Material 3 issued to Oven 900 production	15,635	Debit
L900	Gross wages of direct labour on Oven 900 production	24,680	Debit
L901	Employer's NIC and pension on Oven 900 production	3,520	Debit
V900	Expenses of Oven 900 production	1,970	Debit

Stock of Oven 900s (at marginal cost)

	£
As at 1 October 2007	13,850
As at 31 October 2007	16,830

PURCHASE ORDER

HIGH HEAT LTD
Grundell Trading Estate,
Andover,
Hants SO9 7DF

Order number: 8094802

Date: 10 October 2007

Order placed by: Pamela Robinson

To: Power Filters
Wallop Industrial Estate
Andover

Order checked by: Karim Huq

Quantity	Ref. no.	Description	Unit price £	Total value £
75	FF783	Hi-grade filters	16.70	1,252.50

VAT at 17.5% is to be added where applicable. Price includes delivery to above address.

PURCHASE ORDER

HIGH HEAT LTD
Grundell Trading Estate,
Andover,
Hants SO9 7DF

Order number: 8097506

Date: 27 October 2007

Order placed by: Pamela Robinson

To: Power Filters
Wallop Industrial Estate
Andover

Order checked by:

Quantity	Ref. no.	Description	Unit price £	Total value £
80	FF783	Hi-grade filters	17.10	1,368.00

VAT at 17.5% is to be added where applicable. Price includes delivery to above address.

GOODS RECEIVED NOTE

HIGH HEAT LIMITD

Number: 05791283
Order ref: 8094802   **Date:** 12 October 2007

Supplier: Power Filters

Quantity	Material code number	Description
75	FF783	Hi-grade filters

Received and checked by: Malcolm Harrison

GOODS RECEIVED NOTE

HIGH HEAT LIMITD

Number: 05792004
Order ref: 8097506

Supplier: Power Filters

Date: 29 October 2007

Quantity	Material code number	Description
80	FF783	Hi-grade filters

MATERIALS REQUISITION

Area: Assembly Shop   **Requisition number:** 165745   **Date:** 15 October 2007

Quantity	Code number	Description	Notes
60	FF783	Hi-grade filters	

Manager signature *Lynn Tilling*

MATERIALS REQUISITION

Area: Assembly Shop   **Requisition number:** 166102   **Date:** 31 October 2007

Quantity	Code number	Description	Notes
90	FF783	Hi-grade filters	

Manager signature *Lynn Tilling*

MEMORANDUM

To: Management Accounts Assistant
From: Ismay Ratliff, Production Director
Subject: Stock valuation October 2006
Date: 3 November 2007

Raw materials stock valuation

The company auditors have been talking to me about alternative methods of identifying the costs of raw materials that we use in our production. They have suggested we look at the Average Cost method (AVCO).

Please prepare example stock records for hi-grade filters for October 2007, using this alternative, so I can assess the impact of the Average Cost methods on valuation.

Part-finished goods valuation

We have also discussed the valuation of part-finished goods in our year-end accounts. Usually we aim to complete all items in the factory as at the year-end, 31 December, in advance of our two-week closure for Christmas and New Year. This year, however, I anticipate that we will have 40 Oven 678s in the Assembly Shop, 100% complete as to materials and machining but only 60% complete as to labour. The costs of a single Oven 678 are as follows:

	£
Materials	565.00
Labour	890.00
Expenses (variable overheads absorbed on machine hour basis)	200.00
	1,655.00

Please calculate the value for part-finished goods that we should show in our accounts.

Finished goods valuation

We have always valued finished goods at their marginal cost of production in the year-end financial accounts, although we use full absorption for management accounting purposes. The auditors have suggested that we should consider moving to a full absorption basis in the financial accounts as well. Please give me your views as to whether this is likely to increase or decrease the value of finished goods stock, and the effect this will have on profit.

HIGH HEAT LTD

Date   1 January 2007   **For year to:** 31 December 2007
Subject: Wages payments
Labour rates: Factory employees

Employee grade	£ per basic hour
A	10.00
B	8.50
C	7.00

All full-time employees are contracted to work 7.5 hours per day for a five day week. All employees get 5 weeks annual leave, plus bank holidays.

All authorised holiday, sick and training time is paid at the employee's basic hourly rate.

Any hours worked in excess of the full-time equivalent of 7.5 per day, as indicated on the authorised Time Sheet, are to be paid as overtime at a rate of time and a half.

Productivity bonuses may be paid at the discretion of Managers, countersigned by the relevant manager on the Time Sheet. Productivity bonuses are expressed in hours and paid at double time.

Analysis of wages

The following are to be treated as direct labour costs:

- payment for time spent on direct tasks
- the basic pay for overtime hours spent on direct tasks

The following are to be treated as indirect labour costs:

- overtime premium payments
- bonus payments
- idle time payments
- holiday pay
- sick pay
- payment for time spent on training

Discrepancies on Time Sheets

Employees will initially be paid for the hours attendance shown at the bottom of their Time Sheet at their basic rate.

Employees know that it is a serious matter if a Time Sheet is submitted to payroll without due authorization and/or which is incorrect. For this reason, overtime rates and all bonus hours will not be paid if the Time Sheet contains a discrepancy. If it has not been authorized no payment can be made until it is so authorised.

MEMORANDUM

To: Management Accounts Assistant
From: Ismay Ratliff, Production Director
Subject: Absorption of production overheads for October 2007
Date: 5 November 2007

I would like you to complete the calculations for absorption of production overheads for October 2006. Here are the data you need:

- Actual production overhead expenditure   £68,750
- Total number of machine hours   4,590
- Absorption rate used for 2007   £13 per machine hour

Under or over-absorbed production overhead is written off to the profit and loss account each month.

Please let me know if you have any queries concerning the data.

MEMORANDUM

To: Management Accounts Assistant
From: Ismay Ratliff, Production Director
Subject: Production overhead absorption rates for 2008
Date: 12 November 2007

We need to get on with calculating the production overhead absorption rate for next year's budget.

As you know we currently use one absorption rate per machine hour for both production departments. I would like you to calculate this single rate for next year and include it in a memo to me.

In our monthly management meeting, the Assembly Shop Manager Lynn Tilling suggested that we should use a separate absorption rate for each of the two production departments: a machine hour rate in the Machine Shop and a direct labour hour rate in the Assembly Shop. I'm afraid to say I am not too sure what this means. In a memo, can you please explain what she meant: why should we change our absorption methods and why are the rates suggested by Ms Tilling likely to be the best in our circumstances?

Thanks for your help.

BUDGETED DATA FOR 2007

1) Budgeted production costs

	£	£
Direct production materials	2,163,000	
Direct labour	1,625,800	
Total budgeted direct cost		3,788,800
Budgeted production overheads:		
Indirect labour: production departments	406,600	
Managers' salaries		
Machine Shop	41,000	
Assembly Shop	41,000	
Testing Centre costs	124,800	
Staff Amenity Centre costs	70,500	
Machinery & equipment depreciation	25,200	
Rent, rates and power costs	101,300	
Other production overheads	44,600	
Total budgeted production overheads		855,000
Total budgeted production cost		4,643,800

2) Other budget data

	Machine shop	Assembly shop	Testing Centre	Staff Amenity Centre	Total
Direct employees	25	40			65
Indirect employees (production)	1	1	6	3	11
Machine hours	41,500	11,100			52,600
Direct labour hours	35,100	85,900			121,000
Testing Centre hours			10,800		
Fixed assets: net book value	85,400	19,500	15,000	6,100	126,000
Floor area (m²)	1,800	3,000	840	360	6,000

MEMORANDUM

To: Management Accounts Assistant
From: Ismay Ratliff, Production Director
Subject: Production overhead absorption rates for 2008
Date: 19 November 2007

Thank you for explaining why we should change our method of overhead absorption.

Please go ahead and calculate the two separate new production overhead absorption rates for 2008, using the following data as well as what you already have.

Bases of allocation and apportionment of production overhead under the new absorption methods

- Rent, rates and power costs are to be apportioned according to the floor area occupied by each cost centre.

- Other production overheads are to be apportioned equally to the two production cost centres.

- Primary cost allocations should be apportioned to production departments using the step down method.

- Testing Centre costs are to be allocated on the basis of 25% machine shop, 75% assembly shop

- Staff Amenity Centre costs are to be apportioned according to the total number of direct and indirect employees in each area.

- Machinery and equipment depreciation will be allocated on the basis of net book value.

Alternative basis

As a matter of interest, I would like to know what difference would be made to the rates if we used the direct method of apportionment of primary allocated costs instead of the step down method. Please make these calculations as well therefore, applying the following rules:

- Testing Centre costs are to be allocated on the basis of 25% machine shop, 75% assembly shop

- Staff Amenity Centre costs are to be apportioned according to the total number of direct and indirect employees in each area.

MEMORANDUM

To: Management Accounts Assistant
From: Ismay Ratliff, Production Director
Subject: New sites and products
Date: 25 November 2007

HIGHLY CONFIDENTIAL

We are considering opening two new factories, one in Scotland and one in Wales. We expect that the move will allow us to expand our product and service range considerably.

The company's policy is to evaluate all capital projects over a four year planning horizon, and we need a maximum payback period of three years. Our cost of capital is 6 per cent.

We have forecast the following cash flows for the expansion.

Year	Cash flows £
0	(1,000,000)
1	250,000
2	350,000
3	500,000
4	650,000

Discount factors at 6%: 0.9434 (year 1); 0.8900 (year 2); 0.8396 (year 3); 0.7920 (year 4).

Please could you work out the payback period and the Net Present Value of the expansion, and let me have your evaluation of the proposal as soon as possible?

MEMORANDUM

To: Management Accounts Assistant
From: Ismay Ratliff, Production Director
Subject: Producing large size dishwashers
Date: 27 November 2007

We are currently working on producing a range of industrial dishwashers, to satisfy demand from our existing customer base, from January 2008. We need you to produce some projections of our profit for the first year of the new product's sales.

Our sales staff say they can sell 150 industrial dishwashers next year at a price of £2,300 per machine to our existing customers. However, as we have capacity to produce rather more than that, and want to sell them to our new clients as well as our old ones, we have decided we can price them lower than that. Our sales staff tell us that we can sell 5 more machines for every £75 reduction in price. We have therefore decided to price them at £2,000 per machine.

We have put together cost estimates for production at two different levels of output. Please prepare a profit projection for 2008, assuming that all sales will be made at a selling price of £2,000 per machine.

Large size industrial dishwasher: unit cost estimates for 2008 production

Production volume	150 machines £ per unit	160 machines £ per unit
Direct materials	880.00	880.00
Direct labour	412.00	412.00
Production overheads	364.00	355.00
Other overheads	50.00	46.88
Total cost	1,706.00	1,693.88

MEMORANDUM

To: Management Accounts Assistant
From: Ismay Ratliff, Production Director
Subject: Producing large size dishwashers, and other matters
Date: 29 November 2007

HIGHLY CONFIDENTIAL

Analysis of dishwasher product

Thank you for your work on the profits that we can make on producing and selling dishwashers.

While we are very happy that the range looks like it will be profitable, we are fairly conservative about risk, and are therefore concerned that there should be a margin of safety of at least 25% of projected sales volume.

Please could you do some further calculations to answer the following questions:

- What is the projected margin of safety at the £2,000 selling price?

- What is the P/V ratio (we usually need a ratio of at least 20%)?

- There is a fair amount of uncertainty surrounding the estimate of production overheads because, as you know, we will probably be opening new sites. What is the maximum percentage increase in production overheads that we could incur before the new product begins to incur losses?

Please let me have your answers, and any comments you have about the proposal, in a memo.

MEMORANDUM

To: Management Accounts Assistant
From: Ismay Ratliff, Production Director
Subject: New products at the new sites
Date: 30 November 2007

HIGHLY CONFIDENTIAL

Contracts required by Welsh consultancy

We are planning a new consultancy service from our Welsh site, which will incur fixed costs of £50,000 in the first year. Each contract we take on is projected to make a contribution of £2,000. Please calculate how many contracts a year we need to take on in order to generate the target profit for the service, which is £80,000.

Limiting factor on production of large electric woks in Scotland

We are planning to make large-scale electric woks at our new site in Scotland. We will have 2,000 hours of the required machine time available, and 4,500 hours of the required labour. Each wok requires 14 hours of machine time and 20 hours of labour. Please identify for me the limiting factor on production of woks, and the maximum number of woks that we can produce.

AAT

PRACTICE SIMULATION
UNIT 6

HIGH HEAT LTD

ANSWER BOOKLET

ANSWER BOOKLET

Task 1

Oven 900 – contribution to fixed costs for October 2007

	£	£
Sales		
Less: cost of sales	_____	
		_____
Contribution to fixed costs		═══════════

Task 2

STOCK RECORD (STOCK CARD)

Part description: Hi-grade filters
Code: FF783
Maximum purchase price: £17.00

Maximum quantity: 100
Minimum quantity: 20
Reorder level: 50
Reorder quantity: 75

	Receipts			Issues			Balance		
Date	Quantity	Price £	Total £	Quantity	Price £	Total £	Quantity	Price £	Total £
1 Oct							20	16.30	326.00
2 Oct	75	16.50	1,237.50				20	16.30	326.00
							75	16.50	1,237.50
							95		1,563.50
8 Oct				20	16.30	326.00			
				30	16.50	495.00			
				50		821.00	45		742.50

Task 3

MEMORANDUM

To: Production Director
From: Management Accounts Assistant
Subject: Stock of hi-grade filters, October 2007
Date: 5 November 2007

Task 4

MEMORANDUM

To: Production Director
From: Management Accounts Assistant
Subject: Stock valuation October 2007
Date: 3 November 2007

Raw materials stock valuation

Part-finished goods valuation

Finished goods valuation

STOCK RECORD

Part description: Hi-grade filters
Code: FF783
Valuation basis: AVCO

Date	Receipts			Issues			Balance		
	Quantity	Price £	Total £	Quantity	Price £	Total £	Quantity	Price £	Total £
1 Oct							20	16.30	326.00
2 Oct	75	16.50	1,237.50				20	16.30	326.00
							75	16.50	1,237.50
							95	16.46	1,563.50
8 Oct				50	16.46	823.00	45	16.46	740.70

Task 5

TIME SHEET						
Week ending 31/10/07						
Name Sanjeev Patel						
Area Machine shop			**Employee number**		M042	
Grade B						
Activity	**MON**	**TUES**	**WED**	**THURS**	**FRI**	**TOTAL**
Oven 900 machining	9		9			
Oven 778 machining		9		3		
Sick				4.5		
Training					7.5	
Hours attendance	9.0	9.0	9.0	7.5	7.5	
Bonus hours	0.5	0.5	0.5			
Employee's signature	Sanjeev Patel					
Manager's signature	Malcolm Harrison					
ANALYSIS OF HOURS						
Basic rate hours						
Overtime hours						
Bonus hours						
ANALYSIS OF GROSS PAY						
	Hours	**Rate £**	**£**	**£**		
Direct hours (25.5 + 4.5)						
Indirect hours						
Sick						
Training						
Overtime hours at premium						
Bonus hours						
Total indirect						
Gross pay						

TIME SHEET						
Week ending 31/10/07						
Name Jacob Ellis						
Area Machine shop			**Employee number** M042			
Grade C						
Activity	**MON**	**TUES**	**WED**	**THURS**	**FRI**	**TOTAL**
Oven 900 machining						
Hours attendance						
Bonus hours						
Employee's signature **Jacob Ellis**						
Manager's signature						
ANALYSIS OF HOURS						
Basic rate hours						
Overtime hours						
Bonus hours						

ANALYSIS OF GROSS PAY

	Hours	**Rate £**	**£**	**£**	
Direct hours					
Indirect hours					
Sick					
Training					
Overtime hours					
Bonus hours					
Total indirect					
Gross pay					

Task 6

MEMORANDUM

To: Malcolm Harrison, Machine Shop Manager
From: Management Accounts Assistant
Subject: Discrepancy on Time Sheet for Jacob Ellis
Date: 2 November 2007

Task 7

Calculation of under-/over-absorption of production overheads

October 2007

Total number of machine hours worked _____

Pre-determined overhead absorption rate per machine hour, 2007 _____

Total production overhead absorbed, October 2007 _____

Actual production overhead incurred _____

Production overhead over/(under) absorbed, October 2007 _____

The amount of £ _____ has been over-/under-* absorbed and will be debited/credited* to the profit and loss account.

(*Delete as applicable.)

Task 8

MEMORANDUM

To: Production Director
From: Management Accounts Assistant
Subject: Production overhead absorption rates for 2008
Date: 14 November 2007

Calculation of single machine hour rate

Problems with the single rate

Task 9

OVERHEAD ANALYSIS SHEET: BUDGET 2008

Rate using step down method of apportionment.

Overhead expense item	Basis of allocation/ apportionment	Total £	Machine Shop £	Assembly Shop £	Testing Centre £	Staff Amenity Centre £
Primary allocations and apportionments						
Indirect labour						
Manager salaries						
Testing Centre costs						
Staff Amenity Centre costs						
Depreciation						
Rent, rates, etc.						
Other o'heads						
Total primary allocation						
Reapportion Staff Amenity Centre						
Re-apportion Testing Centre						
Total production cost centre overhead allocation						

SPACE FOR CALCULATION OF ABSORPTION RATES
FOR EACH PRODUCTION DEPARTMENT USING STEP DOWN METHOD:

Machine Shop =

Assembly Shop =

Alternative rates using direct method of apportionment

Overhead expense item	Basis of allocation/ apportionment	Total £	Machine Shop £	Assembly Shop £	Testing Centre £	Staff Amenity Centre £
Total primary allocations						
Apportion Test Centre costs						
Apportion Staff Amendity Centre costs						
Total production cost centre overhead allocation						

**SPACE FOR CALCULATION OF ABSORPTION RATES
FOR EACH PRODUCTION DEPARTMENT USING DIRECT APPORTIONMENT:**

Machine Shop =

Assembly Shop =

Task 10

Working paper for calculation of payback period and net present value

Payback period

Net present value

MEMORANDUM

To: Production Director
From: Management Accounts Assistant
Subject: New sites and products
Date: 25 November 2007

HIGHLY CONFIDENTIAL

Task 11

Working paper to determine sales volume, cost behaviour patterns and projected costs and revenues

Projected sales volume

Analysis of cost behaviour

Projected costs and revenues for new product range next year

Output volume (machines)

	£	£
Sales revenue		
Projected costs		
Direct material		
Direct labour		
Production overhead		
Other overhead		
Total projected cost		
Projected annual profit		

Task 12

Working paper to calculate margin of safety, P/V ratio and maximum possible change in fixed production overheads

Margin of safety

Profit/volume (P/V) ratio

Possible change in fixed production overheads

MEMORANDUM

To: Production Director
From: Management Accounts Assistant
Subject: New sites and products
Date: 30 November 2007

HIGHLY CONFIDENTIAL

I attach the calculations that I have made in response to your memo of today's date.

Analysis of dishwasher product

Task 13

MEMORANDUM

To: Production Director
From: Management Accounts Assistant
Subject: New products at the new site
Date: 30 November 2007

HIGHLY CONFIDENTIAL

Contracts required by Welsh consultancy

Limiting factor on production of large electric woks in Scotland

AAT

SAMPLE SIMULATION
UNIT 7

HOMER LTD

COVERAGE OF PERFORMANCE CRITERIA AND RANGE STATEMENTS

All performance criteria are covered in this simulation.

Element	PC Coverage
7.1	**Prepare and present periodic performance reports**
A	Consolidate **information** derived from different units of the organisation into the appropriate form.
B	Reconcile **information** derived from different information systems within the organisation.
C	Compare results over time using an appropriate method that allows for changing price levels.
D	Account for transactions between separate units of the organisation in accordance with the organisation's procedures.
E	Calculate **ratios** and **performance indicators** in accordance with the organisation's procedures.
F	Prepare reports in the appropriate form and present them to management within the required timescales.
7.2	**Prepare reports and returns for outside agencies**
A	Identify, collate and present relevant information in accordance with the conventions and definitions used by outside agencies.
B	Ensure calculations of **ratios** and performance indicators are accurate.
C	Obtain authorisation for the despatch of completed **reports and returns** from the appropriate person.
D	Present **reports and returns** in accordance with outside agencies' requirements and deadlines.
7.3	**Prepare VAT returns**
A	Complete and submit VAT returns correctly, using data from the appropriate **recording systems**, within the statutory time limits.
B	Correctly identify and calculate relevant **inputs and outputs**.
C	Ensure submissions are made in accordance with current legislation.
D	Ensure guidance is sought from the VAT office when required, in a professional manner.

Any missing range statements should be assessed separately.

INSTRUCTIONS

This simulation is designed to let you show your ability to prepare reports and returns.

You should read the whole simulation before you start work, so that you are fully aware of what you will have to do.

You are allowed **three hours** to complete your work.

Write your answers in the Answer Booklet provided on pages 259 to 269. If you need more paper for your answers, ask the person in charge.

You should write your answers in blue or black ink, **not** pencil.

You may use correcting fluid, but in moderation. You should cross out your errors neatly and clearly.

Your work must be accurate, so check your work carefully before handing it in.

Coverage of performance criteria and range statements

It is not always possible to cover all performance criteria and range statements in a single simulation. Any performance criteria and range statements not covered must be assessed by other means by the assessor before a candidate can be considered competent.

Performance criteria and range statement coverage for this simulation is shown on page 250.

THE SITUATION

Your name is Amir Pindhi and you work as an Accounts Assistant for Homer Limited, Sestos Drive, Pantile Trading Estate CV32 1AW.

Homer Limited is a manufacturing company, producing a single product, the 'Bart'. The company's year end is 31 March.

Today's date is Monday 14 April 2007.

Divisional structure of Homer Limited

All production activities are carried out in the Manufacturing division. This division transfers most of its output to the Sales Division, which sells the output to external customers.

The Manufacturing Division transfers finished output to the Sales division at full production cost, but without any mark-up for profit. The Manufacturing division also sells some of its finished output direct to external customers.

Accounting for VAT

Homer Limited is registered for VAT.

Sales of Barts to UK customers are subject to VAT at the standard rate of 17.5%.

The company also exports to other countries within the European Union (EU). Such exports qualify as zero-rated. The company does not export to countries outside the EU. The company does not import any goods or services.

The local VAT office for Homer Limited is at Bell House, 33 Lambert Road, Coventry CV12 8TR.

Application for bank loan

The company is about to seek a long-term loan from its bankers to finance expansion plans.

The bank has requested some financial information in support of this application, and one of your responsibilities will be to present this information in the form required by the bank.

Presenting your work

Unless you are told otherwise:

- all ratios and statistics should be computed and presented to two decimal places;
- monetary amounts should be computed and presented to the nearest penny.

THE TASKS TO BE COMPLETED

1. Refer to the table on page 255 of this book which analyses monthly sales achieved by each of the company's two divisions during the years ended 31 March 2006 and 31 March 2007.

    ■   Consolidate these figures to arrive at the monthly sales and cumulative sales for each month in the two year period. Note that this task relates only to sales made to external customers, not to transfers within the company from the Manufacturing division to the Sales division. You should set out your answer on the schedule on page 261 of the Answer Booklet.

2. Using the figures calculated in Task 1, plot a line graph on page 262 of the Answer Booklet. The graph should show the cumulative sales achieved month by month during the year ended 31 March 2006 and, as a separate line, the cumulative sales achieved month by month during the year ended 31 March 2007. As in Task 1, you are concerned only with the sales to external customers, not with internal transfers from Manufacturing to Sales.

3. On page 256 of this book you will find month-by-month values of an index appropriate to the industry in which Homer operates. The values given are stated by reference to a base figure of 100, which was the value of the index in the base period January 2002.

    ■   Calculate the indexed value of the monthly sales to external customers, in March 2007 terms, for each month's sales in the year ended 31 March 2007. Your answer should be set out on page 263 of the Answer Booklet in accordance with the notes on that page.

4. Refer to the information on page 256 of this book.

    ■   Complete the loan application form on page 264 of the Answer Booklet.

    ■   Write a memo to the Accountant, Sonia Liesl, enclosing the form for her attention and approval prior to its submission to the bank. Use the blank memo form on page 265 of the Answer Booklet and date your memo 14 April 2007.

5. Write a memo to Sonia Liesl, presenting the following statistics for her information, and very briefly suggesting a possible reason for the movement in each statistic's value since year ended 31 March 2006. (The 2006 values are given in brackets below.)

    ■   The gross profit percentage for year ended 31 March 2007 (The percentage in year ended 31 March 2006 was 43.15%).

    ■   The net profit percentage for year ended 31 March 2007 (2006: 7.84%).

    ■   The production cost per 'Bart' produced and sold in year ended 31 March 2007 (2006: £10.83).

    ■   The value of sales earned per employee in year ended 31 March 2007 (2006: £26,018.13).

    Use the memo form on page 266 of the Answer Booklet and date your memo 14 April 2007.

6. Refer to the information on pages 256 and 257 of this book that relates to the company's VAT return for the quarter ended on 31 March 2007.

- Complete the blank return on page 267 of the Answer Booklet. Note that the return is to be signed by the Accountant, Sonia Liesl, and that payment of any balance due to HMRC will be made by cheque.

7. Refer to the memo from Sonia Liesl on page 257 of this booklet.

- Draft a letter to your local VAT Office (in the name of Sonia Liesl) asking for the required information. Use the letterhead on page 268 of the Answer Booklet.

8. Reply to Sonia Liesl's memo giving her the brief details she requests, and enclosing the draft letter prepared in Task 7 above. Use the blank memo form on page 269 of the Answer Booklet.

Monthly sales during the years ended 31 March 2006 and 31 March 2007

All figures in £000. All figures exclude VAT.

	Sales Division	Manufacturing Division		
	Total	To external customers	To Sales Division	Total
2005/2006				
April	350	34	185	219
May	225	46	128	174
June	190	32	96	128
July	255	54	138	192
August	310	36	166	202
September	238	24	148	172
October	220	20	125	145
November	295	34	172	206
December	240	39	182	221
January	257	20	150	170
February	230	14	155	169
March	340	45	218	263
2006/2007				
April	339	42	197	239
May	189	53	119	172
June	223	14	109	123
July	295	44	214	258
August	280	50	176	226
September	265	34	138	172
October	219	12	119	131
November	322	50	170	220
December	316	39	180	219
January	281	29	148	177
February	248	24	168	192
March	240	51	185	236

Industrial index: base = 100 (January 2002)

2006	April	123.8
	May	124.4
	June	124.9
	July	125.7
	August	126.3
	September	127.0
	October	127.5
	November	128.1
	December	128.9
2007	January	129.6
	February	130.2
	March	131.0

Statistical information relating to year ended 31 March 2007

Production cost of Barts produced and sold in the year	£2,190,000
Gross profit for the year	£1,470,000
Administration costs for the year	£580,000
Distribution costs for the year	£430,000
Total of all other costs for the year	£150,000
Net profit for the year before taxation	£310,000
Net profit for the previous year before taxation	£278,000
Total capital employed	£6,590,000
Number of Barts produced and sold in the year	199,000
Average number of employees in the year	143

The following details have been extracted from the company's daybooks. (All figures are exclusive of VAT.)

SALES DAY BOOK TOTALS
QUARTER ENDED 31 MARCH 2007

	January £	February £	March £	Total £
UK sales: standard rated	282,862.57	245,871.89	269,088.11	797,822.57
EU sales: zero-rated	27,143.05	26,126.66	21,920.34	75,190.05
Total	310,005.62	271,998.55	291,008.45	873,012.62
VAT on UK sales	49,500.95	43,027.58	47,090.42	139,618.95

PURCHASES DAY BOOK TOTALS
QUARTER ENDED 31 MARCH 2007

	January £	February £	March £	Total £
Purchases/expenses	186,007.66	163,265.69	171,295.45	520,568.80
VAT on purchases/expenses	32,551.34	28,571.50	29,976.70	91,099.54

A debt of £658, inclusive of VAT, was written off as bad in March 2007. The related sale was made in June 2006. Bad debt relief is now to be claimed.

MEMO

To: Amir Pindhi
From: Sonia Liesl
Subject: VAT on imports
Date: 11 April 2007

As you may know, we have been in discussions with a supplier based in the Far East. We are considering importing certain components in future for use in our manufacturing activities.

Please could you remind me very briefly of the VAT implications if we decide to proceed with this. Please also draft a letter to the VAT Office, in my name, requesting relevant publications so that we can be sure we account for the VAT correctly.

Thanks for your help.

AAT

SAMPLE SIMULATION
UNIT 7

HOMER LTD

ANSWER BOOKLET

Task 1

Sales to external customers
Manufacturing and Sales divisions combined

	Monthly totals £'000	Cumulative total for the year £'000
2005/2006		
April		
May		
June		
July		
August		
September		
October		
November		
December		
January		
February		
March		
2006/2007		
April		
May		
June		
July		
August		
September		
October		
November		
December		
January		
February		
March		

Notes

1.   In the first column, enter the monthly total of external sales achieved by the two divisions.
2.   In the second column, enter the cumulative total of external sales in the accounting year.

Task 2

Task 3

Indexed sales to external customers
Manufacturing and Sales divisions combined

	Unadjusted totals £'000	Index factor	Indexed totals £'000
2006/2007			
April			
May			
June			
July			
August			
September			
October			
November			
December			
January			
February			
March			

Notes

1. In the first column, insert the monthly totals of external sales calculated in Task 1.
2. In the second column, insert the index factor required to convert to March 2007 values.
3. In the third column, calculate the monthly sales in March 2007 terms (to the nearest £1,000).

Task 4

LOAN APPLICATION (extract)

Name of applicant company _____

Latest year for which accounting information is available _____

Total sales revenue

In latest year for which accounts are available   £ _____

In previous year   £ _____

Percentage change (+/-) _____

Net profit after all expenses, before taxation

In latest year for which accounts are available   £ _____

In previous year   £ _____

Percentage change (+/-) _____

Gross profit margin (%) _____

Net profit margin (%) _____

Return on capital employed (%) _____

Notes

1.　In the case of a company with a divisional structure, all figures should refer to the results of the company as a whole, not to individual divisions within the company.

2.　Unless otherwise stated, all questions relate to the latest year for which accounting information is available.

3.　Figures should be actual historical values, with no indexing for inflation.

4.　Return on capital employed is defined as net profit for the year before taxation, divided by total capital employed.

Task 4 (continued)

MEMO

To:

From:

Subject:

Date:

_____

_____

_____

_____

_____

_____

_____

_____

_____

_____

_____

_____

_____

_____

_____

_____

_____

_____

_____

_____

_____

_____

_____

_____

Task 5

MEMO

To:

From:

Subject:

Date:

Task 6

Value Added Tax Return

For the period
01 01 07 to 31 03 07

For Official Use

Registration number	Period
625 7816 29	03 07

You could be liable to a financial penalty if your completed return and all the VAT payable are not received by the due date.

Due date: 30.04.07

HOMER LIMITED
SESTOS DRIVE
PANTILE TRADING ESTATE
CV32 1AW

| For Official Use | |

ATTENTION

If you have a general enquiry or need advice please call our National Advice Service on 0845 010 9000

If this return and any tax due are not received by the due date you may be liable to a surcharge.

If you make supplies of goods to another EC Member State you are required to complete an EC Sales List (VAT 101).

Before you fill in this form please read the notes on the back and the VAT Leaflet "*Filling in your VAT return*" and "*Flat rate schemes for small businesses*", if you use the scheme. Fill in all boxes clearly in ink, and write 'none' where necessary. Don't put a dash or leave any box blank. If there are no pence write "00" in the pence column. Do not enter more than one amount in any box.

For official use		£	p
	VAT due in this period on sales and other outputs **1**		
	VAT due in this period on acquisitions from other EC Member States **2**		
	Total VAT due (the sum of boxes 1 and 2) **3**		
	VAT reclaimed in this period on purchases and other inputs (including acquisitions from the EC) **4**		
	Net VAT to be paid to Customs or reclaimed by you (Difference between boxes 3 and 4) **5**		
	Total value of sales and all other outputs excluding any VAT. Include your box 8 figure **6**		
	Total value of purchases and all other inputs excluding any VAT. Include your box 9 figure **7**		
	Total value of all supplies of goods and related services, excluding any VAT, to other EC Member States **8**		
	Total value of all acquisitions of goods and related services, excluding any VAT, from other EC Member States **9**		

If you are enclosing a payment please tick this box.

DECLARATION: You, or someone on your behalf, must sign below.

I, _____ declare that the
(Full name of signatory in BLOCK LETTERS)
information given above is true and complete.

Signature_____ Date _____ 20 _____

A false declaration can result in prosecution.

Task 7

HOMER LIMITED
Sestos Drive, Pantile Trading Estate CV32 1AW
Telephone: 02467 881235

_____

_____

_____

_____

_____

_____

_____

_____

_____

_____

_____

_____

_____

_____

_____

_____

_____

_____

_____

_____

_____

_____

Registered office: Sestos Drive, Pantile Trading Estate CV32 1AW
Registered in England, number 2007814

Task 8

MEMO

To:

From:

Subject:

Date:

_____

_____

_____

_____

_____

_____

_____

_____

_____

_____

_____

_____

_____

_____

_____

_____

_____

_____

_____

AAT PRACTICE SIMULATION
UNIT 7

DONALD RATHERSON & CO

PERFORMANCE CRITERIA

The following performance criteria are covered in this skills test.

Element	PC Coverage

7.1   **Prepare and present periodic performance reports**

A   Consolidate **information** derived from different units of the organisation into the appropriate form.

B   Reconcile **information** derived from different information systems within the organisation.

C   Compare results over time using an appropriate method that allows for changing price levels.

D   Account for transactions between separate units of the organisation in accordance with the organisation's procedures.

E   Calculate **ratios** and **performance indicators** in accordance with the organisation's procedures.

F   Prepare reports in the appropriate form and present them to management within the required timescales.

7.2   **Prepare reports and returns for outside agencies**

A   Identify, collate and present relevant information in accordance with the conventions and definitions used by outside agencies.

B   Ensure calculations of **ratios** and performance indicators are accurate.

C   Obtain authorisation for the despatch of completed **reports and returns** from the appropriate person.

D   Present **reports and returns** in accordance with outside agencies' requirements and deadlines.

7.3   **Prepare VAT returns**

A   Complete and submit VAT returns correctly, using data from the appropriate **recording systems**, within the statutory time limits.

B   Correctly identify and calculate relevant **inputs and outputs**.

C   Ensure submissions are made in accordance with current legislation.

D   Ensure guidance is sought from the VAT office when required, in a professional manner.

Any missing range statements should be assessed separately.

INSTRUCTIONS

This simulation is designed to test your ability to prepare reports and returns.

This simulation is divided into 10 tasks. You are advised to look through the whole simulation first to gain a general appreciation of your tasks.

The situation is provided on below. The tasks to be completed are set out on pages 274 to 276.

Your answers should be set out in the Answer Booklet provided.

You are allowed three hours to complete your work.

A high level of accuracy is required. Check your work carefully before handing it in.

Correcting fluid may be used but it should be used in moderation. Errors should be crossed out neatly and clearly. You should write in blue or black ink, not pencil.

THE SITUATION

Introduction

Donald Ratherson & Co is a business which makes and sells equipment for professional decorators, such as ladders, internal scaffolding and paintguns. Its premises are in Ascot in Berkshire, with a showroom in London

The business has three business units (plus an accounting and administration section).

- The Manufacturing Unit in Ascot buys in materials from suppliers and makes equipment, which is then transferred either to the Mail Order Unit or to the Showroom. In both cases items are transferred at full production cost, so there is no inter-departmental profit.

- The Mail Order Unit in Ascot buys in equipment for resale from outside suppliers and also sources them internally from the Manufacturing Unit. It then sells to customers who order by post, phone or internet.

- The Showroom operates from premises in London. It displays equipment bought in from outside and also sources internally from the Manufacturing Unit. Its customers tend to be large retailers who require specialist equipment and service in respect of large window displays in their shops.

You work as Deputy Accountant for the business. The people with whom you deal are as follows:

Ian Yates   Chief Accountant

Donald Ratherson   Owner

The simulation requires you to perform tasks relating to the previous full financial year ended 30 September 2007. You also need to look at data relating to the month ending 31 October 2007 and to complete the business's VAT return for the quarter ending on that date. Today's date is 12 November 2007.

Accounts and reports

In the business's accounting system, costs are attributed to the different business units as follows.

- Direct manufacturing costs, including raw materials, wages and expenses, to the Manufacturing Unit

- Direct mail order and showroom costs, including goods for resale, wages and expenses, to the Mail Order Unit and Showroom respectively

- Other overheads of the Ascot site, including all accounting and administration costs, to the three business units according to an agreed ratio

Each month and year the cost and revenue statements for each of the three Business Units are added together in a standard form to produce a consolidated statement of costs and revenue. The balances that exist between the Manufacturing Unit and the Mail Order Unit and the Showroom must be reconciled before this consolidated statement can be finalised.

The business is a member of the Institute of Decorators. Data from the statement of costs and revenue, plus other data, is provided to the Institute annually.

Accounting for VAT

Donald Ratherson & Co is registered for VAT. All sales to UK customers are standard-rated for VAT. Supplies to EU countries qualify as zero-rated. The company does not export to non-EU countries. It does not import any of its goods or services from outside the EU, nor does it make taxable acquisitions from EU countries.

The local VAT office for Donald Ratherson & Co is at Lyle House, Henry Road, Guildford GU8 5CM.

THE TASKS TO BE COMPLETED

Note that in all tasks monetary amounts are to be calculated to the nearest £, and ratios and percentages are to be calculated to two places of decimals.

Task 1

The company's owner, Donald Ratherson, feels that in the most recent year ending 30 September 2007, the business was more profitable than he had expected, but he wonders how far inflation accounts for this and how far it was as a result of improved efficiency. Ian Yates has handed you details of the business's annual costs and revenues for the previous year ended 30 September 2006, which are given on page 284 in the Answer Booklet. He has also identified some data, plus two indices that specifically relate to the full year's figures, which he has set out in a memo to you on page 277 in this booklet.

You are required to complete the table on page 284 in the Answer Booklet by re-stating the business's revenues and costs for the year ended 30 September 2007 in line with Ian Yates's memo.

Task 2

Use the data on pages 278 and 279 in this booklet to produce the consolidated costs and revenues statement for the business for the year ending 30 September 2007, on page 285 in the Answer Booklet.

Task 3

Refer to the memo dated 11 November 2007 from Ian Yates on page 280 in this booklet.

You are required to prepare a memo to Ian Yates providing the information requested. Use the blank memo form on page 286 in the Answer Booklet, the table on page 287 in the Answer Booklet, the time series graph on page 288 and the sheet of graph paper on page 289 in the Answer Booklet.

Task 4

For some years, Donald Ratherson & Co's most popular product has been the LadderPaint modular system. Data related to LadderPaint's production and saleS is shown on page 281 in this booklet. For the year ended 30 September 2007:

You are required to:

a)	calculate the production cost per LadderPaint system transferred from the Manufacturing Unit

b)	calculate the percentage of manufacturing costs represented by LadderPaint systems

c)	calculate the sales value per unit of LadderPaint sold

d)	calculate the gross profit margin per unit of LadderPaint

e)	calculate the percentage of total Mail Order and Showroom revenue represented by LadderPaint sales in the year

f)	complete the comparison of actual and budgeted manufacturing costs for LadderPaint and calculate the productivity ratio.

Set out your answers on page 290 in the Answer Booklet, where you will find comparative figures for 2006.

Task 5

On page 291 in the Answer Booklet there is an extract from the standard form issued by the Institute of Decorators.

You are required to complete the standard form by inserting the relevant accounting figures, ratios and statistics required by the Institute.

Task 6

You are required to send a memo to Ian Yates, enclosing the completed form and report, and requesting him to authorise them before despatch to the Institute. Use the blank memo form on page 292 in the Answer Booklet.

Task 7

Refer to the extracts from Business Unit cost and revenue statements for October 2007, and the further data relating to transactions at the end of the month, on page 281 in this booklet.

You are required to prepare a reconciliation between the inter-unit balances using the format on page 293 in the Answer Booklet.

Task 8

Refer to the data on page 282 in this booklet.

You are required to:

a)   complete the business's VAT control account on page 293 in the Answer Booklet.

b)   complete the business's VAT return for the quarter ended 31 October 2007 on page 294 in the Answer Booklet. You are not required to sign the VAT return.

Task 9

The Showroom of Donald Ratherson & Co sold some goods with a market value of £15,000 to a customer, GHA Stores plc, in February 2007 on 30 days credit. Donald Ratherson was informed yesterday that GHA Stores plc had ceased trading and the debt is irrecoverable. This is the first time that Donald Ratherson & Co has had a substantial bad debt.

You are required to write to the local VAT Office, seeking confirmation of your understanding of the steps that Donald Ratherson & Co needs to take in order to claim bad debt relief for the VAT element of this debt, and the timescale in which the steps should be taken so that relief is obtained as soon as possible. Use page 295 in the Answer Booklet.

Task 10

Donald Ratherson has been talking to his personal accountant and has realised that there are a few issues to do with VAT with which he is unfamiliar. His personal accountant began to put a checklist of points together for Donald, but this is still incomplete.

You are required to complete the checklist for Donald on pages 296 and 297 in the Answer Booklet.

Data for Task 1

MEMO

To: Deputy Accountant
From: Ian Yates
Subject: Trends affecting Donald Ratherson & Co's performance
Date: 11 November 2007

I have identified the following specific factors that have affected our performance over the year from 1 October 2006 to 30 September 2007:

–   Showroom prices to customers have risen by 8% on average, but Mail Order prices have only risen by 4%.

–   In the Manufacturing Unit, raw materials prices have risen by 3% on average.

–   The prices paid by Mail Order and Showroom for goods for resale have risen 2% on average

–   Wage rates in the Manufacturing Unit and the Mail Order Unit rose by 5%

–   Wage rates in the Showroom rose by 7%

–   Expenses in the Mail Order Unit and Showroom rose by 3% on average

–   Expenses in the Manufacturing Unit rose on average by 4%

–   Overheads of the Ascot site, including accounting and administration costs, have been on average 5% higher.

I also attach some relevant indices from the Institute of Decorators relating to our business.

Institute of Decorators

Indices for manufacturers of decorating equipment

Years ending in	Revenue	Gross profit
2003	100.0	100
2004	104.2	103.9
2005	108.3	107.8
2006	109.7	108.1
2007	111.5	109.6

Data for Task 2

Cost statement: Manufacturing Unit

Year ended 30 September 2007

	£
Raw materials	
Opening stock	14,016
Purchases	134,352
Total actual fixed overheads	148,368
Closing stock	(20,736)
Cost of raw materials used in year	127,632
Wages	178,685
Expenses	19,145
Transfer cost to Mail Order Unit and Showroom (= production cost)	325,462
Allocated costs of Ascot site, including accounting and administration costs (65%)	60,125
Total Manufacturing Unit costs	385,587
Average number of employees	**12**

Cost and revenue statement: Mail Order Unit

	£	£
Sales		1,146,354
Goods for resale		
Opening stock	24,130	
Purchases	289,645	
Closing stock	(21,717)	
	292,058	
Transfer cost of goods for resale from Manufacturing Unit	260,369	
Cost of goods sold in year		(552,427)
Mail Order Unit gross profit		593,927
Wages		(165,728)
Expenses		(55,242)
Allocated costs of Ascot site, including accounting and administration costs (20%)		(18,500)
Mail Order Unit net profit		354,457
Average number of employees		11

Cost and revenue statement: Showroom

Year ended 30 September 2007

	£	£
Sales		1,092,240
Goods for resale	37,620	
Opening stock	228,840	
Purchases	(41,382)	
	225,078	
Transfer cost of goods for resale from Manufacturing Unit	65,093	
Cost of goods sold in year		290,171
Showroom gross profit		802,069
Wages		(144,000)
Expenses		(57,600)
Allocated costs of Ascot site, including accounting and administration costs (15%)		(13,875)
Showroom net profit		586,594
Average number of employees		8

Data for Task 3

MEMO

To: Deputy Accountant
From: Ian Yates
Subject: Results for the year ended 30 September 2007
Date: 11 November 2007

I would like you to prepare a report for me, which I shall show to Donald Ratherson. Use the table that I have supplied to you.

Please set out in the table the consolidated figures for costs and revenues for the year ended 30 September 2007 against the full comparable figures (inflation-adjusted) for the year ended 30 September 2007 (ignore the figures adjusted using the Institute of Decorators indices). Set out the differences between the two sets of figures, both in monetary amount and in percentage terms, and a calculation of the gross profit margin, net profit margin and return on capital employed percentages for both years (I have included figures on average capital employed for both years in the table).

Please also construct a component bar chart for the 2007 figures and the inflation-adjusted 2006 figures, breaking down total sales revenue for the two periods into:

- net profit
- cost of sales
- wages
- expenses
- accounting and administration costs.

Finally, I attach the time series graph that we prepared this time last year, showing the total revenue and profit figures for the business since 2001. Please complete the graph for the year ended 31 October 2007, and then extend the trend line by eye to give me an idea of what sales and profit should be in the year ended 31 October 2008. Enter your estimates of these two figures in the space provided beneath the graph.

Please include an accompanying introductory memo, highlighting the profitability ratios you have calculated, and referring to the table, the bar chart and the time series graph.

Data for Task 4

LadderPaint

Production and sales data for the year ended 30 September 2007

	Units	£
Sales	988	151,164
By Mail Order Unit	762	116,586
BY Showroom		267,750
Production costs	1,750	
Metal		13,875
Resins		2,740
Cord		3,655
Paint		3,950
Packaging		1,265
		25,485
		77,760
Wages (8,750)		77,760
Expenses		11,520
		114,765

Note. There were no opening or closing stocks of LadderPaint or the relevant raw materials in any unit.

Budgeted production for the year was 1,500 units, produced in 6,000 hours

Data for Task 7

Cost statement extract: Manufacturing unit

Month ended 31 October 2007

	£
Production cost of items transferred to Mail Order Unit and Showroom	27,122

Cost and revenue statement extract: Mail Order Unit

Month ended 31 October 2007

	£
Transfer cost of goods for resale from Manufacturing Unit	15,985

Cost and revenue statement extract: Showroom

Month ended 31 October 2007

	£
Transfer cost of goods for resale from Maufacturing Unit	10,644

On further investigation, it is found that some goods have been transferred from Manufacturing but have not been recorded in the other units. The production cost of the goods are as follows.

	£
Goods transferred to Mail Order Unit	107
Goods transferred to Showroom	386

Data for Task 8

Donald Ratherson & Co

Sales Day Book (SDB) summary Auguast to October 2007

	Aug £	Sept £	Oct £	Total £
UK: Standard-rated	185,463	186,795	189,674	561,932
Other EU: Zero-rated	10,856	9,745	8,796	29,397
VAT	32,456	32,689	33,193	98,338
Total	228,775	229,229	231,663	389,667

Donald Ratherson & Co

Purchases Day Book (PDB) summary Auguast to October 2007

	Aug £	Sept £	Oct £	Total £
Purchases	185,463	56,745	57,912	170,060
Expenses	7,355	7,496	8,001	22,852
VAT	13,673	9,115	7,596	30,384
Total	76,431	73,356	73,509	389,667

Donald Ratherson & Co

Cash Book (CB) summary Auguast to October 2007

	Aug £	Sept £	Oct £	Total £
Expenses	286	195	23	504
VAT	25	17	2	44
Total	331	212	25	548

AAT

PRACTICE SIMULATION
UNIT 7

DONALD RATHERSON & CO

ANSWER BOOKLET

ANSWER BOOKLET

Task 1

	Actual 2006		Factor	Restated 2006	
	£	£		£	£
Sales					
Mail Order		1,001,456	☐		☐
Showroom		924,763	☐		☐
		1,926,219			
Cost of sales					
Raw materials	125,896		☐		☐
Goods for resale					
Mail Order	281,546		☐		☐
Showroom	216,875		☐		☐
		(624,317)			
Gross profit		1,301,902			
Wages					
Manufacturing Unit	169,842		☐	☐	
Mail Order	155,246		☐	☐	
Showroom	139,000		☐	☐	
		(464,088)			
Expenses					
Manufacturing Unit	15,746		☐	☐	
Mail Order	52,463		☐	☐	
Showroom	55,126		☐	☐	
		(123,335)			
Costs of Ascot site, including accounting and admin		(89,750)	☐	☐	
Net profit		624,729		☐	

Restatement using Institute of Decorators indices

	2006	Index factor	Adjusted 2006 figure
	£		£
Total revenue	1,926,219	☐	☐
Total gross profit	1,301,902	☐	☐

Task 2

Donald Ratherson & Co
Consolidated statement of revenues and costs for the year ended 30 September 2007

	£	£	£
Sales			
Cost of sales			
Raw materials			
Opening stock			
Purchases			
Closing stock			
	——————		
Goods for resale			
Opening stock			
Purchases			
Closing stock			
	——————		
		——————	
			——————
Gross profit			
Wages			
Expenses			
Costs of Ascot site, including accounting and administration costs			
			——————
Net profit			══════

Task 3

MEMO

To:	Ian Yates
From:	Deputy Accountant
Subject:	Report on results for year ended 30 September 2007
Date:	12 November 2007

Task 3 (continued)

Donald Ratherson & Co
Report on the comparison of revenues and costs for the
year end 31 October 2007 with inflation-adjusted figures for 2006

	2007		Adjusted 2006		Difference	
	£	£	£	£	£	%
Sales						
Mail Order						
Showroom		_____		_____		
Cost of sales						
Raw materials						
Goods for resale						
Mail Order						
Showroom	_____		_____			
		_____		_____		
Gross profit						
Wages						
Manufacturing Unit						
Mail Order						
Showroom	_____		_____			
Expenses						
Manufacturing Unit						
Mail Order						
Showroom	_____		_____			
Cost of Ascot site, including accounting and administration		_____		_____		
Net profit		_____		_____		
Average capital employed	12,650,000		12,000,000			

Workings

			%	%
Gross profit margin				
Net profit margin				
Return on capital employed				

Task 3

Time series 2001–08

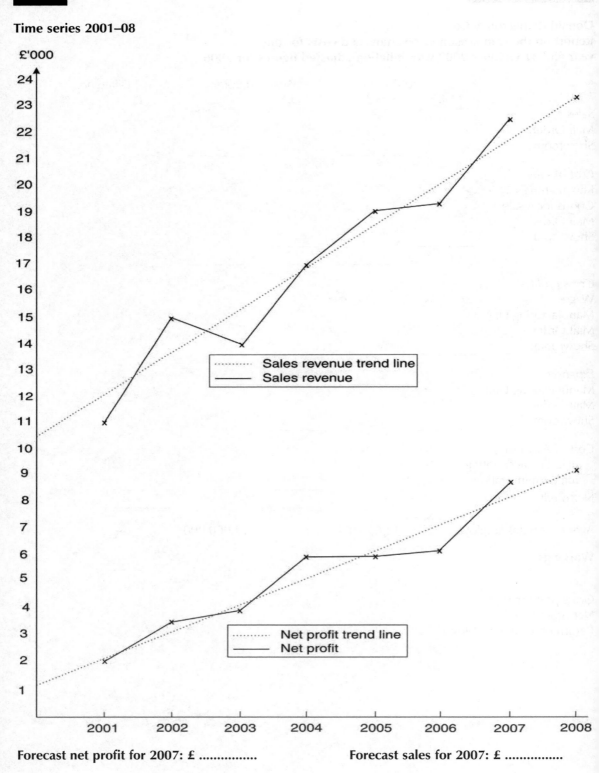

£'000

Sales revenue trend line
Sales revenue

Net profit trend line
Net profit

Forecast net profit for 2007: £ ....   **Forecast sales for 2007: £ ....**

Task 3 (continued)

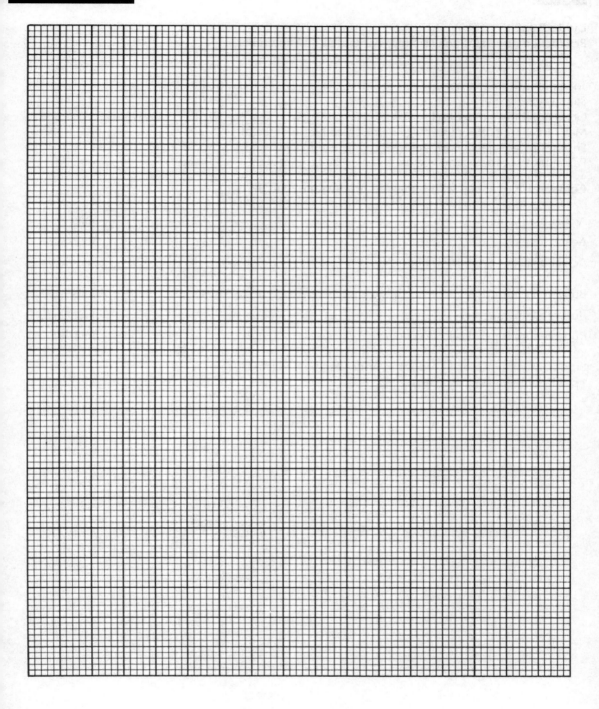

Task 4

LadderPaint
Production and sales analysis for year ended 30 September

	2006	2007	Workings
Total production cost per unit	£62.30	£	
Sales value per unit	£149.00	£	
Gross profit margin per unit	58.19%	%	
Mail Order Unit sales percentage represented by LadderPaint	15.20%	%	
Showroom sales percentage represented by LadderPaint	12.85%	%	
Percentage of production costs represented by LadderPaint	35.47%	%	

Comparison of actual with budgeted production 2006/07

Actual production ☐ units

Actual hours ☐ hours

Actual units per production hour ☐ units/hr

Budgeted production ☐ units

Budgeted hours ☐ hours

Budgeted units per production hour ☐ units/hr

Productivity ratio: actual production/hr divided by budgeted
production per hour × 100% ☐ %

Task 5

Institue of Decorators – standard form of return 2007

Name of business:: Donald Ratherson & Co

	Actual current year 30 September 2007	% of sales (1)	Actual prior year 30 September 2006	% of sales (1)
Year ended				
Average number of employees	31		32	
	£		£	
Sales		100		
Sales per employee				
Gross profit				
Net profit before taxation				
Average capital employed				
	%		%	
Return on capital employed (2)				

	Inflation-adjusted prior year £
Prior year sales revenue adjusted for inflation using Institute index	
Prior year gross profit adjusted for inflation using Institute index	

		Comparison £	% of prior year actual figure
Current year actual sales exceed prior year actual sales by	Box 1		
Amount of increase accounted for by inflation (4)	Box 2		
Amount of increase in real terms	Box 1 – Box 2		
Current year actual gross profits exceed prior year's actual gross profits by	Box 3		
Amount of increase accounted for by inflation (4)	Box 4		
Amount of increase in real terms	Box 3 – Box 4		

Notes

1) All percentages are to be expressed to two decimal places

2) Return on capital employed is the net profit, divided by the average capital employed for the year, expressed as a percentage to two decimal places

3) All entries are to be based on figures for the business as a whole, excluding any transactions between divisions or business units within the business

4) Deduct actual results from inflation-adjusted results

Task 6

```
                                    MEMO
To:          Ian Yates
From:        Deputy Accountant
Subject:     Institute of Decorators' return and report
Date:        11 November 2007
```

Task 7

Reconciliation of business units balances as at 31 October 2007

	£	£
Mail Order Unit balance brought forward		
Add: transfer from Manufacturing		
Closing Mail Order balance with Manufacturing		
Showroom Unit balance brought forward		
Add: transfer from Manufacturing		
Closing Showroom balance with Manufacturing		
Production cost of items transferred to Mail Order Unit and Showroom		

Task 8

Donald Ratherson & Co

VAT Control Account

Administration/overheads

Date	Description	Debit £	Date	Description	Debit £
2007			2007		
31 Aug	Pay HMRC	49,654	1 Aug	B/d	49,654

Value Added Tax Return

For the period

to

For Official Use

Registration number

Period

You could be liable to a financial penalty if your completed return and all the VAT payable are not received by the due date.

Due date:

For Official Use

If you have a general enquiry or need advice please call our National Advice Service on 0845 010 9000

ATTENTION

If this return and any tax due are not received by the due date you may be liable to a surcharge.

If you make supplies of goods to another EC Member State you are required to complete an EC Sales List (VAT 101).

Before you fill in this form please read the notes on the back and the VAT Leaflet *"Filling in your VAT return"*. Fill in all boxes clearly in ink, and write 'none' where necessary. Don't put a dash or leave any box blank. If there are no pence write "00" in the pence column. Do not enter more than one amount in any box.

For official use		£	p
	VAT due in this period on sales and other outputs **1**		
	VAT due in this period on acquisitions from other EC Member States **2**		
	Total VAT due (the sum of boxes 1 and 2) **3**		
	VAT reclaimed in this period on purchases and other inputs (including acquisitions from the EC) **4**		
	Net VAT to be paid to Customs or reclaimed by you (Difference between boxes 3 and 4) **5**		
	Total value of sales and all other outputs excluding any VAT. Include your box 8 figure **6**		00
	Total value of purchases and all other inputs excluding any VAT. Include your box 9 figure **7**		00
	Total value of all supplies of goods and related services, excluding any VAT, to other EC Member States **8**		00
	Total value of all acquisitions of goods and related services, excluding any VAT, from other EC Member States **9**		00

If you are enclosing a payment please tick this box.

DECLARATION: You, or someone on your behalf, must sign below.

I, ... declare that the
(Full name of signatory in BLOCK LETTERS)
information given above is true and complete.

Signature.. Date .... 20 ....

A false declaration can result in prosecution.

F

0196929   IB (October 2000)

VAT 100 (Half)

Task 9

DONALD RATHERSON & CO

Park Drive Trading Estate, Sunninghill Road, Ascot, Berks GU8 5ZD
Telephone: 01344 627896

Task 10

Checklist re VAT

Prepared for: Donald Ratherson

By: A N Accountant

1   The three types of supply for VAT purposes are: _____, _____ and _____ supplies.

2   A taxable person who makes only zero-rated outputs *can/cannot reclaim input tax on their purchases. (*Delete as applicable.)

3   In a month when the VAT registration limit is exceeded, a trader must notify HMRC within:

_____

4   The effects of registration for VAT are that the trader:

1   _____

2   _____

3   _____

5   A VAT invoice must show:

information about the supplier: _____

information about the invoice: _____

information about the customer: _____

6   A less detailed VAT invoice can be issued where the total including VAT is less than £_____

7   The basic tax point for a VAT invoice is: _____

_____

8   An earlier tax point than the basic tax point applies if: _____

_____

9   To find out more detail about VAT without reference to the VAT Office one should refer to:

_____

10   If we import raw materials from outside the EU we *must/need not pay input VAT on them. (*Delete as applicable.)

11   If we export goods to buyers outside the EU we must treat them as *standard rated/zero rated/exempt supplies. (*Delete as applicable.)

12   We would get automatic bad debt relief if we could be part of the _____ scheme, but our annual taxable turnover is too high.

13   We would only have to complete one VAT return per year if we were part of the _____ scheme, but our taxable turnover is too high.

14   In any dispute with the local VAT Office we would need to decide between:

    1   _____

    2   _____

15   If we submit our VAT return late, HMRC will issue us with a _____

_____

You also asked me for some information on other matters:

16   The government body responsible for publishing government statistics is: _____

_____

17   An example of a regulatory body seeking a report or return is: _____

_____

18   Other types of outside organisation which may seek a report or return from us are:

    1   _____

    2   _____

    3   _____

ANSWERS

answers to chapter 1:
COSTING INFORMATION

1   Financial accounting is the recording of historical, or past, transactions of the business in order to be able to produce a set of financial statements in accordance with legal and accounting professional requirements. These financial statements are required by law for limited companies and are prepared for the use of those outside the business such as shareholders, lenders, customers and suppliers.

Cost accounting is the recording of historical, or past, transactions of the business in order to provide useful information for the management of the business in order to carry out their functions of decision making, planning and control. The costing information can be presented in any manner which is useful to management as it is used solely by the management team within the business.

2   **Decision making** – many of the decisions that management will be required to make will be to do with production and sales of their products. Decisions will have to be made as to whether to produce a product in the first place – for this it will be necessary to know what the product is going to cost to make, what selling price can be set for it and therefore whether it is going to be profitable. Costing information will show the anticipated cost of the product and can also be used to set the selling price of the product if this is not dependent on market forces. In other instances management may have to make decisions about the levels of production for which they will need costs for different amounts of production. Management may also have to choose between products if there is competition for resources such as factory space or labour hours. Again detailed information about the costs of the products is required if an informed decision is to be made.

Planning – once a decision has been taken to make a new product in the next period or to continue production of an existing one then a plan or budget will be drawn up. Budgets contain the details of the quantities and costs of production. They will include budgets for the quantity of materials required, the cost of those materials, the number of labour hours required, the cost of the labour and estimates of all the overheads of the business for the period.

Control – control of costs is a vital element of management's role. One method of control is to compare the actual costs for a period to the budgeted costs for the same period. Any differences between actual cost and budgeted costs are known as variances and any significant variances should be investigated in order to determine their cause and to alter either the budgets or future operations in the light of the variances.

3　a)　The expenditure of a business can be classified as either capital expenditure or revenue expenditure. Capital expenditure is expenditure on the purchase of assets for long term use within the business, fixed assets. Revenue expenditure is all other expenditure of the business, the day to day purchases and running costs of the business.

　b)　Costs of a business can also be classified according to the function of the business that caused the cost. The main functions in manufacturing businesses are usually production, selling and distribution and administration. Costs will therefore be classified as production costs, selling and distribution costs or administration costs.

　c)　Costs can be classified according to their relationship with the product that a business makes or the unit of service that it provides. If the cost can be directly identified with a unit of production or service then it is known as a direct cost. All other costs which cannot be directly identified with the unit of production or service are known as indirect costs. When classifying costs in this manner it is usual to split the direct and indirect costs into three categories, materials, labour and expenses.

　d)　Some costs of a business will tend to alter as activity levels change whilst others will remain constant despite a change in activity levels. This is what is meant by analysing costs according to behaviour. If a cost remains constant irrespective of the level of activity then it is known as a fixed cost. If the cost varies directly with the level of activity then it is classified as a variable cost. Some costs have both a fixed and a variable element - this means that there is a fixed element that must be paid no matter what the level of activity and then there is a further element of the cost which will alter as activity levels alter. These costs are known as semi-variable costs. A further classification of cost is a step fixed cost. This is a cost that is fixed for a range of activity levels but outside this range will alter and then remain fixed for a further range of activity levels.

4

	Capital	Revenue
Purchase of a car for resale by a car dealer		✓
Purchase of a car for use by a salesman	✓	
Road tax payable on purchase of a car for use by a salesman		✓
Redecorating head office		✓
Installing new machinery	✓	
Cleaning of new machinery after initial use		✓

5

	Production cost	Selling and distribution cost	Administration cost
Depreciation of salesmen's cars		✓	
Production manager's salary	✓		
Depreciation of machinery	✓		
Rent of office space			✓
Depreciation of delivery vans		✓	
CD-Roms for office computer			✓

6

	Direct cost	Indirect cost
Wages of factory supervisor		✓
Hire of plant for construction of a building by a building firm	✓	
Cleaning materials used in the factory		✓
Factory rent		✓
Wages of a trainee accountant in an accountancy firm	✓	
Cement used for construction of a building by a building firm	✓	

7
a)   Semi-variable cost
b)   Fixed cost
c)   Variable cost
d)   Fixed cost
e)   Step fixed cost

8

	Units	Cost £
Highest level – June	145,000	424,000
Lowest level – April	110,000	340,000
Increase	35,000	84,000

Variable element of cost	=	$\dfrac{£84,000}{35,000 \text{ units}}$
	=	£2.40 per unit

	£
June production – variable costs (145,000 x £2.40)	348,000
Fixed costs (balancing figure)	76,000
Total production cost	424,000

9

	80,000 units £	130,000 units £	180,000 units £
Variable costs – production costs (£3.80 + 1.40 + 0.30 = £5.50)	440,000	715,000	990,000
Fixed cost – depreciation	30,000	30,000	30,000
Step fixed cost – rent	150,000	190,000	190,000
	620,000	935,000	1,210,000

10   a)   Individual contracts
       b)   A passenger mile (or passenger kilometre)

11

	Total £	Prime cost £	Production expense £	Admin. expense £	Selling and distribution expense £
Wages of assembly employees	6,750	6,750			
Wages of stores employees	3,250		3,250		
Tyres for toy wheels	1,420	1,420			
Safety goggles for operators	810		810		
Job advert for new employees	84			84	
Depreciation of delivery vehicles	125				125
Depreciation of production machines	264		264		
Cost of trade exhibition	1,200				1,200
Computer stationery	130			130	
Course fee for AAT training	295			295	
Royalty for the design of wheel 1477	240	240			
	14,568	8,410	4,324	509	1,325

12 Cost behaviour patterns

a)

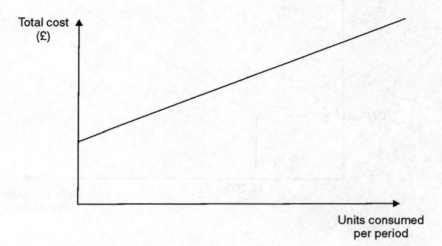

b)

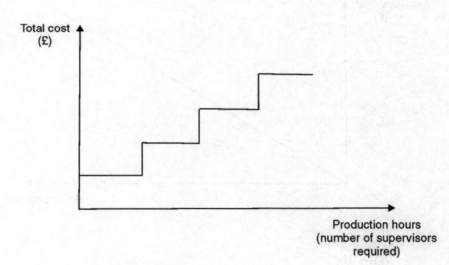

c)

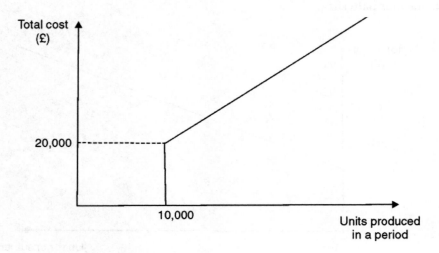

d)

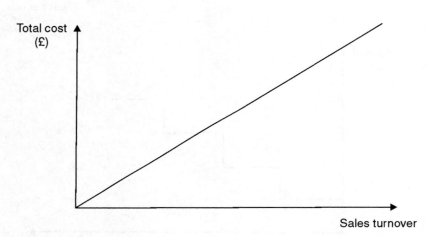

e)

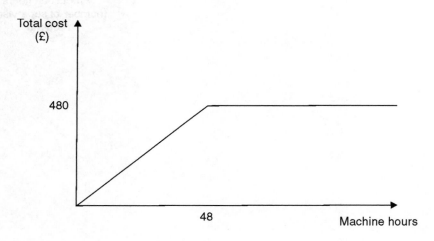

13

REPORT

To: Managing Director
From: Accounting Technician
Subject: Cost behaviour   **Date:** 18 May 2007

The classification of costs by their behaviour

Costs may be classified in many different ways, but one of the most important ways from the point of view of managing a business is classification according to how costs change in response to changes in the level of activity. The main distinction is between **fixed costs** and **variable costs**.

Fixed costs are those that do not change whatever the level of activity. The cost of rental of a business premises is a common example: this is a constant amount (at least within a stated time period) that does not vary with the level of activity conducted on the premises. Other examples are business rates, salaries, buildings insurance and so on.

A sketch graph of a fixed cost would look like this.

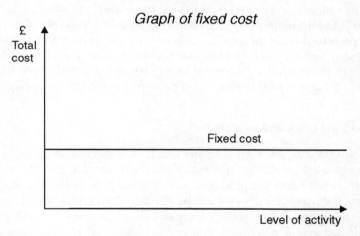

Graph of fixed cost

Variable costs, of course, are those that do vary with the level of activity: if a business produces two widgets, for example, it uses twice as many materials as it does for one widget. Similarly if it sells more goods, its sales administration costs like stationery and postage will vary proportionately.

A sketch graph of a variable cost would look like this.

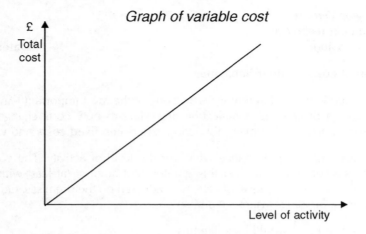

Graph of variable cost

£
Total
cost

Level of activity

Many costs behave in a more complicated fashion than these simple models suggest. For example, a telephone bill has a **fixed element** (the standing charge) and a **variable element** (the cost of calls). These are called **mixed costs** (or semi-variable or semi-fixed costs). Other costs are stepped: that is, they are fixed within a certain level of activity but increase above or below that level at certain levels of activity. For example, if a second factory has to be rented to produce the required volume of output the cost of rent will double. Other patterns are exhibited when quantity discounts are available.

Cost behaviour and total costs and unit costs

If the variable cost of producing a widget is £5 per unit then it will remain at that cost per unit no matter how many widgets are produced. However if the fixed costs are £5,000 then the fixed cost per unit will decrease as more units are produced: one unit will have fixed costs of £5,000 per unit; if 2,500 are produced the fixed cost per unit will be £2; if 5,000 are produced fixed costs per unit will be only £1. Thus as the level of activity increases the total costs per unit (fixed costs plus variable costs) will decrease.

In sketch graph form this may be illustrated as follows.

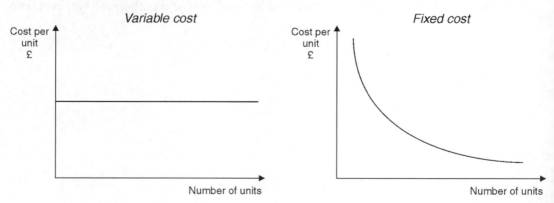

Variable cost

Cost per
unit
£

Number of units

Fixed cost

Cost per
unit
£

Number of units

The importance of cost behaviour

The classification of costs according to behaviour serves a number of purposes, notably the following.

a)   In **planning** it is necessary to know the cost that will be incurred at various possible levels of activity so that a level appropriate to the overall resources of the business may be chosen.

b)   To **maintain control** of the business it is necessary to compare actual results achieved to those expected and this will require adjustments depending upon actual and expected levels of activity.

c)   When **marginal costing** is used, for example for **decision making**, the distinction between fixed and variable costs is fundamental to this approach.

Signed: Accounting Technician

answers to chapter 2:
MATERIALS COSTS

1   a)   The three main categories of stock for a manufacturing business are **raw materials, work in progress** and **finished goods**

    b)   The internal document used to record the quantity of materials received from a supplier is known as a **goods received note**

    c)   The initial internal document that starts the purchasing process for materials is known as a **purchase requisition**

    d)   A **purchase order** is the document that is sent to a supplier to request the supply of materials

    e)   When materials are required from stores by the factory a **materials requisition** is filled out

    f)   A **purchase invoice** is the document received from a supplier of materials requesting payment

2

STOCK CARD

Description: 23 Electrical component EC23   **Bin No:**   413

Code No:

Receipts			Issues			Balance
Date	Reference	Quantity	Date	Reference	Quantity	Quantity
2007 1 June						50
3 June	GRN0326	340				390
			5 June	MR0295	150	240
			10 June	MR0307	190	50
12 June	GRN0348	300				350
			20 June	MR0315	180	170
			25 June	MR0320	100	70
28 June	GRN0363	320				390

3

STORES LEDGER ACCOUNT

Stock item ____LRM____

Code ____8888____

Date	Receipts Qty	Receipts Unit price £	Receipts £	Issues Qty	Issues Unit price £	Issues £	Balance Qty	Balance Unit cost £	Balance £
Op bal							100	2.00	200
3 Sept	400	2.10	840				500	2.08	1,040
4 Sept				200	2.08	416	300	2.08	624
9 Sept	300	2.12	636				600	2.10	1,260
11 Sept				400	2.10	840	200	2.10	420
18 Sept	100	2.40	240				300	2.20	660
20 Sept				100	2.20	220	200	2.20	440

Workings

With the weighted average cost method, a weighted average cost is calculated each time a new delivery is received. The weighting is provided by the number of units at each price brought into the calculation. The general formula is as follows:

$$\text{Average price per unit} = \frac{\text{Total value of existing stock} + \text{Total value of goods added to stock}}{\text{Units of existing stock} + \text{units added to stock}}$$

4 a)

STORES LEDGER ACCOUNT

Stock item ___XK2___

Code ___041861___

FIFO basis

Date	Receipts				Issues				Balance	
	GRN	Qty	Unit price £	£	Req No	Qty	Unit price £	£	Qty	£
1 July									400	1,200.00
4 July					416	320	3.00	960	80	240.00
7 July	668	500	3.20	1,600					580	1,840.00
12 July					422	80	3.00	240		
						100	3.20	320	400	1,280.00
16 July					428	300	3.20	960	100	320.00
19 July	674	500	3.50	1,750					600	2,070.00
23 July					433	100	3.20	320		
28 July						130	3.50	455	370	1,295.00
					440	300	3.50	1,050	70	245.00

b)

STORES LEDGER ACCOUNT

Stock item ___XK2___

Code ___041861___

LIFO basis

Date	Receipts				Issues				Balance	
	GRN	Qty	Unit price £	£	Req No	Qty	Unit price £	£	Qty	£
1 July									400	1,200.00
4 July					416	320	3.00	960	80	240.00
7 July	668	500	3.20	1,600					580	1,840.00
12 July					422	180	3.20	576	400	1,264.00
16 July					428	300	3.20	960	100	304.00
19 July	674	500	3.50	1,750					600	2,054.00
23 July					433	230	3.50	805	370	1,249.00
28 July					440	270	3.50	945		
						20	3.20	64	70	
						10	3.00	30		210.00

c)

	STORES LEDGER ACCOUNT									

Stock item ___XK2___

Code ___041861___

AVCO basis

Date	Receipts				Issues				Balance	
	GRN	Qty	Unit price £	£	Req No	Qty	Unit price £	£	Qty	£
1 July									400	1,200.00
4 July					416	320	3.00	960	80	240.00
7 July	668	500	3.20	1,600					580	1,840.00
12 July					422	180	3.17	570	400	1,269.40
16 July					428	300	3.17	951	100	318.40
19 July	674	500	3.50	1,750					600	2,068.40
23 July					433	230	3.45	793	370	1,274.90
28 July					440	300	3.45	1,035	70	239.90

Workings

Calculation of weighted average price:

				£
4 July	80	@	3.00	240.00
7 July	500	@	3.20	1,600.00
	580		3.17	1,840.00
12 July	(180)	@	3.17	(570.60)
16 July	(300)	@	3.17	(951.00)
19 July	500	@	3.50	1,750.00
	600	@	3.45	2,068.40
23 July	(230)	@	3.45	(793.50)
28 July	(300)	@	3.45	(1,035.00)
	70	@	3.45	239.90

5   FIFO

		Units		Cost	Total cost £
1 July	Opening balance	220	@	5.60	1,232.00
3 July	Issue	(160)	@	5.60	(896.00)
		60			336.00
7 July	Purchase	300	@	6.00	1,800.00
		360			2,136.00
10 July	Issue	(60)	@	5.60	(336.00)
		(110)	@	6.00	(660.00)
		190			1,140.00
15 July	Issue	(100)	@	6.00	(600.00)
		90			540.00
20 July	Purchase	250	@	6.30	1,575.00
		340			2,115.00
24 July	Issue	(90)	@	6.00	(540.00)
		(110)	@	6.30	(693.00)
		140			882.00

a)   Cost of issues (£896.00 + 336.00 + 660.00 + 600.00 + 540.00 + 693.00) = £3,725.00

b)   Closing stock value = £882.00

LIFO

		Units		Cost	Total cost £
1 July	Opening balance	220	@	5.60	1,232.00
3 July	Issue	(160)	@	5.60	(896.00)
		60			336.00
7 July	Purchase	300	@	6.00	1,800.00
		360			2,136.00
10 July	Issue	(170)	@	6.00	(1,020.00)
		190			1,116.00
15 July	Issue	(100)	@	6.00	(600.00)
		90			516.00
20 July	Purchase	250	@	6.30	1,575.00
		340			2,091.00
24 July	Issue	(200)	@	6.30	(1,260.00)
		140			831.00

a)   Cost of issues (£896.00 + 1,020.00 + 600.00 + 1,260.00) = £3,776.00

b)   Closing stock value = £831.00

AVCO

		Units		Cost	Total cost £
1 July	Opening balance	220	@	5.60	1,232.00
3 July	Issue	(160)	@	5.60	(896.00)
		60			336.00
7 July	Purchase	300	@	6.00	1,800.00
		360		5.93	2,136.00
10 July	Issue	(170)	@	5.93	(1,008.10)
15 July	Issue	(100)	@	5.93	(593.00)
20 July	Purchase	250	@	6.30	1,575.00
		340		6.21	2,109.90
24 July	Issue	(200)	@	6.21	(1,242.00)
		140	@	6.21	867.90

a) Cost of issues (£896.00 + 1,008.10 + 593.00 + 1,242.00) = £3,739.10

b) Closing stock value = £867.90

6 The FIFO method of stock valuation makes the assumption that each time an issue is made from stock that this issue is of the earliest purchases which will often reflect the actual usage pattern as the oldest stocks will often be used first. This means that at the end of the period the closing stocks are valued at the most recent up-to-date prices. However this method also means that the cost of issues to production are made at varying different and possibly out-of -date prices – this in turn means that the profit shown, if prices are rising, will be higher than that under the LIFO method.

The LIFO method of stock valuation makes the assumption that each time an issue is made from stock that this issue is of the most recent purchases – effectively therefore the issue is being made from the top of the pile of stock which may reflect actual practice. Issues are therefore made at current up-to-date prices which means that managers are more aware of current prices as these are the ones that their department is being charged. However as with FIFO it does mean that the price being charged for issues is constantly changing. The closing stock under LIFO is valued at the earliest prices and therefore may be an extremely out of date figure. As issues are charged at current prices the profit shown under LIFO, if prices are rising, will be lower than that under FIFO and indeed this method is not recommended for use in the financial statements by SSAP 9.

7

Materials control account

	£		£
Opening stock	12,523	WIP	79,247
Creditors	83,469	Production overhead control	6,248
		Closing stock	10,497
	95,992		95,992

Work in progress control account

	£		£
Materials control	79,247		

Production overhead control account

	£		£
Materials control	6,248		

8

a) Re-order level = maximum demand x maximum lead time

= 200 x 8

= 1,600 units

b) EOQ = $\sqrt{\dfrac{2cd}{h}}$

= $\sqrt{\dfrac{2\times £100\times 40,000}{2}}$

= 2,000 units

c) Minimum stock level = re-order level – (average usage x average lead time)

= 1,600 – (160 x 5)

= 800 units

d) Maximum stock level = re-order level + re-order quantity – (minimum usage x minimum lead time)

= 1,600 + 2,000 – (130 x 2)

= 3,340 units

3 September

Average price per unit $= \dfrac{(100 \times £2) + (400 \times £2.10)}{(100 + 400)\,\text{units}}$

$= \dfrac{£(200 + 840)}{500\,\text{units}}$

$= \dfrac{£1,040}{500\,\text{units}}$

$= £2.08$

4 September

The 200 units issued on 4 September will be valued at £2.08 per unit.

200 × £2.08 = £416

Therefore balance = 300 × £2.08 = £624

9 September

The 300 units received on this date have a total value of £636 (300 × £2.12).

Average price per unit $= \dfrac{£(624 + 636)}{(300 + 300)\,\text{units}}$

$= \dfrac{£1,260}{600\,\text{units}}$

$= £2.10$

11 September

The 400 units issued on 11 September will be valued at £2.10 per unit.

400 × £2.10 = £420

Therefore balance = 200 × £2.10 = £420

18 September

The 100 units received on 18 September have a total value of £240 (100 × £2.40).

Average price per unit $= \dfrac{£(420 + 240)}{(200 + 100)\,\text{units}}$

$= \dfrac{£660}{300\,\text{units}}$

$= £2.20$

20 September

The 100 units issued on 20 September will be valued at £2.20 per unit

100 × £2.20 = £220

Therefore balance = 200 × £2.20 = £440

9 FIFO to LIFO

a) Changing from FIFO to LIFO during a period of rapidly rising prices would result in lower stock valuations.

b) Changing from FIFO to LIFO during a period of rapidly rising prices would result in higher costs of materials charged to production.

10 Protective gloves

Closing stock = Opening stock + purchases – issues
                 = 100 + 200 – 150 = 150 pairs

Value of closing stock = 150 pairs x £1.90 (purchase price on 7 November)
                      = £285

11 Wiggles plc

STORES RECORD CARD (STOCK CARD)

Material description: *Paper*

Code no: *1564A*

Date	Details	Receipts Sheets	Receipts £	Issues Sheets	Issues Unit price £	Issues £	Balance Sheets	Balance £
	Opening stock						10,000	3,000
3 May	Purchase	4,000	1,600				14,000	4,600
6 May	Issue			7,000	0.33	2,310	7,000	2,290
12 May	Purchase	10,000	3,100				17,000	5,390
15 May	Issue			6,000	0.32	1,920	11,000	3,470
22 May	Issue			7,200	0.32	2,304	3,800	1,166
25 May	Purchase	10,000	3,200				13,800	4,366

12

STOCK RECORD CARD

Product: Motor oil

Centre: Servicing

Date	Receipts			Issues			Balance	
	Quantity	Cost per litre	Total cost	Quantity	Cost per litre	Total cost	Quantity	Total cost
	litres	£	£	litres	£	£	litres	£
b/f 1 May							2,100	2,100
4 May	2,400	1.20	2,880				4,500	4,980
8 May				3,300	2,400 x £1.20 900 x £1.00	3,780	1,200	1,200
10 May	3,000	1.10	3,300				4,200	4,500
11 May				3,200	3,000 x £1.10 200 x £1.00	3,500	1,000	1,000
17 May	5,000	1.00	5,000				6,000	6,000
18 May				5,400	5,000 x £1.00 400 x £1.00	5,400	600	600
23 May	6,400	0.95	6,080				7,000	6,680
24 May				4,420	4,420 x £0.95	4,199	2,580	2,481

Proof

600 litres @ £1.00 = £600
1,980 litres @ £0.95 = £1,881

Therefore, quantity of stock on 24 May = 600 litres + 1,980 litres = 2,580 litres at a value of £2,481 (£600 + £1,881).

answers to chapter 3:
LABOUR COSTS AND EXPENSES

1 a)

	£
Basic pay 37 hours @ £6.80	251.60
Overtime pay 6 hours @ £6.80 x 1.5	61.20
Total gross pay	312.80

b) Overtime payment   £61.20

c) Overtime premium £6.80 x 0.5 x 6 hours   £20.40

2

	£
300 units @ £1.00	300.00
100 units @ £1.15	115.00
30 units @ £1.35	40.50
Total gross pay	455.50

3 a) Harry

	£
Product A £10.40 x 22	228.80
Product B £18.60 x 7	130.20
Total gross pay	359.00

b) Stella

	£
Basic pay 35 hours @ £8.40	294.00
Overtime pay 8 hours @ £8.40 x 1 1/3	89.60
Total gross pay	383.60

c) Yvette

	£
Basic salary £20,000/12	1,666.67
Bonus £20,000 x 5%	1,000.00
Total gross pay	2,666.67

4

Wages control account

	£		£
Bank	24,700	WIP	20,900
HMRC	6,200	Production overheads	12,400
Pension scheme	2,400		
	33,300		33,300

Work in progress control account

	£		£
Wages control	20,900		

Production overhead control account

	£		£
Wages control	12,400		

5   Freehold building $= \dfrac{£450,000 - 50,000}{40 \text{ years}}$

$= £10,000$

Machinery $= (£220,000 - 20,000) \times \dfrac{4,200}{32,000}$

$= £26,250$

Cars $= (£120,000 - 52,500) \times 25\%$

$= £16,875$

6

Work in progress control account

	£		£
Direct production costs	7,200		

Production overhead control account

	£		£
Indirect production costs	39,256		

7

Job no	Employee name	Number of hours	Rate £	Total cost £
N172	N Davies	2.25	6.60	14.85
	R Khan	1.00	6.80	6.80
				21.65
N174	J Pitman	6.00	10.00	60.00
M215	N Davies	2.00	6.60	13.20
	Y Chang	1.50	6.50	9.75
	R Khan	3.75	6.80	25.50
				48.45

8

a) False.

b) True. Most expenses are the costs of other functions such as distribution, administration and finance.

c) False. Power to run machines is only a direct expense if the machine is dedicated to producing a particular product.

d) True.

answers to chapter 4:
OVERHEADS

1

	Total £	Assembly £	Finishing £	Stores £	Maintenance £
Indirect materials	18,700	16,500	2,200		
Indirect labour	22,800	7,500	6,200	4,500	4,600
Rent and rates	10,000	3,000	2,000	2,500	2,500
Heat and light	7,400	2,220	1,480	1,850	1,850
Supervisor's wages	9,880	5,720	4,160	–	–
Depreciation of machinery	8,400	5,250	1,750	525	875
	77,180	40,190	17,790	9,375	9,825
Stores		6,875	2,500	(9,375)	
Maintenance		5,731	4,094		(9,825)
		52,796	24,384	–	–

Workings

Rent and rates and light and heat are apportioned on the basis of floor area – assembly 30%, finishing 20%, stores and maintenance 25% each.

Supervisor's wages are apportioned on the basis of the supervisor's time in each department – 22:16

Depreciation is apportioned on the basis of net book value – 150:50:15:25

The stores overheads are then reapportioned on the basis of the number of materials requisitions and the maintenance overheads on the basis of the number of maintenance hours required.

2

	Total £	A £	B £	Stores £	Canteen £
Indirect wages	75,700	7,800	4,700	21,200	42,000
Rent	24,000	9,600	6,400	3,200	4,800
Buildings insurance	2,000	800	533	267	400
Power	6,400	2,880	1,920	320	1,280
Heat and light	4,000	1,600	1,066	534	800
Supervisor's wages	10,000	10,000	–	–	–
Machinery depreciation	3,200	1,493	1,280	160	267
Machinery insurance	2,200	1,027	880	110	183
	127,500	35,200	16,779	25,791	49,730
Canteen		29,009	16,577	4,144	(49,730)
				29,935	
Stores		17,961	11,974	(29,935)	
		82,170	45,330	–	–

Workings

Rent, buildings insurance and heat and light are apportioned on the basis of floor area – 12:8:4:6

Power is apportioned using the percentages given

Supervisor's wages are allocated directly to department A.

Machinery depreciation and insurance are apportioned on the basis of the net book value of the machinery – 140:120:15:25

Canteen costs are apportioned according to the number of staff that use it – 70:40:10

The stores costs are apportioned on the basis of the number of materials requisitions.

3

	Total £	Assembly £	Polishing £	Stores £	Maintenance £
	130,000	60,000	40,000	20,000	10,000
Stores		10,000	8,000	(20,000)	2,000
				–	12,000
Maintenance		7,200	4,800		(12,000)
	130,000	77,200	52,800	–	–

4

		Cutting	Finishing
a)	Rate per unit	$\dfrac{58,600}{10,000}$	$\dfrac{42,400}{10,000}$
		= £5.86 per unit	= £4.24 per unit

can be used where all products are of similar size and require a similar input in terms of time and resources of the departments

		Cutting	Finishing
b)	Rate per direct labour hour	$\dfrac{58,600}{4,000}$	$\dfrac{42,400}{24,000}$
		= £14.65 per labour hour	= £1.77 per labour hour

most appropriate in labour intensive departments where most of the overhead relates to labour

		Cutting	Finishing
c)	Rate per machine hour	$\dfrac{58,600}{12,000}$	$\dfrac{42,400}{2,000}$
		= £4.88 per machine hour	£21.20 per machine hour

most appropriate in a largely mechanised department where most of the overhead relates to machinery costs

5 a) $C = \dfrac{£125,000}{100,000}$

= £1.25 per machine hour

as C is a highly mechanised department most of the overhead will relate to the machinery therefore machine hours have been used to absorb the overhead.

$D = \dfrac{£180,000}{80,000}$

= £2.25 per direct labour hour

as D is a highly labour intensive department then most of the overhead will relate to the hours that are worked by the labour force therefore labour hours are used to absorb the overhead.

b)   Product P – department C overhead   £1.25 x 5   =   £ 6.25
                   department D overhead   £2.25 x 7   =   £15.75

6 a) Overhead absorption rate = $\dfrac{£5,400}{1,200}$

= £4.50 per unit

Overhead incurred = £5,000
Overhead absorbed
1,000 units x £4.50 = £4,500

Under-absorbed overhead = £500 – a further expense in the P&L

b) Overhead absorption rate = $\dfrac{£5,040}{1,800}$

= £2.80 per direct labour hour

Overhead incurred = £5,100
Overhead absorbed
2,200 hours x £2.80 = £6,160

Over-absorbed overhead = £1,060 – a credit to the P&L

c) Overhead absorption rate = $\dfrac{£320,000}{80,000}$

= £4.00 per machine hour

Overhead incurred = £320,000
Overhead absorbed
82,000 x £4.00 = £328,000

Over-absorbed overhead = £8,000 – a credit to the P&L

7 a)

Production overhead control account

	£		£
Creditors/cash – overheads incurred	5,000	WIP – overheads absorbed	4,500
		P&L – under absorbed	500

b)

Production overhead control account

	£		£
Creditors/cash – overheads incurred	5,100	WIP – overheads absorbed	6,160
P&L – over absorbed	1,060		
	6,160		6,160

c)

Production overhead control account

	£		£
Creditors/cash – overheads incurred	320,000	WIP – overheads absorbed	328,000
P&L – over absorbed	8,000		
	328,000		328,000

8 Overhead absorption rates are calculated as follows:

$$\text{Overhead absorption rate} = \frac{\text{Budgeted overheads}}{\text{Budgeted activity level}}$$

Using budgeted figures means that the actual overhead cost is unlikely to be the same as the overheads actually absorbed into production, as we are relying on two estimated figures (overheads and activity levels). These estimates are likely to differ from the actual values that are experienced during the period. Consequently, at the end of the period when the profit and loss account is drawn up, the profit figure will be wrong as the overhead charge will be the absorbed amount rather than the actual amount. The error in the profit figure will result from one of two possibilities.

a) If more overheads are absorbed than have actually been incurred, this is known as **over-absorption**.

b) If fewer overheads are absorbed than have actually been incurred, this is known as **under-absorption**.

The amount over- or under-absorbed is adjusted for in the profit and loss account after the production cost has been charged. Under-absorption means that too little overhead has been charged in the production cost, so a deduction is made from profit. Over-absorption means that too much overhead has been charged, so there is a compensating addition to profit.

9 Machining department

		£
Overheads incurred		9,322
Overheads absorbed (£5 × 1,753)		8,765
Under-absorbed overhead		557

10 Happy Ltd

Actual fixed overheads for November	Basis	Total £	Warehouse £	Manufacturing £	Sales £	Administration £
Depreciation	Net book value	14,600	2,920	10,220	730	730
Rent	% floor space	48,000	9,600	31,200	2,400	4,800
Other property overheads	% floor space	12,800	2,560	8,320	640	1,280
Administration overheads	allocation	28,800	–	–	–	28,800
Staff costs	allocation	39,800	4,800	14,340	12,250	8,410
		144,000	19,880	64,080	16,020	44,020

1   Trident Ltd

Marginal Costing Statement for March

	£	£
Sales revenue (4,000 × £40)		160,000
Variable costs		
Direct materials	25,000	
Direct labour	50,000	
Variable overheads	15,000	
Total variable costs		(90,000)
Total contribution for the period		70,000

The total contribution for the period is therefore £70,000. Fixed costs are treated as a period cost and are not included in the total contribution calculation.

2   a)   **Absorption costing**

	£
Direct materials	12.00
Direct labour – cutting (2 x £7.40)	14.80
finishing	6.80
Variable overheads:	
Cutting ((£336,000/240,000) x 2)	2.80
Finishing (£132,000/120,000)	1.10
Fixed overheads:	
Cutting ((£144,000/240,000) x 2)	1.20
Finishing (£96,000/120,000)	0.80
	39.50

     b)   **Marginal costing**

	£
Direct materials	12.00
Direct labour – cutting (2 x £7.40)	14.80
finishing	6.80
Variable overheads:	
Cutting (£336,000/240,000 x 2)	2.80
Finishing (£132,000/120,000)	1.10
	37.50

3 Cost per unit – absorption costing

	£
Direct materials	6.80
Direct labour	3.60
Variable costs (£32,400/24,000)	1.35
Fixed costs (£44,400/24,000)	1.85
	13.60

Cost per unit – marginal costing

	£
Direct materials	6.80
Direct labour	3.60
Variable costs (£32,400/24,000)	1.35
	11.75

a) Absorption costing – profit and loss account

	July £	July £	August £	August £
Sales (22,000 x £16)		352,000		
(25,000 x £16)				400,000
Less: cost of sales				
Opening stock (1,500 x £13.60)	20,400			
(3,500 x £13.60)			47,600	
Production (24,000 x £13.60)	326,400		326,400	
	346,800		374,000	
Less: closing stock (3,500 x £13.60)	(47,600)			
(2,500 x £13.60)			(34,000)	
		299,200		340,000
Profit		52,800		60,000

Marginal costing – profit and loss account

		July		August	
		£	£	£	£
Sales	(22,000 x £16)		352,000		
	(25,000 x £16)				400,000
Less: cost of sales					
Opening stock	(1,500 x £11.75)	17,625			
	(3,500 x £11.75)			41,125	
Production (24,000 x £11.75)		282,000		282,000	
		299,625		323,125	
Less: closing stock	(3,500 x £11.75)	(41,125)			
	(2,500 x £11.75)			(29,375)	
			258,500		293,750
Contribution			93,500		106,250
Fixed costs			44,400		44,400
			49,100		61,850

b) **Reconciliation of profit figures**

		July £	August £
Absorption cost profit		52,800	60,000
Increase in stock	(3,500 – 1,500)		
x fixed c.p.u.	2,000 x £1.85	(3,700)	
Decrease in stock	(3,500 – 2,500)		
x fixed c.p.u.	1,000 x £1.85		1,850
		49,100	61,850

4 Unit cost – absorption costing

	£
Direct materials	23.60
Direct labour (4 x £5.80)	23.20
Variable overheads (£88,000/8,000)	11.00
Fixed overheads (£51,200/8,000)	6.40
	64.20

Unit cost – marginal costing

	£
Direct materials	23.60
Direct labour (4 x £5.80)	23.20
Variable overheads (£88,000/8,000)	11.00
	57.80

a) **Absorption costing – profit and loss account**

	£	£
Sales (8,200 x £70)		574,000
Less: cost of sales		
Opening stock (840 x £64.20)	53,928	
Production cost (8,000 x £64.20)	513,600	
	567,528	
Less: closing stock (640 x £64.20)	41,088	
		526,440
Profit		47,560

Marginal costing – profit and loss account

	£	£
Sales (8,200 x £70)		574,000
Less: cost of sales		
Opening stock (840 x £57.80)	48,552	
Production cost (8,000 x £57.80)	462,400	
	510,952	
Less: closing stock (640 x £57.80)	36,992	
		473,960
Contribution		100,040
Less: fixed costs		51,200
Profit		48,840

b)

	£
Absorption costing profit	47,560
Decrease in stocks x fixed cost per unit (200 x £6.40)	1,280
Marginal costing profit	48,840

5   Absorption costing has the advantage of allowing managers to see whether the sales of their products are covering all of the production costs of those products. However, due to the different nature of fixed costs compared with variable costs, it is argued that contribution is a much more useful figure for management than a profit figure after production overheads have been apportioned. If fixed costs are included in the cost per unit then the unit cost will fall as activity levels increase simply due to the nature of the fixed cost not changing but being spread over more units of activity.

A further argument for the use of marginal costing rather than absorption costing for cost reporting purposes is to do with the profit differences and stock levels. Under absorption costing we have seen that it is possible to report a higher profit figure by increasing the closing stock levels. If a manager is assessed and possibly remunerated on the basis of the figure that he reports for profit then the profit can be manipulated by over producing and building up stock levels. Although this will increase absorption costing profit it may not be in the best interests of the organisation. This type of manipulation of profit cannot take place if marginal costing is used.

answers to chapter 6:
COSTING SYSTEMS

1 **Batch costing** is a form of costing that is similar to **job costing**, except that costs are collected for a **batch of items**. The cost unit is the **batch**. A **cost per unit** is calculated by **dividing the total batch cost by the number of units in the batch.**

2 **Costing methods**

a) Job costing
b) Batch costing
c) Job costing

3 Job costing is an appropriate costing system in the type of business where the product that is produced is a 'one-off' job for a customer. Each individual job will tend to be different and have different materials, labour and expenses inputs. Therefore the costs of each individual job need to be specified.

4 **Job costing schedule**

	£
Direct materials	2,800.00
Direct labour	526.50
Overheads	234.90
Total costs	3,561.40
Profit (20% x 3,561.40)	712.28
	4,273.68
VAT	747.89
Total price	5,021.57

5

JOB NUMBER 2856

	Budget £	Actual £	Variance £
Direct materials			
▪ wood	1,650.00	1,830.00	180.00 ADV
▪ components	830.00	755.00	75.00 FAV
▪ plastic	320.00	300.00	20.00 FAV
Direct labour			
▪ Grade I - 30hours	414.00	478.50	64.50 ADV
▪ Grade III - 12 hours	132.00	77.00	55.00 FAV
Direct expenses			
▪ hire of equipment	300.00	380.00	80.00 ADV
Overheads 42 x £4.60	193.20		
40 x £4.60		184.00	9.20 FAV
Total cost	3,839.20	4,004.50	165.30 ADV
Profit (3,839.20 x 25%)	959.80		
(4,799.00 – 4,004.50)		794.50	
	4,799.00	4,799.00	
VAT@ 17.5%	839.82	839.82	
Job cost	5,638.82	5,638.82	

6 **Step 1** Calculate the number of normal loss units:
100,000 kg x 6% = 6,000 kg

Step 2 Calculate the expected output from the process:
100,000 kg – 6,000 kg = 94,000 kg

Step 3 Total the process costs:
£287,000 + 138,000 + 82,600 = £507,600

Step 4 Calculate the cost per unit of expected output:

$$\frac{£507,600}{94,000} = £5.40 \text{ per kg}$$

Process account

	kg	£		kg	£
Materials	100,000	287,000	Normal loss	6,000	-
Labour		138,000	Abnormal loss	2,000	10,800
Overheads		82,600	Output	92,000	496,800
	100,000	507,600		100,000	507,600

Abnormal loss account

	kg	£		kg	£
Process account	2,000	10,800	Profit and loss	2,000	10,800

7

Step 1   Calculate the number of normal loss units:
18,000 ltr x 5% = 900 ltr

Step 2   Calculate the expected output from the process:
18,000 ltr – 900 ltr = 17,100 ltr

Step 3   Total the process costs:
£35,800 + 7,200 + 11,720 = £54,720

Step 4   Calculate the cost per unit of expected output:
$$\frac{£54,720}{17,100} = £3.20 \text{ per litre}$$

Process account

	ltr	£		ltr	£
Materials	18,000	35,800	Normal loss	900	-
Labour		7,200	Output	17,500	56,000
Overheads		11,720			
Abnormal gain	400	1,280			
	18,400	56,000		18,400	56,000

Abnormal gain account

	ltr	£		ltr	£
Profit and loss	400	1,280	Process account	400	1,280

1

Production overhead control account

	£		£
Overheads incurred	4,720	Overheads absorbed	
		1,400 x £3.20	4,480
		Under-absorbed overhead	240
	4,720		4,720

The under-absorbed overhead of £240 is debited to the profit and loss account as an additional cost.

2

Production overhead control account

	£		£
Overheads incurred	5,840	Overheads absorbed	
Over-absorbed overhead	223	940 x £6.45	6,063
	6,063		6,063

The over-absorbed overhead of £223 will be credited to the profit and loss account.

3

Materials control account

	£		£
Creditors	14,365	WIP control	11,632
		Closing stock	2,733
	14,365		14,365

Wages control account

	£		£
Gross wages (18,375 + 2,682)	21,057	WIP control	18,375
		Production overhead control	2,682
	21,057		21,057

Production overhead control account

	£		£
Wages control	2,682	Overhead absorbed – WIP	
Bank	6,243	1,530 x £5.20	7,956
		Under-absorbed overhead	969
	8,925		8,925

Work in progress control account

	£		£
Materials control	11,632	Finished goods	36,540
Wages control	18,375		
Production overhead	7,956	Closing stock	1,423
	37,963		37,963

4 a) & b)

Materials control account

	£		£
Opening stock	1,290	WIP control	6,620
Creditors	7,640	Administration overhead	990
		Closing stock	1,320
	8,930		8,930

Wages control account

	£		£
Gross wages (£5,430 + £1,460)	6,890	WIP control	5,430
		Production overhead control	1,460
	6,890		6,890

Production overhead control account

	£		£
Wages control	1,460	Overhead absorbed – WIP	
Cash	4,290	490 x £11.10	5,439
		Under-absorbed overhead	311
		(P&L)	
	5,750		5,750

Work in progress control account

	£		£
Opening balance	1,540	Finished goods	12,200
Materials control	6,620		
Production overhead	5,439	Closing balance	1,399
	13,599		13,599

Finished goods control account

	£		£
Opening stock	1,830	P&L (bal fig)	12,380
WIP control	12,200	Closing stock	1,650
	14,030		14,030

Debtors control account

	£		£
Opening balance	7,200	Cash	6,800
Sales	14,700	Closing balance	15,100
	21,900		21,900

Creditors control account

	£		£
Cash	4,900	Opening balance	5,460
Closing balance	8,200	Materials	7,640
	13,100		13,100

Cash at bank account

	£		£
Opening balance	3,070	Creditors	4,900
Debtors	6,800	Production overheads	4,290
Closing balance	530	Administration overheads	1,210
	10,400		10,400

Administration overheads account

	£		£
Materials control	990		
Cash	1,210	P&L	2,200
	2,200		2,200

Sales account

	£		£
P&L	14,700	Debtors	14,700

c) **Profit and loss account for August**

	£
Sales	14,700
Cost of goods sold (finished goods)	(12,380)
Gross profit	2,320
Under absorbed overhead	(311)
Administration overheads	(2,200)
Net loss	(191)

1 Provided that the selling price and the variable costs remain constant then contribution per unit will also be constant no matter what the level of activity. However full production cost per unit will decrease as production levels increase as the fixed costs are spread over more units. Therefore the constant figure of contribution per unit is more useful in the decision making process.

2 a) Break-even point $= \dfrac{£1,100,000}{£28-17}$

$\quad\quad\quad = 100,000$ units

b) i) Margin of safety (units) $=$ Budgeted sales – breakeven sales

$\quad\quad\quad\quad\quad = (115,000 - 100,000)$ units

$\quad\quad\quad\quad\quad = 15,000$ units

ii) Margin of safety (% budgeted sales) $= \dfrac{115,000 - 100,000}{115,000} \times 100\%$

$\quad\quad\quad\quad\quad = 13\%$

3 Contribution per unit $= £(16 - 8) = £8$

Contribution required to breakeven $=$ fixed costs $= £40,000$

Breakeven point $= \dfrac{\text{Fixed costs}}{\text{Contribution per unit}}$

$\quad\quad\quad = \dfrac{£40,000}{£8}$

$\quad\quad\quad = 5,000$ units

Sales revenue at breakeven point $= 5,000$ units x £16 per unit
$\quad\quad\quad\quad\quad\quad\quad = £80,000$

4   Margin of safety = Budgeted sales volume – breakeven sales volume

Breakeven sales volume = $\dfrac{\text{Fixed costs}}{\text{Contribution per unit}}$

$$= \dfrac{£110,000}{£55}$$

$$= 2,000 \text{ units}$$

Therefore, margin of safety (units) = 2,500 units – 2,000 units
                                    = 500 units

Therefore, margin of safety (sales revenue) = margin of safety (units) x selling price per unit
                                            = 500 units x £80
                                            = £40,000

5   Target profit units = $\dfrac{£540,000+300,000}{£83-65}$

$$= 46,667 \text{ units}$$

6   Profit volume ratio = $\dfrac{£40-28}{£40} \times 100\%$

$$= 30\%$$

Target profit sales revenue = $\dfrac{£518,000+250,000}{0.3}$

$$= £2,560,000$$

7   **Identify the limiting factor**

Materials – at maximum demand

(4 x 20,000) + (5 x 25,000) + (3 x 8,000) = 229,000 kg

Labour hours – at maximum demand

(2 x 20,000) + (3 x 25,000) + (3 x 8,000) = 139,000 hours

Machine hours - at maximum demand

(4 x 20,000) + (3 x 25,000) + (2 x 8,000) = 171,000 hours

Therefore the only limiting factor is labour hours.

Contribution per labour hour

	R	S	T
Contribution	£11	£14	£19
Labour hours	2	3	3
Contribution per labour hour	£5.50	£4.67	£6.33
Ranking	2	3	1

Production plan

	Units	Labour hours used	Cumulative labour hours used
T	8,000	24,000	24,000
R	20,000	40,000	64,000
S (balance)	12,000	36,000	100,000
		100,000	

Contribution earned

	£
R (20,000 x £11)	220,000
S (12,000 x £14)	168,000
T (8,000 x £19)	152,000
	540,000

8

Sauce	Fudge	Butterscotch	Chocolate
	£	£	£
Selling price per bottle (W1)	2.00	2.00	1.00
Less: Unit variable costs			
Direct materials (W2)	0.20	0.25	0.10
Direct labour (W3)	0.60	0.50	0.25
Variable overheads (W4)	0.05	0.10	0.05
Contribution per bottle*	1.15	1.15	0.60
Profit volume ratio (%)**	57.5%	57.5%	60%

* Contribution = Selling price – Variable costs
** Profit volume ratio =   x 100%

Workings

1   **Selling price per bottle**

$$\text{Selling price per bottle} = \frac{\text{Total sales revenue}}{\text{Sales (bottles)}}$$

$$\text{Fudge sauce} = \frac{£1,000}{500} = £2 \text{ per bottle}$$

$$\text{Butterscotch sauce} = \frac{£1,400}{700} = £2 \text{ per bottle}$$

$$\text{Chocolate sauce} = \frac{£600}{600} = £1 \text{ per bottle}$$

2   **Direct materials per bottle**

$$\text{Direct materials per bottle} = \frac{\text{Total direct material costs}}{\text{Production volume (bottles)}}$$

$$\text{Fudge sauce} = \frac{£100}{500} = £0.20 \text{ per bottle}$$

$$\text{Butterscotch sauce} = \frac{£175}{700} = £0.25 \text{ per bottle}$$

$$\text{Chocolate sauce} = \frac{£60}{600} = £0.10 \text{ per bottle}$$

3   **Direct labour cost per bottle**

$$\text{Direct labour cost per bottle} = \frac{\text{Total direct labour costs}}{\text{Production volume (bottles)}}$$

$$\text{Fudge sauce} = \frac{£300}{500} = £0.60 \text{ per bottle}$$

$$\text{Butterscotch sauce} = \frac{£350}{700} = £0.50 \text{ per bottle}$$

$$\text{Chocolate sauce} = \frac{£150}{600} = £0.25 \text{ per bottle}$$

4   **Variable overheads per bottle**

Variable overheads per bottle $= \dfrac{\text{Total variable overhead costs}}{\text{Production volume (bottles)}}$

Fudge sauce $= \dfrac{£25}{500} = £0.05$ per bottle

Butterscotch sauce $= \dfrac{£70}{700} = £0.10$ per bottle

Chocolate sauce $= \dfrac{£30}{600} = £0.05$ per bottle

If the company only manufactures chocolate sauce, the sales revenue that it would need to earn each month to cover the fixed costs of £300 is:

$$\dfrac{\text{Fixed costs}}{\text{P/V ratio for chocolate sauce}} = \dfrac{£300}{60\%}$$

$$= \dfrac{£300}{60\%}$$

$$= £500$$

b)   Therefore, the sales revenue required = £500 (which is 500 bottles of chocolate sauce at £1 each).

Alternatively, you could have calculated the breakeven point in volume terms ie the point at which fixed costs are covered.

$$\text{Breakeven point} = \dfrac{\text{Fixed costs}}{\text{Contribution per bottle of chocolate sauce}}$$

$$= \dfrac{£300}{£0.60} = 500 \text{ bottles}$$

Each bottle sells for £1, therefore sales revenue required to cover fixed costs = 500 x £1 = £500.

1 The time value of money is the principle that a sum of money received now is worth more than the same sum received at some time in the future due to the fact that this sum could be invested now to earn interest. This means that a sum of money receivable or payable at some time in the future is worth less than its face value now due to the interest that is lost on not investing. Therefore future cash flows must be discounted in order to determine their present value.

2 a) **Payback period**

	Cash inflows	Cumulative cash inflows
	£	£
31 Dec 2008	15,000	15,000
31 Dec 2009	25,000	40,000
31 Dec 2010	35,000	75,000
31 Dec 2011	30,000	105,000

The payback period is 4 years if the cash flows are assumed to take place at the year end. Therefore the project should be rejected by the managers as it does not meet their payback criteria.

Even if the cash flows were assumed to occur evenly the payback period would still be more than three years.

b) **Net present value**

Year	Cash flow	Discount factor	Present value
	£	@ 10%	£
0	(95,000)	1.0000	(95,000)
1	15,000	0.9090	13,635
2	25,000	0.8264	20,660
3	35,000	0.7513	26,295
4	30,000	0.6830	20,490
5	30,000	0.6209	18,627
Net present value			4,707

As the project has a positive net present value then the managers should invest in the new plant and machinery as even after taking account of the time value of money the project shows a surplus.

c) In both calculations the cash flows have been assumed to occur at the end of the year.

d) The payback period investment criteria showed that the project should be rejected as the payback period method only considers the cash flows within the payback period limit. In fact in this case there are substantial cash flows later in this project's life. The net present value method takes account of all of the cash flows of the project and discounts each year's cash flows to take account of the time value of money. In this case the net present value is positive and therefore the investment is worthwhile even though it takes four years to payback the initial investment cost.

3 a) £24,000 x 0.8734 = £20,9652

b) £1,500 x 2.408 = £3,603

c) $\dfrac{£2,000}{0.06}$ = £33,333

d) £30,000 x 1.000 = £30,000

4   Net present value

Year	Cash flow £	Discount factor @ 7%	Present value £
0	(84,000)	1.000	(84,000)
1	26,000	0.9346	24,300
2	30,000	0.8734	26,202
3	21,000	0.8163	17,142
4	14,000	0.7629	10,681
Net present value			(5,675)

On the basis of the net present value calculations, as the net present value of the business is negative, the directors should not purchase the sole trader's business.

5 a) **Net present value**

Year	Cash flow £	Discount factor @ 12%	Present value £
0	(355,000)	1.0000	(355,000)
1 (47 + 60)	107,000	0.8929	95,540
2 (55 + 60)	115,000	0.7972	91,678
3 (68 + 60)	128,000	0.7118	91,110
4 (53 + 60)	113,000	0.6355	71,811
5 (22 + 60)	82,000	0.5674	46,527
Net present value			41,666

Note that depreciation is not a cash flow and having been charged in arriving at the profit figure must be added back to find the cash inflow in each year.

b) It has been assumed that the profit is earned on the last day of each year.

c) The net present value of the investment is positive and on this basis the potential investment is worthwhile.

6 a) **Net present value at 15%**

Year	Cash flow £	Discount factor @ 15%	Present value £
0	(180,000)	1.000	(180,000)
1	42,000	0.8696	36,523
2	50,000	0.7561	37,805
3	75,000	0.6575	49,312
4	80,000	0.5717	45,736
Net present value			(10,624)

At the cost of capital of 15% the project has a negative net present value, and should therefore be rejected.

b) **Net present value at 10%**

Year	Cash flow £	Discount factor @ 10%	Present value £
0	(180,000)	1.0000	(180,000)
1	42,000	0.9090	38,178
2	50,000	0.8264	41,320
3	75,000	0.7513	56,347
4	80,000	0.6830	54,640
Net present value			10,485

If the project can be financed at 10%, it should be accepted as it has a positive NPV.

c) The IRR is the discount rate or cost of capital at which the NPV of the project is zero. It tells a business the maximum discount rate at which the project is worthwhile.

7 **Confectioners Unlimited**

a)

	Year 2 £	Year 3 £	Year 4 £
Sales revenues	60,000	100,000	320,000
Variable costs	(30,000)	(50,000)	(160,000)
Net cash flows	30,000	50,000	160,000

	Net cashflows £	Cumulative cashflow £
Sales revenues	30,000	30,000
Variable costs	50,000	80,000
Net cash flows	50,000	240,000

The set-up costs of £160,000 are repaid at the end of year 4 (cash flows are received at the end of each year). The payback period is therefore 4 years.

b)

	Year 1	Year 2	Year 3	Year 4	Year 5
	£'000	£'000	£'000	£'000	£'000
Set-up cost	(160)				
Sales revenue		60	100	320	100
Variable costs		(30)	(50)	(160)	(50)
Net cashflows	(160)	30	50	160	50
Present value factor	0.870	0.756	0.658	0.572	0.497
Present value*	(139.2)	22.68	32.90	91.52	24.85

*Present value = net cash flows × present value factor

Net present value (in £'000) = (139.2) + 22.68 + 32.90 + 91.52 + 24.85
= 32.75
= £32,750

REPORT

To: Managing Director

From: Accounting Technician

Date: December 2007

Net present value

The financial effects of setting up a new ice-cream parlour have been appraised and the project has been found to have a net present value of £32,750. The project has a positive NPV at 15% and based on this, I would recommend that the project is accepted.

Internal rate of return

The company requires an annual rate of return of 15% on any new project and therefore a project such as this which has an IRR of 26% should be accepted.

(Based on the IRR alone, it is recommended that the company should accept any project which has an IRR greater than 15%.)

1 a) The factory Supervisor will be concerned about the day to day operations of the factory employees. The type of information that he might require would include:

- schedules of production for each day/week in order to schedule the employees suitably
- details of employee's holidays in order to help to schedule the work
- details of absentees
- details of hours worked by each employee and in particular overtime hours
- whether production schedules are met
- requirements for any additional overtime

  b) The Manufacturing Director will be concerned more about the costs and overall performance of the labour force. The type of information that he might require would include:

- summaries of hours worked in each period including overtime hours
- the breakdown of overtime hours into week day and weekend overtime
- whether production targets have been met
- total labour cost in each period
- all variances from budget for the labour force

  c) The Managing Director will only really be concerned with any problem areas with the labour force. He will leave all other aspects to the factory supervisor and manufacturing director. The type of information that he might require would include:

- any significant labour variances from budget
- any excessive overtime worked
- any delays that have meant that production schedules have not been met

2 The general requirements for useful information is that it must be relevant, reliable, consistent and prompt. Each of these will be considered in turn.

Relevant – Information will be relevant if it is information that that particular person requires – not all personnel in the organisation will require the same amount of detailed information. The more junior management will require details about the day to day running of their part of the organisation but further up the management levels less detailed information will be required -the relevant information for higher levels of management will be overviews, summaries, variances and problem areas.

Reliable – In order to be useful information must be reliable – this means that it must be as accurate as possible. Some information is factual, such as the number of hours of overtime worked in a week – this must be correct. Other information may be more subjective, such as the possible reasons for more materials being used in a period than was budgeted for – however again this should be as accurate as is possible given the circumstances.

Consistent – Information that is provided within an organisation will tend to be provided on a regular basis, weekly, monthly, quarterly etc and this information will often be compared over time. It is therefore important that each time the information is provided that it is provided on a consistent basis - the same format and with the same bases for all calculations, otherwise a comparison of one period's information to that of another would not be of use.

Prompt – When management require internal information about their business then they require it in order to be able to make decisions and to plan and control the business. In order to be able to do this the information that they require must be up to date. If figures for production in the factory for a week are required they will normally be required early in the following week not two or three weeks later.

3   **Internal sources**

- Invoices
- Orders
- Delivery notes
- Job cards

4   **Cost accounting**

- Information about product costs and profitability
- Information about departmental costs and profitability
- Cost information to help with pricing decisions
- Budgets and standard costs
- Actual performance and variances between actual and budget
- Information to help with the evaluation of one-off decisions

5   The typical type of information that might be required by the partners of a firm of solicitors in order to be able to appraise the performance of the firm for the last month might include:

- chargeable hours of all levels of staff
- amounts billed to clients during the month
- amounts of overtime worked by staff
- levels of overheads for the month
- potential new clients gained in the month
- absentee/illness rates
- amounts billed per chargeable hour

6

	Abberville £	Bacup £	Calver £	Total £
Sales	137,489	195,374	104,328	437,191
Cost of sales	53,621	72,288	41,731	167,640
Gross profit	83,868	123,086	62,597	269,551
Expenses	33,373	37,121	22,952	93,446
Net profit	50,495	85,965	39,645	176,105

1   Production and productivity

Production is the quantity or volume of output produced. It is the number of units produced, or the actual number of units produced converted into an equivalent number of 'standard hours of production'.

Productivity is the measure of the efficiency with which output has been produced.

2

	Quarter ending 30 June 2007	*Quarter ending 31 March 2007*
Cost per unit	$\dfrac{£567,900}{330,000} = £1.72$	$\dfrac{£580,400}{332,000} = £1.75$
Labour productivity	$\dfrac{330,000}{12,600 \text{ hours}} = 26.2$ units per hour	$\dfrac{332,000}{12,300} = 27$ units per hour
Productivity index	$\dfrac{330,000}{350,000} = 94.3\%$	$\dfrac{332,000}{320,000} = 103.8\%$

3   FACTORY

Cost per unit	$\dfrac{£557,800}{128,700} = £4.33$ per unit
Labour productivity	$\dfrac{128,700}{39,400} = 3.27$ units per hour
Labour productivity	$\dfrac{128,700}{280} = 460$ units per employee
Productivity index	$\dfrac{128,700}{120,000} = 107.3\%$

TELEPHONE SALES

Cost per order	$\dfrac{£14,560}{9,180} = £1.59$ per order
Labour productivity	$\dfrac{9,180}{27} = 340$ orders per person

4 Idle time is the time that the production workers are on the factory floor but are not actually producing the products of the organisation. Some idle time is necessary for Health and Safety reasons - workers must have time for coffee breaks, lunch breaks etc. This is known as unavoidable idle time as it is a necessary part of working life.

Other idle time however is a consequence of the manufacturing process. There may be bottlenecks in production which mean that some production workers are not able to work when they should. There may be machine breakdowns or a lack of materials that mean that there is no production to work on. The workers may have finished the assigned tasks for the day and no other task is available. This is all known as avoidable idle time as it is not strictly necessary although it is a practical aspect of factory life.

5

	Jan	Feb	Mar	Apr	May	June
Labour utilisation %	$\frac{2,100}{2,190}$	$\frac{2,050}{2,130}$	$\frac{2,220}{2,240}$	$\frac{2,200}{2,300}$	$\frac{2,310}{2,430}$	$\frac{2,250}{2,350}$
	95.9%	96.2%	99.1%	95.7%	95.1%	95.7%

6

	May	June	July
Fixed asset utilisation	$\frac{£360,000}{£210,000}$	$\frac{£402,000}{£190,000}$	$\frac{£398,000}{£200,000}$
	£1.71	£2.11	£1.99
Machinery utilisation	$\frac{£360,000}{28,000 \text{ hours}}$	$\frac{£402,000}{32,000 \text{ hours}}$	$\frac{£398,000}{31,000 \text{ hours}}$
	£12.86 per machine hour	£12.56 per machine hour	£12.84 per machine hour
Asset turnover	$\frac{£360,000}{£300,000}$	$\frac{£402,000}{£310,000}$	$\frac{£398,000}{£320,000}$
	£1.20	£1.30	£1.24

7 **Return on capital employed (ROCE)** also called return on investment, (ROI) is calculated as a percentage, as profit/capital employed × 100 and it shows how much profit has been made in relation to the amount of the resources invested.

8

	May	June	July
Gross profit margin	$\dfrac{530}{1,320}$	$\dfrac{570}{1,420}$	$\dfrac{530}{1,500}$
	40.2%	40.1%	35.3%
Net profit margin	$\dfrac{240}{1,320}$	$\dfrac{240}{1,420}$	$\dfrac{240}{1,500}$
	18.2%	16.9%	16.0%
ROCE	$\dfrac{240}{2,600}$	$\dfrac{240}{2,840}$	$\dfrac{240}{3,080}$
	9.2%	8.5%	7.8%

The gross profit margin has shown a significant decrease in July. The net profit margin decreased in June even though the gross profit margin was similar to that of May indicating an increase in expenses. The net profit margin again decreases in July largely due to the deteriorating gross profit margin.

The return on capital employed has decreased each month due to a combination of the gross and net profit margin decreases.

9

		May	June	July
a)	Cost per unit	$\dfrac{£416,000}{220,000}$	$\dfrac{£402,000}{215,000}$	$\dfrac{£403,000}{216,000}$
		1.89	£1.87	£1.87
b)	Labour productivity	$\dfrac{220,000}{1,400}$	$\dfrac{£215,000}{1,360}$	$\dfrac{216,000}{1,430}$
		157 per hour	158 per hour	151 per hour
c)	Productivity index	$\dfrac{220,000}{220,000}$	$\dfrac{215,000}{220,000}$	$\dfrac{216,000}{220,000}$
		100%	97.7%	98.2%
d)	Labour utilisation %	$\dfrac{1,400}{1,400}$	$\dfrac{1,360}{1,400}$	$\dfrac{1,430}{1,400}$
		100%	97.1%	102.1%

e)	Fixed asset utilisation	$\dfrac{£595,000}{£320,000}$	$\dfrac{£600,000}{£300,000}$	$\dfrac{£610,000}{340,000}$
		£1.86	£2.00	£1.79
f)	Asset turnover	$\dfrac{£595,000}{460,000}$	$\dfrac{£600,000}{£508,000}$	$\dfrac{£610,000}{£562,000}$
		£1.29	£1.18	£1.09
g)	Gross profit margin	$\dfrac{£179,000}{595,000}$	$\dfrac{£198,000}{£600,000}$	$\dfrac{£207,000}{£610,000}$
		30.1%	33.0%	33.9%
h)	Net profit margin	$\dfrac{£48,000}{£595,000}$	$\dfrac{£54,000}{600,000}$	$\dfrac{£58,000}{610,000}$
		8.1%	9.0%	9.5%
i)	ROCE	$\dfrac{£48,000}{460,000}$	$\dfrac{£54,000}{508,000}$	$\dfrac{£58,000}{562,000}$
		10.4%	10.6%	10.3%

There have been few major changes over the three month period although perhaps the most notable is the increase in gross profit margin in June and July. This has led to an increased net profit margin in those months although no increase in return on capital employed.

On the whole the performance in June and July has not been as good as in May although one area of improvement is the decrease in the cost per unit in the last two months. However in July labour productivity decreased even though the labour utilisation level was good. However both fixed asset utilisation and asset turnover decreased contributing to the decrease in return on capital employed in July.

10 Net profit margin

$$\text{Net profit margin} = \frac{\text{Net profit}}{\text{Turnover}} \times 100$$

2006 $\dfrac{75,000}{600,000} \times 100 = 12.5\%$

2007 $\dfrac{80,000}{800,000} \times 100 = 10\%$

answers to chapter 12:
WRITING A REPORT

1 ■ Title of the report
   ■ Who the report is from and to
   ■ Date
   ■ Terms of reference
   ■ Summary
   ■ Main body of the report
   ■ Conclusion
   ■ Recommendations
   ■ Appendix

2   **REPORT**

To: Sales Director
From: Accountant
Date: 19 August 2007
Subject: Shop Profitability

Terms of reference

This report on the profitability of the shop for the last six months has been requested by the sales director. A number of performance measures for profitability have been calculated and are shown in the appendix to this report.

Summary

The performance measures indicate not only a substantial increase in sales over the first six months of the year but also a healthy increase in all areas of profitability.

Findings

The major change in the shop performance has been a 50% increase in turnover in the six month period from January to June 2007. However this appears to have been achieved with an increase in profitability as well.

The gross profit margin has increased gradually each month from 40.9% in January to 45.2% in June. The net profit margin has also increased over the period from 14.8% to highs of 15.5% although there was a sharp decrease in March and April. This may have been due to costs incurred as part of the expansion such as advertising costs which then reverted to normal levels in later months.

The return on capital employed has largely followed the pattern of the net profit margin although over the period has shown a healthy increase from 9.4% to 10.6%. This increase has been helped by an increased asset turnover, or capital utilisation, which has leapt from 64 pence of sales per £1 of capital to 70 pence in June.

Conclusion

All profitability performance measures show a significant increase over the period combined with a large increase in turnover over the six months.

APPENDIX

Performance measures

	Jan	Feb	Mar	Apr	May	June
Gross profit margin	40.9%	42.0%	43.0%	43.6%	44.0%	45.2%
Net profit margin	14.8%	15.5%	14.0%	14.5%	15.5%	15.1%
Return on capital employed	9.4%	9.7%	9.0%	9.9%	10.7%	10.6%
Asset turnover	0.64	0.63	0.64	0.68	0.69	0.70

3

REPORT

To:	Manufacturing Director
From:	Accountant
Date:	20 July 2007
Subject:	Productivity of divisions

Terms of reference

This report on productivity in each of the three manufacturing divisions has been prepared for the manufacturing director. The findings of the report are based upon the performance measures shown in the appendix to this report.

Summary

There are no significant differences between the performance of the three divisions although on the whole the most productive division is Division B and the least productive Division A. The most concerning factor is probably the fact that both units produced and hours worked are below budget in all three divisions.

Findings

The cost per unit figures do not differ significantly between the three divisions although the range is £3.12 to £3.05 in Division C. If all three divisions could produce the products at a cost of £3.05 this would clearly help the profitability of the organisation as a whole.

The productivity per labour hour again shows no huge differences but only Division B has achieved the budgeted productivity of 30 units per labour hour.

The productivity index shows that all of the Divisions have produced less than the units that were budgeted for. In line with this the labour utilisation figures show that less hours were worked than were budgeted for. This may need to be investigated.

Of the three Divisions, Division B appears to have performed the best with a fairly low cost per unit together with budgeted productivity per hour and the best performance in terms of productivity index and labour utilisation. Division A appears to have performed less well than the other two divisions with all performance measures being lower.

Conclusion

There are no dramatic differences in the performance of the three divisions although on balance Division B appears to be the most productive and Division A the least.

APPENDIX

Performance measures

	Division A	Division B	Division C
Cost per unit	£3.12	£3.08	£3.05
Productivity per labour hour	28.6	30.0	28.8
Productivity index	88.9%	96.0%	90.9%
Labour utilisation	93.3%	96.0%	94.5%

1 **Significant digits**

a) 2,197.28
b) 2,197.3
c) 2,197

2 **Decimal places**

a) 38.178
b) 38.18
c) 38.2

3 An **independent variable** is a variable whose value affects the value of the dependent variable. On a graph, the **x axis** is used to represent the independent variable.

4 A **scattergraph** is a graph which is used to exhibit data, rather than equations which produce simple lines or curves, in order to compare the way in which the variables vary with each other.

5 a)

	A	B	C	D	E
1		June	July	August	September
2	Sales	48,700	50,200	45,600	46,800
3	Cost of sales	30,200	31,600	29,200	30,000
4	Gross profit	= B2 - B3	= C2 - C3	= D2 - D3	= E2 - E3
5	Expenses	12,200	12,500	11,400	11,700
6	Net profit	= B4 - B5	= C4 - C5	= D4 - D5	= E4 - E5
7	Capital	52,500	52,500	55,000	55,000
8	Gross profit %	=(B4/B2)*100	=(C4/C2)*100	=(D4/D2)*100	=(E4/E2)*100
9	Net profit %	=(B6/B2)*100	=(C6/C2)*100	=(D6/D2)*100	=(E6/E2)*100
10	ROCE	=(B6/B7)*100	=(C6/C7)*100	=(D6/D7)*100	=(E6/E7)*100
11	Asset turnover	=B2/B7	=C2/C7	=D2/D7	=E4/E7

b)

	A	B	C	D	E
1		June	July	August	September
2	Sales	48,700	50,200	45,600	46,800
3	Cost of sales	30,200	31,600	29,200	30,000
4	Gross profit	18,500	18,600	16,400	16,800
5	Expenses	12,200	12,500	11,400	11,700
6	Net profit	6,300	6,100	5,000	5,100
7	Capital	52,500	52,500	55,000	55,000
8	Gross profit %	38.0	37.1	36.0	35.9
9	Net profit %	12.9	12.2	11.0	10.9
10	ROCE	12.0	11.6	9.1	9.3
11	Asset turnover	0.93	0.96	0.83	0.85

6

	A	B	C
1		Quarter ending 30/3	Quarter ending 30/6
2	Budgeted production	320,000	350,000
3	Actual production	332,000	330,000
4	Production cost	£580,400	£567,900
5	Hours worked	12,300	12,600
6	Cost per unit	=B4/B3	=C4/C3
7	Labour productivity	=B3/B5	=C3/C5
8	Productivity index	=(B3/B2)*100	=(C3/C2)*100

7   MONTHLY SALES FIGURES

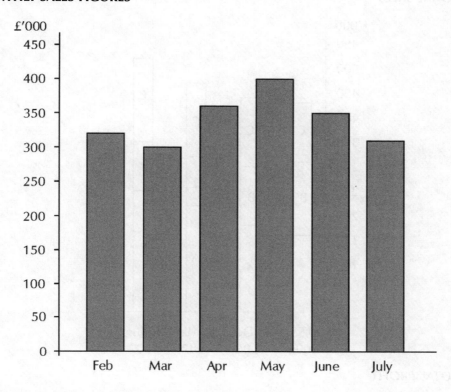

8   SALES, GROSS PROFIT, NET PROFIT

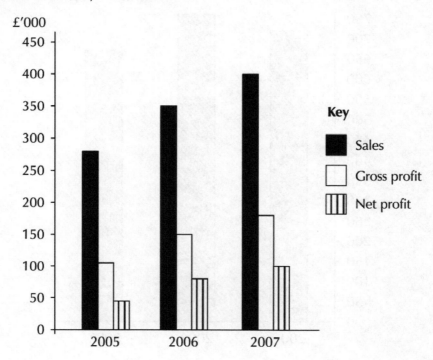

9   DIVISIONAL SALES

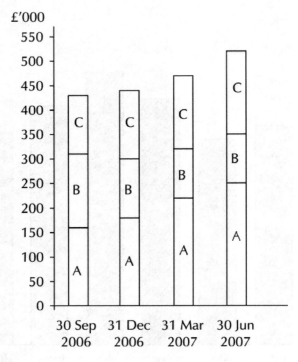

10   a)   TOTAL PROFIT

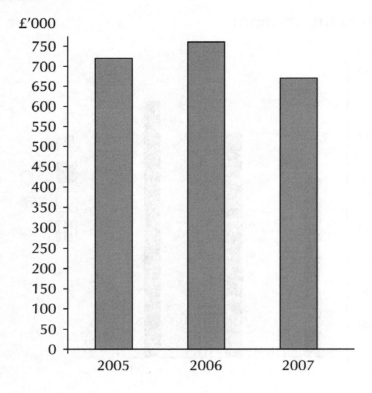

b) **PROFIT BREAKDOWN**

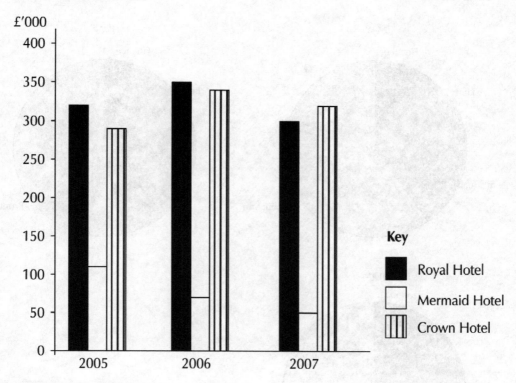

c) **PROFIT BREAKDOWN**

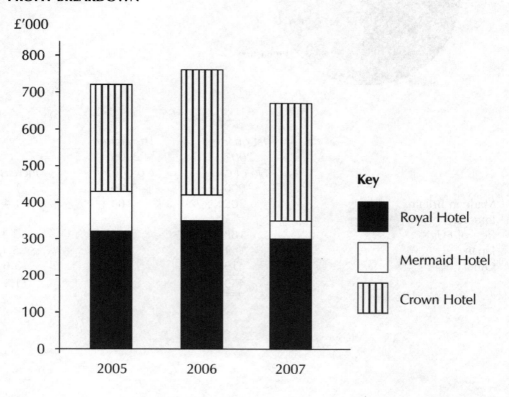

11   TOTAL COSTS

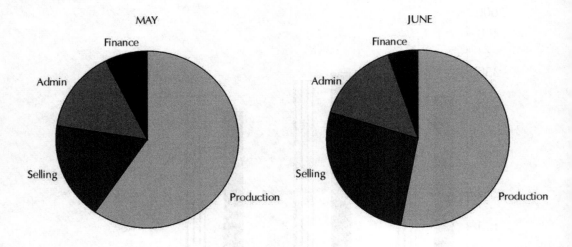

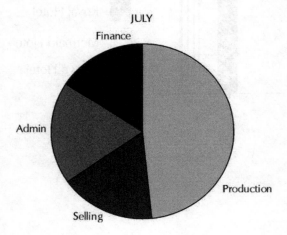

12	1st quarter 2007	1st quarter 2006	
	No of cars ('000)	No of cars ('000)	Increase %
Made in Britain	205	184	11.4
Imports			
Rest of EU	188	166	13.3
Japan	41	39	5.1
Other	19	18	5.6
	453	407	11.3

13 a) AT Engineering Ltd

Sheet Metal Work Department
Wages for week ended 12 June

Operative	Total hours worked	Basic hourly rate £	Basic wages £	Hrs	Overtime premium One third £	Hrs	Double basic £	Total wages £
M	46	7.20	331.20	2	4.80	4	28.80	364.80
N	39	7.50	292.50	3	7.50			300.00
O	40	7.20	288.00					288.00
P	51	7.50	382.50	7	17.50	4	30.00	430.00
Q	52	8.40	436.80	8	22.40	4	33.60	492.80
R	34	7.20	244.80					244.80
	262		1,975.80		52.20		92.40	2,120.40

b) Weighted average wages cost $= \dfrac{£2,120.40}{262}$

$= £8.09$ per operative hour, to the nearest penny.

1   a)   **The mean**

The arithmetic mean is the best known and most widely used average. The arithmetic mean of some data is the sum of the data, divided by the number of items in the data. It is widely used because it gives a convenient and readily understood indication of the general size of the data, it takes account of all items of data and it is suitable for further mathematical analysis. On the other hand, its value can be unduly influenced by a few very large or very small items of data.

b)   **The median**

The median is the value of the middle member of a set of data, once the data have been arranged in either ascending or descending order. It is one sort of average and it has the following properties.

- It is fairly easy to obtain.
- It is not affected very much by extreme values.
- It is not generally suitable for further statistical analysis.

The median may be more useful than the arithmetic mean in certain circumstances, for instance when determining the average salary of the employees in a company. Since a few employees might have very high salaries, the arithmetic mean could be drawn upwards by these, out of the range of salaries earned by most employees. The mean would then not be representative. The median, however, would be the item in the middle of the ranking, which would be within the range of salaries earned by most employees.

c)   **Time series**

A time series is simply a series of values recorded over time. Examples of a time series are:

i)   output at a factory each day for the last month
ii)   monthly sales over the last two years
iii)   the number of people employed by a company each year for the last 20 years

Time series are often shown on a graph, with time always being the independent variable shown along the x axis, and the values at each time shown along the y axis.

The features of a time series are normally taken to be:

- A trend
- Cyclical variations
- Seasonal variations
- Random variations

2 $$\frac{159+62+55+86+104+168+192}{7} = \frac{826}{7}$$

$$= \textbf{118 per day}$$

3

	£	3-month moving average £
July 2006	337,600	
August 2006	415,300	347,466.66
September 2006	289,500	323,733.33
October 2006	266,400	251,533.33
November 2006	198,700	241,233.33
December 2006	258,600	211,500.00
January 2007	177,200	211,700.00
February 2007	199,300	199,800.00
March 2007	222,900	226,100.00
April 2007	256,100	248,266.66
May 2007	265,800	295,866.66
June 2007	365,700	

4	Week	Costs	4-week moving average
		£	£
	1	128,500	
	2	195,400	
			162,575
	3	148,600	
			164,825
	4	177,800	
			157,400
	5	137,500	
			157,300
	6	165,700	
			158,700
	7	148,200	
			168,650
	8	183,400	
			168,400
	9	177,300	
			170,200
	10	164,700	
			172,750
	11	155,400	
			167,950
	12	193,600	
			170,400
	13	158,100	
			172,275
	14	174,500	
			163,725
	15	162,900	
	16	159,400	

5

	A	B	C	D
1	Week 1	128,500		
2				
3	Week 2	195,400		
4			=(B1+B3+B5+B7)/4	
5	Week 3	148,600		=(C4+C6)/2
6			=(B3+B5+B7+B9)/4	
7	Week 4	177,800		=(C6+C8)/2
8			=(B5+B7+B9+B11)/4	
9	Week 5	137,500		=(C8+C10)/2
10			=(B7+B9+B11+B13)/4	
11	Week 6	165,700		=(C10+C12)/2
12			=(B9+B11+B13+B15)/4	
13	Week 7	148,200		=(C12+C14)/2
14			=(B11+B13+B15+B17)/4	
15	Week 8	183,400		=(C14+C16)/2
16			=(B13+B15+B17+B19)/4	
17	Week 9	177,300		=(C16+C18)/2
18			=(B15+B17+B19+B21)/4	
19	Week 10	164,700		=(C18+C20)/2
20			=(B17+B19+B21+B23)/4	
21	Week 11	155,400		=(C20+C22)/2
22			=(B19+B21+B23+B25)/4	
23	Week 12	193,600		=(C22+C24)/2
24			=(B21+B23+B25+B27)/4	
25	Week 13	158,100		=(C24+C26)/2
26			=(B23+B25+B27+B29)/4	
27	Week 14	174,500		=(C26+C28)/2
28			=(B25+B27+B29+B31)/4	
29	Week 15	162,900		
30				
31	Week 16	159,400		

6 a)

	£	3-month moving average £
2006		
January	55,600	
February	52,700	54,800.00
March	56,100	55,200.00
April	56,800	57,066.67
May	58,300	58,533.33
June	60,500	59,233.33
July	58,900	59,533.33
August	59,200	59,800.00
September	61,300	60,866.67
October	62,100	62,266.67
November	63,400	62,733.33
December	62,700	62,466.67
2007		
January	61,300	62,166.67
February	62,500	62,633.33
March	64,100	63,933.33
April	65,200	64,733.33
May	64,900	65,600.00
June	66,700	

b) **MONTHLY SALES AND TREND**

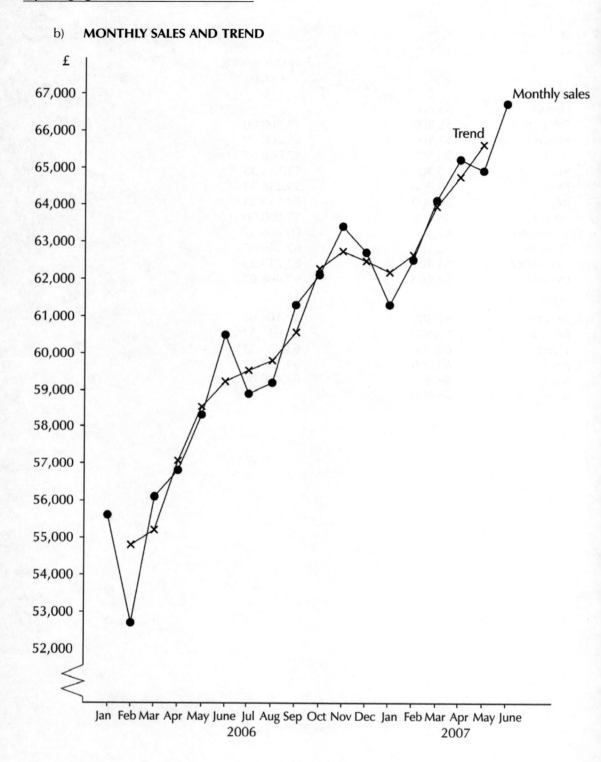

7   **Interpolation** is a method of estimating a figure within a range of figures already available. Therefore if the costs of production for a factory range from £126,700 for 30,000 units to £193,500 for 40,000 units then if an estimate were required for the production cost of 37,500 units this could be found from a graph of these costs by reading off the anticipated cost figure for 37,500 units.

Extrapolation however is a method of estimating a figure that is outside the range of figures already available. Using the same production cost example, if an estimate was required for the production cost of 45,000 units then the graph line would have to be extended and the estimated cost figure read off from the extended graph.

8   A **price index** is an index which measures the change in the money value of a group of items over a period of time.

9

2006	£		Index
August	527,500		100.00
September	513,400	513,400/527,500 x 100	97.33
October	556,700	556,700/527,500 x 100	105.54
November	523,400	523,400/527,500 x 100	99.22
December	582,300	582,300/527,500 x 100	110.39
2007			
January	561,300	561,300/527,500 x 100	106.41
February	532,600	532,600/527,500 x 100	100.97
March	524,300	524,300/527,500 x 100	99.39
April	515,700	515,700/527,500 x 100	97.76
May	529,600	529,600/527,500 x 100	100.40
June	538,200	538,200/527,500 x 100	102.03

10   If £35,000 = 100%, then:

$$£42,000 = \frac{42,000}{35,000} \times 100\% = 120\%$$

$$£40,000 = \frac{40,000}{35,000} \times 100\% = 114\%$$

$$£45,000 = \frac{45,000}{35,000} \times 100\% = 129\%$$

$$£50,000 = \frac{50,000}{35,000} \, 100\% = 143\%$$

The table showing sales for the last five years can now be completed, taking 2003 as the base year.

Year	Sales (£'000)	Index
2003	35	100
2004	42	120
2005	40	114
2006	45	129
2007	50	143

11 a)   RPI adjusted sales

January		162,400
February	163,800 x 171.1/172.0	162,943
March	165,900 x 171.1/172.2	164,840
April	167,200 x 171.1/173.0	165,364
May	166,200 x 171.1/172.1	165,234
June	164,100 x 171.1/171.3	163,908
July	162,300 x 171.1/171.0	162,395
August	160,500 x 171.1/170.3	161,254

b)   Index

January		100.0
February	162,943/162.400 x 100	100.3
March	164,840/162.400 x 100	101.5
April	165,364/162,400 x 100	101.8
May	165,234/162,400 x 100	101.7
June	163,908/162,400 x 100	100.9
July	162,395/162,400 x 100	100.0
August	161,254/162,400 x 100	99.3

c)

	A	B	C	D	E
1	January	162,400	171.1	=B1*(C1/C1)	=(D1/D1)*100
2	February	163,800	172.0	=B2*(C1/C2)	=(D2/D1)*100
3	March	165,900	172.2	=B3*(C1/C3)	=(D3/D1)*100
4	April	167,200	173.0	=B4*(C1/C4)	=(D4/D1)*100
5	May	166,200	172.1	=B5*(C1/C5)	=(D5/D1)*100
6	June	164,100	171.3	=B6*(C1/C6)	=(D6/D1)*100
7	July	162,300	171.0	=B7*(C1/C7)	=(D7/D1)*100
8	August	160,500	170.3	=B8*(C1/C8)	=(D8/D1)*100

12

		2005	2006	2007
a)	Receipts per loaded coach km (£)	1.62	1.93	2.09
b)	Receipts per passenger km (pence)	5.70	6.20	6.40
c)	Passenger kms per loaded coach km (average coach load) (passengers)	28.50	31.20	32.70
d)	Total operating expenses per loaded coach km (£)	1.21	1.25	1.28

13 a)

	2005	2006	2007
Receipts per loaded coach km (2006 £)	1.74	2.01	2.09
Receipts per passenger km (2006 pence)	6.10	6.50	6.40
Total operating expenses per loaded coach km (2007 £)	1.30	1.30	1.28
Conversion factor	100.00	100.00	1.00
	93.20	96.10	

b) There was a real increase in fares per passenger kilometre in 2006; the slight decline in 2007 may partly reflect the impact of the new competitor. In spite of this new competition, real receipts per loaded coach kilometre increased by 20% between 2005 and 2007. There have been greater numbers travelling on each coach, in spite of the new competitor on the main routes: the average coach load has risen to 32.7 (approximately 70% of capacity, up 15% on 2005). Over the period, operating expenses per loaded coach kilometre have been contained, and indeed showed a drop of almost 2% in real terms in 2007. Profit, if measured as fares less operating expenses, has shown a substantial increase from £792,000 in 2005 (in money terms) to £1,613,000 in 2007.

1   The National Statistics 'themes' are:

- agriculture, fishing and forestry
- commerce, energy and industry
- compendia and reference
- crime and justice
- economy
- education and training
- health and care
- labour market
- natural and built environment
- population and migration
- social and welfare
- transport, travel and tourism
- other

2

BARDEN LOCAL DISTRICT COUNCIL
GRANT APPLICATION

PART 1 BUSINESS DETAILS

Business name ...... D. & G. Harper ....

....

Business address .... Harper House ....

.... East Park Road ....

.... Barden BD4 6GK ....

Business telephone ... 02185 3743 ....

Business fax ...... 02185 3264 ....

Owner's name ...... David and Gareth Harper ....

....

Email address ...... dgh@dandgharper.co.uk ....

Type of business ..... Curtain and blind manufacturer ....

....

....

....

PART 2 FINANCIAL DETAILS

2A TURNOVER AND PROFIT

Figures are to be provided for annual turnover and reported net profit for the last three complete financial years

Financial year ended:		UK turnover £	Export turnover £	Net profit £
Month	Year			
June	2005	378,690	10,580	74,110
June	2006	735,400	38,600	162,540
June	2007	882,400	48,340	204,770

2B WORKING CAPITAL

Figures are to be provided for working capital at the end of the most recent financial year.

Year ending: 30 June 2007

£

Current assets	97,470
Minus: current liabilities	(42,170)
Working capital	55,300

2C FIXED ASSETS

Figures are to be provided for fixed asset totals at the end of the most recent financial year.

Year ending: 30 June 2007

£

Land and buildings	184,500
Plant and machinery	190,400
Other	97,700
Total fixed assets	472,600

PART 3 NON FINANCIAL DETAILS

3A EMPLOYMENT DETAILS

Figures are to be provided for the number of employees for the last three financial years.

Financial year ended:		Number of full time employees	Number of part time employees
Month	Year		
June	2005	9	1
June	2006	14	3
June	2007	14	3

3B BUSINESS DETAILS

Date business started: . .1998. . . . .

Business type -   Sole trader   ☐

Partnership   ☑

Company   ☐

PART 4 GRANT APPLICATION

Indicate in the space provided the reasons for the grant application. If the grant application is processed further more detail will be requested at a later date.

. . Grant application for £15,000 to help fund additional factory space and potential . . . . .

. . employment of 6 additional full time employees. . . . .

. . . .

. . . .

. . . .

. . . .

. . . .

3

CHAMBER OF COMMERCE
ANNUAL ECONOMIC REVIEW

Please tick the appropriate box in answer to each question - all answers will be treated in the strictest confidence. All answers should be based upon the business performance for the last full financial year.

1   BUSINESS DETAILS

End of last full financial year:

Turnover range:

Upto £50,000 ☐

£50,000 - £100,000 ☐

£100,000 - £250,000 ☐

£250,000 - £500,000 ☑

£500,000 - £1,000,000 ☐

Over £1,000,000 ☐

Main business activity:

Engineering ☐		Health ☐	
Construction ☑		Art and design ☐	
Agriculture ☐		Transport ☐	
Energy ☐		Tourism ☐	
Retail ☐		Other (please state)	
Education ☐		. . . .	

2 TURNOVER

Percentage of total turnover accounted for by export sales:

0%	☑	30% to 50%	☐
upto 10%	☐	50% to 75%	☐
10% to 20%	☐	75% to 100%	☐
20% to 30%	☐		

Percentage increase/decrease in turnover compared to previous financial year:

Decrease upto 20%	☐	Increase upto 20%	☐
Decrease of 20% to 50%	☐	Increase of 20% to 50%	☑
Decrease of more than 50%	☐	Increase of more than 50%	☐

Percentage increase/decrease in net profit compared to previous financial year:

Decrease upto 20%	☐	Increase upto 20%	☐
Decrease of 20% to 50%	☐	Increase of 20% to 50%	☑
Decrease of more than 50%	☐	Increase of more than 50%	☐

3 BUSINESS CONFIDENCE

Do you consider that over the following 12 months:

Turnover	will increase	☑	Profitability	will increase	☑
	remain the same	☐		remain the same	☐
	decrease	☐		decrease	☐

answers to chapter 16:
VALUE ADDED TAX

1
a) From 1 April 2007 the VAT registration threshold is **£64,000**
b) From 1 April 2007 the VAT deregistration limit is **£61,000** for taxable supplies
c) VAT on purchases is known as **input** tax
d) VAT on sales is known as **output** tax
e) A VAT return is normally completed every **3** months

2
Standard rate of 17.5%

Reduced rate of 5% on domestic fuel

Zero rate 0%

3
a) £15,862.50 – as a business making exempt supplies cannot reclaim any input VAT
b) £13,500.00 – as a business making zero-rated supplies can reclaim input VAT

4
If the business makes zero-rated supplies then it will not have to pay VAT over to HMRC but as a VAT registered business will be able to reclaim any input VAT suffered.

5
a) £16,685.00 – the VAT on cars for use in a business is not reclaimable

b) £141.00 – the VAT on business entertaining is not reclaimable

6
a) 13 August 2007 – actual tax point
b) 15 August 2007 – basic tax point
c) 12 August 2007 – actual tax point
d) 20 August 2007 – actual tax point

7
a) £25.69
b) £34.65
c) £33.95
d) £43.90

8 a) VAT   £64.36
           Net of VAT   £367.80

    b) VAT   £39.13
        Net of VAT   £223.64

    c) VAT   £32.30
        Net of VAT   £184.60

    d) VAT   £46.19
        Net of VAT   £263.99

9 ■ The business name, address and VAT registration number
    ■ The date of supply
    ■ Description of goods/services
    ■ For each applicable VAT rate the total including VAT and the VAT rate

10 All the invoices except d) look superficially plausible, but in fact d) is the only valid invoice. This shows the importance of attention to detail in applying VAT law.

    a) The invoice from Jupiter plc is invalid because the invoice number has been omitted.

    b) The invoice from Hillside Ltd is invalid because it does not show the supplier's address. In all other respects it meets the requirements for a valid VAT invoice.

    c) The invoice from Generous plc is invalid because the supplier's VAT registration number is not shown. Finally, the invoice is invalid because the applicable rates of VAT (17.5% and 0%) are not shown.

    d) The total value of the supply by Jewels & Co, including VAT, does not exceed £250, so a less detailed invoice is permissible.

        The invoice is valid, because it includes all the information which must be shown on a less detailed invoice.

answers to chapter 17:
VAT RECORDS

1 The errors in the previous period may be corrected through the VAT account (and on the VAT return) because the net error is £(700 + 800) = £1,500, which does not exceed £2,000.

Standard rated purchases total £(9,950 + 5,792 + 8,168) = £23,910.

Standard rated sales total £(6,237 + 19,008 + 1,084) = £26,329.

PETER PERFECT
VAT ACCOUNT FOR THE VAT PERIOD FROM 1.1.2007 TO 31.3.2007

VAT allowable	£	*VAT payable*	£
Input VAT allowable		Output VAT due	
£23,910 × 17.5%	4,184.25	£26,329 × 17.5%	4,607.58
Adjustment for credits		Adjustment for returned	
received (178 + 743) × 17.5%	(161.18)	sale £505 ´ 17.5%	(88.38)
Correction of error	800.00	Correction of error	(700.00)
	4,823.07		3,819.20
		Cash (receipt from	
		HM Revenue & Customs)	1,003.87
	4,823.07		4,823.07

2 The sale of plant (capital item) is excluded from the calculation of the partial exemption percentage.

Output VAT	£	£
£6,000,000 × 17.5%		1,050,000
		1,050,000
Input VAT		
Attributable to taxable supplies	600,000	
Unattributable £96,000 × 73% (see below)	70,080	
		670,080
Amount due to HM Revenue & Customs		379,920

The **partial exemption fraction** is $\dfrac{6,000+1,500-20}{6,000+1,500+2,800-20} = 0.727$, rounded up to 73%.

3

VAT account

VAT deductible – input tax	£	VAT payable – output tax	£
Purchases day book	2,485.61	Sales day book	3,474.89
Cash payments book	624.78	Cash receipts book	993.57
EU acquisitions	925.47	EU acquisitions	925.47
	4,035.86		5,393.93
Less: credit notes received	210.68	Less: credit notes issued	441.46
Total VAT deductible	3,825.18	Total VAT payable	4,952.47
		Less: VAT deductible	3,825.18
		Due to HMRC	1,127.29

4

VAT account

VAT deductible – input tax	£	VAT payable – output tax	£
Purchases day book	4,668.14	Sales day book	6,275.78
Cash payments book	936.47	Cash receipts book	1,447.30
EU acquisitions	772.46	EU acquisitions	772.46
Bad debt relief	284.67		
Net overcharge for previous period (221.68 – 126.57)	95.11		
	6,756.85		8,495.54
Less: credit notes received	510.36	Less: credit notes issued	726.58
Total VAT deductible	6,246.49	Total VAT payable	7,768.96
		Less: VAT deductible	6,246.49
		Due to HMRC	1,522.47

5

Value Added Tax Return
For the period
01 04 07 to 30 06 07

For Official Use

Registration number	Period
234 4576 12	06 07

You could be liable to a financial penalty if your completed return and all the VAT payable are not received by the due date.

Due date: 31 July 2007

For Official Use

Waltzer Enterprises
Adam Industrial Park
Yarden
LR3 9GS

If you have a general enquiry or need advice please call our National Advice Service on 0845 010 9000

ATTENTION

If this return and any tax due are not received by the due date you may be liable to a surcharge.

If you make supplies of goods to another EC Member State you are required to complete an EC Sales List (VAT 101).

Before you fill in this form please read the notes on the back and the VAT Leaflet *"Filling in your VAT return"*. Fill in all boxes clearly in ink, and write 'none' where necessary. Don't put a dash or leave any box blank. If there are no pence write "00" in the pence column. Do not enter more than one amount in any box.

			£	p
For official use	VAT due in this period on sales and other outputs	1	10,177	80
	VAT due in this period on acquisitions from other EC Member States	2	275	17
	Total VAT due (the sum of boxes 1 and 2)	3	10,452	97
	VAT reclaimed in this period on purchases and other inputs (including acquisitions from the EC)	4	6,163	12
	Net VAT to be paid to Customs or reclaimed by you (Difference between boxes 3 and 4)	5	4,289	85
	Total value of sales and all other outputs excluding any VAT. Include your box 8 figure	6	61,551	00
	Total value of purchases and all other inputs excluding any VAT. Include your box 9 figure	7	37,729	00
	Total value of all supplies of goods and related services, excluding any VAT, to other EC Member States	8	NONE	00
	Total value of all acquisitions of goods and related services, excluding any VAT, from other EC Member States	9	1,572	00

If you are enclosing a payment please tick this box.

✔

DECLARATION: You, or someone on your behalf, must sign below.

I, ... declare that the
(Full name of signatory in BLOCK LETTERS)
information given above is true and complete.

Signature .... Date ....

A false declaration can result in prosecution.

Workings

		£
Box 1	Sales day book	10,082.76
	Cash receipts book	931.98
	Sales returns day book	(836.94)
		10,177.80
Box 4	Purchases day book – EU	275.17
	Purchases day book – UK	5,892.69
	Cash payments book	552.55
	Purchases returns day book	(557.29)
		6,163.12
Box 6	Sales day book – zero rated	3,628.47
	Sales day book – standard	57,615.80
	Cash receipts book	5,325.65
	Sales returns day book – zero	(236.34)
	Sales returns – standard	(4,782.57)
		61,551.01
Box 7	Purchases day book – EU	1,572.45
	Purchases day book – zero	2,636.47
	Purchases day book – standard	33,672.57
	Cash payments book	3,157.46
	Purchases returns – zero	(125.34)
	Purchases returns – standard	(3,184.57)
		37,729.04

6   If a net error of more than £2,000 is discovered then this cannot be adjusted for on the VAT return. Instead voluntary disclosure must be made to the local VAT Business Advice Centre using Form VAT 652 or in a letter.

7   If you have been registered for VAT for at least 12 months and the annual value of your taxable supplies, excluding VAT, is below £1,350,000 then you may be able to use the annual accounting scheme.

Under this scheme you make 9 monthly direct debit payments based upon an estimate of the amount of VAT due. You must then prepare a VAT return for the year and send it in with the tenth balancing payment, by two months after the year end.

A different system is also available if the annual turnover is less than £100,000 and the net liability for VAT is less than £2,000 per annum. Under this scheme you will not be required to make any interim payments. If your net liability exceeds £2,000 per annum then you will only be required to make quarterly interim payments. The annual VAT return and balancing payment are again due within two months of the year end.

8   Because Zag plc makes some exempt supplies, not all the VAT on purchases can be recovered. The VAT on purchases which is not attributable to either taxable supplies or exempt supplies must be apportioned.

a)   Box 1: VAT due on outputs

The figure is £877,500 × 17.5% = £153,562.50

b)   Box 2: VAT due on acquisitions

None.

c)   Box 3: sum of Boxes 1 and 2 = £153,562.50

d)   Box 4: VAT reclaimed on inputs

The figure is as follows.

Apportionment percentage = (877,500 + 462,150)/(877,500 + 462,150 + 327,600) = 80.35%, rounded up to 81%.

	£
Tax on purchases attributable to taxable supplies £585,000 × 17.5%	102,375.00
Tax on unattributable purchases	
£468,000 × 17.5% × 81%	66,339.00
	168,714.00

Zag plc will need to consider the standard method override if the above attribution differs substantially from one based on the use to which the inputs are put.

e)   Box 5: net VAT to be paid or reclaimed

The amount reclaimable is £(168,714 – 153,562.50) = £15,151.50.

Value Added Tax Return

For the period
01 04 07 to 30 06 07

For Official Use

Registration number	Period
483 8611 98	06 07

You could be liable to a financial penalty if your completed return and all the VAT payable are not received by the due date.

Due date: 31 July 2007

For Official Use

ATTENTION

If this return and any tax due are not received by the due date you may be liable to a surcharge.

If you make supplies of goods to another EC Member State you are required to complete an EC Sales List (VAT 101).

ZAG PLC
32 CASE STREET
ZEDTOWN
ZY4 3JN

If you have a general enquiry or need advice please call our National Advice Service on 0845 010 9000

Before you fill in this form please read the notes on the back and the VAT Leaflet *"Filling in your VAT return"*. Fill in all boxes clearly in ink, and write 'none' where necessary. Don't put a dash or leave any box blank. If there are no pence write "00" in the pence column. Do not enter more than one amount in any box.

For official use			£	p
VAT due in this period on sales and other outputs	1		153,562	50
VAT due in this period on acquisitions from other EC Member States	2		NONE	
Total VAT due (the sum of boxes 1 and 2)	3		153,562	50
VAT reclaimed in this period on purchases and other inputs (including acquisitions from the EC)	4		168,714	00
Net VAT to be paid to Customs or reclaimed by you (Difference between boxes 3 and 4)	5		15,151	50
Total value of sales and all other outputs excluding any VAT. Include your box 8 figure	6			00
Total value of purchases and all other inputs excluding any VAT. Include your box 9 figure	7			00
Total value of all supplies of goods and related services, excluding any VAT, to other EC Member States	8			00
Total value of all acquisitions of goods and related services, excluding any VAT, from other EC Member States	9			00

If you are enclosing a payment please tick this box.

DECLARATION: You, or someone on your behalf, must sign below.

I, ... declare that the
(Full name of signatory in BLOCK LETTERS)
information given above is true and complete.

Signature .... Date ....

A false declaration can result in prosecution.

PRACTICE EXAM 1
UNIT 6

BRECKVILLE DAIRIES LTD

SECTION 1

Task 1.1

a) and b)

STOCK RECORD CARD								
	Receipts			Issues			Balance	
Date	Quantity (litres)	Cost per litre (£)	Total cost (£)	Quantity (litres)	Cost per litre (£)	Total cost (£)	Quantity (litres)	Total cost £
Balance as at 1 Nov							2,000	4,000
6 Nov	1,000	2.60	2,600				3,000	6,600
14 Nov				1,000	$\frac{6,600}{3,000} = 2.20$	2,200	2,000	4,400
22 Nov	1,000	3.40	3,400				3,000	7,800
27 Nov				2,000	$\frac{7,800}{3,000} = 2.6$	5,200	1,000	2,600

c) Another method of stock issue and valuation is LIFO (last in first out).

d) FIFO would lead to a lower valuation of the stock balance at 27 November.

Tutorial note. This is because the stock values are based on older costs which are lower than the more up-to-date costs.

Task 1.2

Date	Code	Dr £	Cr £
6 November	2004	2,600	
6 November	6030		2,600
14 November	7012	2,200	
14 November	2004		2,200
22 November	2004	3,400	
22 November	6030		3,400
27 November	7039	5,200	
27 November	2004		5,200

Task 1.3

		£
Normal hours	350 hours x £8	2,800
Overtime:		
Time and a half	60 hours x £12	720
Double time	40 hours x £16	640
Total direct labour cost		4,160

Task 1.4

Fixed overhead	Basis of allocation or apportionment	Total cost £	Materials Mixing £	Product Packing £	Maintenance £
Insurance of machinery	NBV (360:180:60)	33,600	20,160	10,080	3,360
Rent and rates	Floor area (550:400:50)	91,200	50,160	36,480	4,560
Indirect labour costs	Allocated	135,450	35,750	87,450	12,250
		260,250	106,070	134,010	20,170
Maintenance	Time spent (60:40)		12,102	8,068	(20,170)
Totals		**260,250**	**118,172**	**142,078**	**0**

Task 1.5

a) Materials mixing fixed overhead absorption rate:

$$\frac{\text{Department fixed overheads}}{\text{Department machine hours}} = \frac{118,172}{3,940}$$

$$= \text{£30 per machine hour}$$

b) Product packing fixed overhead absorption rate:

$$\frac{\text{Department fixed overheads}}{\text{Department labour hours}} = \frac{142,078}{10,920}$$

$$= \text{£13 per labour hour}$$

Task 1.6

a) i) Variable (marginal) cost per unit:

	£
Direct materials	12.20
Direct labour	27.80
Prime cost	40.00
Variable overheads (20,000/1,000)	20.00
Variable cost per unit	60.00

ii) Full absorption cost per unit:

	£
Direct materials	12.20
Direct labour	27.80
Prime cost	40.00
Variable overheads (20,000/1,000)	20.00
Fixed overheads (50,000/1,000)	50.00
Variable cost per unit	110.00

b) The closing stock of 200 units would be valued at £12,000 (200 x £60) under marginal costing, and £22,000 (200 x £110) under full absorption costing. This means that an extra £10,000 is deducted from the cost of sales, making the profit £10,000 greater under full absorption costing.

SECTION 2

Task 2.1

a)

Units made	1,000	1,200	1,500
Costs	£	£	£
Variable costs:			
▪ direct materials	3,000	3,600	4,500
▪ direct labour	7,000	8,400	10,500
▪ overheads	6,000	7,200	9,000
Fixed costs:			
▪ indirect labour	9,800	9,800	9,800
▪ overheads	19,000	19,000	19,000
Total cost	44,800	48,000	52,800
Cost per unit	44.80	40.00	35.20

b) i) Fixed costs are only fixed over a certain range of activity, and they may well rise if such a large rise in production were to occur, causing a rise in the cost per unit.

ii) Variable costs per unit might also change. For example, quantity discounts might be obtained on bulk purchases of material which would reduce cost per unit.

iii) Without further information it is not possible to extrapolate to estimate a new cost per unit as the new production level is so far beyond the current production range.

Task 2.2

a) Breakeven sales $= \dfrac{\text{Fixed costs}}{\text{Contribution per unit}}$

$= \dfrac{£28,800}{£24\ (\text{working})}$

$=$ 1,200 units

Working

Contribution per unit $= \dfrac{£3,000 + £7,000 + £6,000}{1,000\ \text{units}}$

$=$ £24 per unit

b)

Forecast sales (units)	1,000	1,200	1,500
Break-even sales (units)	1,200	1,200	1,200
Margin of safety (units)	(200)	0	300
Margin of safety (%)	–	0%	20%

c) i) **1,000 units**

At this level of forecast sales the company is selling 200 units below what it needs to break even, so there is no margin of safety; it is already making a loss.

ii) **1,200 units**

At this forecast level of sales the margin of safety is zero as this is the break even level. Sales cannot fall below this level or else a loss will be made.

iii) **1,500 units**

At this forecast level of sales the company is making a profit. Sales could drop by 20% before a profit would no longer be made.

The company needs to sell more than 1,200 units.

Task 2.3

a) Cost per litre of output $= \dfrac{£12,000 - (200 \times £5)}{1,000 \, litres}$

$= £11$

b)

Process account: Product T

	Litres	Unit cost £	Total cost £		Litres	Unit cost £	Total cost £
Input to process	1,200	10	12,000	Normal loss	200	5	1,000
				Output from process	1,000	11	11,000
			12,000				12,000

Task 2.4

Product	V	W	Total
Contribution/unit (£)	10	15	
Machine hours/unit	2	5	
Contribution/machine hour (£)	5	3	
Product ranking	1	2	
Machine hours available			
Machine hours allocated to: Product...V... Product...W..	2,000	1,000	3,000
Units made	1,000	200	
Total contribution earned (£)	10,000	3,000	13,000
Less: Fixed costs (£)			9,000
Profit/loss made (£)			4,000

Task 2.5

REPORT	

To:	Chief Accountant	**Subject:**	Appraisal of investment in mixing machine
From:	Chief Accountant	**Date:**	28 November 2007

The payback period for the purchase of the mixing machine is 3.6 years, which is within our required limit of four years. On this basis we would accept the investment.

The NPV of the investment project is negative at our cost of capital of 15%, the IRR being only 12%. On these criteria we should not accept the investment proposed.

Although the different bases appear to conflict, the correct decision will be made only if we base our decision on NPV. We should therefore reject the investment proposal as it would mean that the company would be £200,000 worse off if it were to go ahead.

PRACTICE EXAM 2
UNIT 6

CASTON FINE FOODS LTD

ANSWERS

SECTION 1

Task 1.1

a) and c)

STOCK RECORD CARD FOR FOOD INGREDIENT RM 1546									
	Receipts			Issues			Balance		
Balance as at	Quantity kg	Cost per kg (£)	Total cost (£)	Quantity kg	Cost per kg (£)	Total cost (£)	Quantity kg	Total cost (£)
16 May							4,000	6,000
20 May	8,000	1.60	12,800				12,000	18,800
25 May				4,000 1,000 5,000	1.50 1.60	6,000 1,600 7,600	7,000	11,200
28 May	8,000	1.70	13,600				15,000	24,800
31 May				6,000	1.60	9,600	9,000	15,200

b)   The method used for valuing stock issues is FIFO.

Tutorial note. At first sight it may seem that there is not enough information to deduce the method of valuing stock issues. However the key is the issue on 25 May which was valued at £7,600. There are only three options for the method FIFO, LIFO and weighted average cost. Try each of them and you will find that the only method which gives an issue value of £7,600 is FIFO.

Task 1.2

Date	Code	Dr £	Cr £
20 May	4320	12,800	
20 May	1100		12,800
25 May	5052	7,600	
25 May	4320		7,600
28 May	4320	13,600	
28 May	1100		13,600
31 May	5038	9,600	
31 May	4320		9,600

Task 1.3

a)

WEEKLY TIMESHEET FOR WEEK ENDING 31 MAY 2007						
Employee: J Stone			**Cost Centre:** Packing			
Employee number: P12			**Basic pay per hour:** £9.00			
	Hours worked on direct work	**Hours worked on indirect work**	**Notes**	**Basic pay £**	**Overtime premium £**	**Total pay £**
Monday	8	–		72		72
Tuesday	6	2		72		72
Wednesday	12			108	18	126
Thursday	10			90	9	99
Friday	5	3		72		72
Saturday	4			36	36	72
Sunday	2			18	18	36
Total	47	5		468	81	549

b) **Analysis of total pay for the week**

	£
Direct labour cost	423
Indirect labour cost	126
Total pay	549

Workings

		£
Direct labour cost	47 hours x £9	423
Indirect labour cost	5 hours x £9	45
Overtime premium		81
		126

Tutorial note. This was a new development in the exam so make sure that you fully understand the calculations and analysis.

Task 1.4

Department	Basis of allocation or apportionment	Ingredients mixing £	Containerisation £	Packing and despatch £	Maintenance £	Stores £	Totals £
Depreciation of machinery	NBV of machinery	480,160	360,120	240,080	60,020	60,020	1,200,400
Rent and rates	Square metres	180,240	150,200	180,240	30,040	60,080	600,800
Light and heat	Square metres	60,000	50,000	60,000	10,000	20,000	200,000
Power	Machine hours	300,000	200,000				500,000
Indirect labour	Allocated	501,644	316,896	558,460	75,800	141,000	1,593,800
Totals		1,522,044	1,077,216	1,038,780	175,860	281,100	4,095,000
Re-apportion maintenance		105,516	70,344		(175,860)		
Re-apportion stores		112,440	112,440	56,220		(281,100)	
Total production cost centres		1,740,000	1,260,000	1,095,000			4,095,000

409

Task 1.5

Ingredients mixing = £1,740,000/3,000 machine hours
= £580 per machine hour

Containerisation = £1,260,000/2,000 machine hours
= £630 per machine hour

Packing and despatch = £1,095,000/5,000 direct labour hours
= £219 per direct labour hour

Task 1.6

a) **Variable (marginal) cost**

	£ per batch
Direct materials	316.80
Direct labour	412.50
Variable overheads $\dfrac{£197,800}{230\,\text{batches}}$	860.00
Total variable cost per batch	1,589.30

b) **Full absorption cost**

	£ per batch
Direct materials	316.80
Direct labour	412.50
Variable overheads $\dfrac{£197,800}{230\,\text{batches}}$	860.00
Total fixed overheads $\dfrac{£278,300}{230\,\text{batches}}$	1,210.00
	2,799.30

SECTION 2

Task 2.1

Batches made and sold

	5,000 £	6,000 £	7,000 £
Sales revenue $\left(\dfrac{30,000}{5,000}=\text{£6 per unit}\right)$	30,000	36,000	42,000
Variable costs:			
direct materials $\left(\dfrac{1,250}{5,000}=0.25\text{ per unit}\right)$	1,250	1,500	1,750
direct labour $\left(\dfrac{3,000}{5,000}=0.60\text{ per unit}\right)$	3,000	3,600	4,200
overheads $\left(\dfrac{7,500}{5,000}=1.50\text{ per unit}\right)$	7,500	9,000	10,500
Fixed costs:			
indirect labour	2,750	2,750	2,750
overheads	8,800	8,800	8,800
Total cost	23,300	25,650	28,000
Total profit	6,700	10,350	14,000
Profit per batch	1.34	1.725	2.00

Tutorial note. Remember only to flex the variable costs and not the fixed costs.

Task 2.2

a) **Batches made and sold**

	5,000	6,000
	£	£
Sales revenue	30,000	36,000
Fixed costs (2,750 + 8,800)	11,550	11,550
Contribution per batch $\left(\dfrac{6,700+11,550}{5,000}\right)$	3.65	
Or $\left(\dfrac{10,350+11,550}{6,000}\right)$		
Break even number of batches $\left(\dfrac{11,550}{3.65}\right)$	3,165 batches	
Break even sales revenue (3,165 x £6)	18,990	
Margin of safety in number of batches		
(5,000 – 3,165)	1,835	
(6,000 – 3,165)		2,835
Margin of safety in sales revenue		
(30,000 – 18,990)	11,010	
(36,000 – 18,990)		17,010
Margin of safety %		
1,835/5,000 x 100	36.7%	
2,835/6,000 x 100		47.25%

Tutorial note. Take care with the contribution per batch. This is the profit per batch plus the fixed costs or alternatively the sales revenue minus the variable costs.

Also remember to round up the break even point rather than rounding down.

b) The budgeted break even volume is the volume of sales at which no profit is made. This means that it is the volume of sales that covers our fixed costs of £11,550 exactly so that budgeted contribution equals budgeted fixed costs. In this case the budgeted break even volume is 3,165 batches or this can be converted into break even sales which are £18,990.

The margin of safety is the amount by which the budgeted sales figure exceeds the break even point. This gives an indication of how close to the break even point the budgeted sales actually are. If budgeted sales are 5,000 units then the margin of safety is 1,835 units or 36.7% which means that sales can fall by 36.7% from budget before a loss is made. If budgeted volume is taken as 6,000 units then this margin of safety increases to 47.25%.

Task 2.3

Normal loss

Normal loss is the expected loss from a process in the form of wastage, evaporation etc. It is part of the manufacturing process and cannot therefore be avoided. It is not controllable but it is expected and can be built into the costing calculations.

For example suppose that a process involving liquids has a normal loss in the form of evaporation of 10% of the liquids input into the process. This means that for every 100 litres input into the process only 90 litres of product are expected. The cost of normal losses is included in the cost of good production, so if each litre of input costs £10, the material cost per litre of output is £1,000/90 litres = £11.11.

Abnormal loss

An abnormal loss is a loss that is over and above the normal or expected loss. It is an unexpected loss which will normally be incurred due to inefficient production. Abnormal losses are controllable and in a perfect world should not occur. For example if the normal loss is 10% and the input to the process is 100 litres and the output is 85 good litres then the abnormal loss is 5 litres. Examples might be due to use of lower grade materials or inefficient cutting of materials.

Abnormal losses do not affect the cost of good production but are removed from the process account and accounted for separately.

Abnormal gain

An abnormal gain is where the actual loss from a process is less than the normal or expected loss. It is an unexpected gain which will normally be due to efficient production. For example if the normal loss is 10% and input to the process is 100 litres and the output is 93 litres then the abnormal gain is 3 litres.

Abnormal gains do not affect the cost of good production but are removed from the process account and accounted for separately.

Tutorial note. This is the first time that process costing has been tested in the exam. This probably means that it will be again so make sure that you are confident with this subject area.

Task 2.4

a) **The net present value**

	Year 0 £'000	Year 1 £'000	Year 2 £'000	Year 3 £'000
Capital expenditure	(600)			
Sales income		760	920	1,060
Operating costs		(456)	(542)	(612)
Net cash flows	(600)	304	378	448
PV factors	1.0000	0.87719	0.76947	0.67497
Discounted cash flows	(600)	266.67	290.86	302.39
Net present value	259.92			

b) **The payback period**

	£'000
Cash outflow	(600)
Year 1 inflow	304
Cumulative cash flow	296
Year 2 inflow	378
Cumulative cash flow	82

$$\text{Payback period} = 1 \text{ year} + \frac{296}{378} \text{ months}$$
$$= 1 \text{ year} + 9.4 \text{ months}$$

Tutorial note. The examiner commented that many students did not show their workings to the payback period. This is a very high risk strategy as if you make just one mistake you will earn no marks, as the marker cannot see what you have done.

Task 2.5

REPORT

To: The Management Accountant

Subject: Proposed investment

From: Accounting Technician

Date: June 2007

The net present value of the proposed new oven-ready meal is positive at almost £260,000 which means that the company would be £260,000 better off in present value terms if the meal was invested in. Therefore on the basis of net present value the project should go ahead.

However the company also has an investment criterion that projects must pay back in a time period of half the expected life of the project. In this case the product life is three years but the payback period is 1 year and just over 9 months. Therefore on the basis of the payback period the project would be rejected.

However the net present value is the more useful investment appraisal technique and as this shows that the present value of the company would increase by almost £260,000 if the investment were made then the investment in the oven-ready meal should be made.

An alternative investment appraisal technique that could have been used to appraise the project is to calculate its internal rate of return (IRR). The IRR is the discount rate at which the project cash flows give a zero net present value. The IRR will give the same investment conclusion as the NPV in this case and will be higher than the cost of capital of 14% and therefore again the decision should be made to invest in the project.

Tutorial note. A further appraisal method, the accounting rate of return (ARR), could also have been discussed. In this calculation the accounting profit (net operating cash flows – depreciation) would be compared to the amount of the investment and a percentage return calculated. This would then be compared to the company's target ARR to determine whether or not the project was acceptable.

PRACTICE EXAM 3
UNIT 6

WRAPWELL LTD

ANSWERS

SECTION 1

Task 1.1

a) The stock method being used to value issues and stocks of Component Z is average cost (AVCO).

b)

	STOCK RECORD CARD FOR PLASTICS COMPONENT 2							
	Receipts			Issues			Balance	
Date 2007	Quantity kg	Cost per kg (£)	Total cost (£)	Quantity kg	Cost per kg (£)	Total cost (£)	Quantity kg	Total cost £
Balance as of 1 Nov							4,000	8,800
11 Nov	12,000	2.00	24,000				16,000	32,800
15 Nov				8,000	2.05	16,400	8,000	16,400
22 Nov	8,000	2.20	17,600				16,000	34,000
29 Nov				4,000	2.125	8,500	12,000	25,500

416

Task 1.2

Date	Code	Dr £	Cr £
11 November	203	24,000	
11 November	600		24,000
15 November	305	16,400	
15 November	203		16,400
22 November	203	17,600	
22 November	600		17,600
29 November	306	8,500	
29 November	203		8,500

Task 1.3

a)

		£
Cost at normal rate	810 × £6	4,860
Time and a half overtime premium	120 × £3	360
Double time overtime premium	90 × £6	540
		5,760

b) Direct labour cost per bottle:
Direct labour cost/actual bottles produced
£5,760/18,000 = 32p per bottle

Task 1.4

Fixed overhead	Basis of allocation or apportionment	Total cost £	Plastics Moulding £	Plastics Extrusion £	Maintenance £
Insurance of machinery	Net book value of fixed assets	22,400	13,400	6,720	2,240
Rent and rates	Square metres occupied	60,800	33,440	24,320	3,040
Indirect labour costs	Allocation	191,600	90,500	78,300	22,800
		274,800	137,380	109,340	28,080
Maintenance		–	19,656	8,424	(28,080)
Totals		**274,800**	**157,036**	**117,764**	**0**

Task 1.5

a) i) Fixed overhead absorbed – Plastics Moulding department
   Actual machine hours × overhead absorption rate
   850 × £60 = £51,000

   ii) Fixed overhead absorbed – Plastics Extrusion department
   Actual labour hours × overhead absorption rate
   1,520 × £25 = £38,000

b) i) Over-/under-absorption of fixed overheads – Moulding
   Actual fixed overheads – overheads absorbed
   £55,000 – £51,000 = £4,000 under-absorbed

   ii) Over-/under-absorption of fixed overheads – Extrusion
   £36,000 – £38,000 = £2,000 over-absorbed

Task 1.6

a) Cost per batch of containers: marginal costing

	£
Direct materials	220.80
Direct labour	386.40
Variable overheads for one batch (£89,000/620)	145.00
Marginal cost per batch	752.20

b) Cost per batch of containers: absorption costing

	£
Marginal cost per batch	752.20
Fixed overheads for one batch (£130,200/620)	210.00
Absorption cost per batch	962.20

SECTION 2

Task 2.1

a)

Units made	10,000	12,000	14,000
Costs	£	£	£
Variable costs			
■ Direct materials	2,200	2,640	3,080
■ Direct labour	3,300	3,960	4,620
■ Overheads	4,200	5,040	5,880
Fixed costs			
■ Indirect labour	1,800	1,800	1,800
■ Overheads	5,600	5,600	5,600
Total cost	17,100	19,040	20,980
Cost per unit	1.71	1.59	1.50

b)   If production volume increased by such a large amount in such a short time, the effect would be to change both fixed and variable costs per unit. Fixed costs would certainly rise, as premises, machinery and supervision would increase. At the point at which these step increases were incurred, the fixed cost per unit would rise, but would fall again as the cost were spread over more units.

If there were shortages of materials and labour, there would be a rise in variable cost per unit as more would have to be paid for both. Discounts on bulk purchases would cause the direct material cost per unit to fall. Otherwise, variable cost per unit would remain constant and would not affect the cost per unit calculations above.

Task 2.2

	N	P	Total (£)
Units selling price (£) Sales revenue/units sold	0.90	0.80	
Less: variable costs per unit			
direct materials (£) direct material/units made	(0.20)	(0.25)	
direct labour (£) variable labour/units made	(0.12)	(0.14)	
variable overheads (£) variable o'heads/units made	(0.15)	(0.19)	
Contribution per unit (£)	0.43	0.22	
Sales volume (units)	150,000	250,000	
Total contribution (£)	64,500	55,000	119,500
Less: fixed costs			(95,600)
Budgeted profit or loss			23,900

Task 2.3

Product	N	P
Fixed costs (£)	51,600	44,000
Unit contribution (£)	0.43	0.22
Break even sales (units)	120,000	200,000
Forecast sales (units)	160,000	240,000
Margin of safety (units)	40,000	40,000
Margin of safety (%) (as a percentage of forecaset sales)	25.00	16.67

Task 2.4

Product	B	C	Total
Contribution/unit (£)	0.43	0.22	
Machine hours/unit Machine hours required/units made	0.002	0.008	
Contribution/machine hr. (£)	215.00	27.50	
Product ranking	1	2	
Machine hours available			2,100

Machine hours allocated to:
  Product   N 0.002 × 150,000
  Product   P Balance
	300	1,800	

Total contribution earned (£)	300 × £215 = 64,500	1,800 × £27.50 = 49,500	114,000
Less: fixed costs (£)			95,600
Profit/loss made (£)			18,400

Task 2.5

a)   The net present value

	Year 0 £'000	Year 1 £'000	Year 2 £'000	Year 3 £'000
Capital expenditure	(800)	0	0	0
Sales income	0	1,200	1,400	1,400
Operating costs	0	(840)	(910)	(860)
Net cash flows	(800)	360	490	540
PV factors	1.0000	0.9009	0.8116	0.7312
Discounted cash flows	(800)	324,324	397.684	394.848
Net present value	315,856			

b)   The payback period

	Year 0 £'000	Year 1 £'000	Year 2 £'000	Year 3 £'000
Net cash flows	(800)	360	490	540
Cumulative	(800)	(440)	50	590

The project pays back during the second year, at 1 year plus (440/490 × 12 months) 10.7 months, ie just under 1 year and 11 months.

Task 2.6

REPORT

To: The Management Accountant **Subject:** Investment appraisal of plastic drink bottle

From: Accounting Technician **Date:** 5 December 2007

---

a) The project has a positive net present value (NPV) when discounted over its life of three years, in the amount of £316,856. On this basis alone it should be pursued, as it results in a significant increase in Wellwrap Ltd's value. In addition the project pays back its initial capital investment well within three years, namely after 1 year and 11 months.

b) Commercial factors that are also relevant to the decision as to whether to proceed are:

- The risks and uncertainties surrounding the project; forecast cash flows and life-span
- How the product will affect sales of existing products
- How competitors will be affected, and how they will react

(Only TWO were required.)

c) The internal rates of return of any capital project is the cost of capital which, if used to appraise the project, would cause the projects. NPV to be zero. This rate can then be compared with the company's cost of capital; if it is higher, then the project should be accepted, and this means that a higher rate of return on capital employed is being achieved than is required, so shareholder value will increase.

PRACTICE EXAM 4
UNIT 6

DELCOM LTD

SECTION 1

Task 1.1

STOCK RECORD CARD FOR STEEL COMPONENT M									
	Receipts			Issues			Balance		
Date	Quantity kg	Cost per kg (£)	Total cost (£)	Quantity kg	Cost per kg (£)	Total cost (£)	Quantity kg	Total cost (£)	
Balance as of 1 May							25,000	50,000	
9 May	30,000	2.30	69,000				55,000	119,000	
12 May				40,000	25,000 × £2 (W1) 15,000 × £2.30	50,000 34,500 ____ 84,500	15,000	34,500	
18 May	20,000	2.50	50,000				35,000	84,500	
27 May				10,000	2.30	23,000	25,000	61,500	

Working 1: Brought forward balance = £50,000/25,000 unit
= £2 per unit

Task 1.2

JOURNAL

Date	Code	Dr (£)	Cr (£)
9 May	306	69,000	
9 May	500		69,000
12 May	401	84,500	
12 May	306		84,500
18 May	306	50,000	
18 May	500		50,000
27 May	402	23,000	
27 May	306		23,000

Task 1.3

Product C: direct labour cost: May

	Hours	Rate £	£
Normal time	8,000	7.00	56,000
Overtime (time and a half)	1,500	10.50 (W2)	15,750
Overtime (double time)	1,000	14.00(W3)	14,000
	10,500		85,750

Working 2: Normal time × 1½ = £7 × 3/2
  = £10.50
Working 3: Normal time × 2 = £7 × 2
  = £14.00

Task 1.4

Fixed overhead	Basis of allocation or apportionment	Total cost (£)	Machining 1 (£)	Machining 2 (£)	Assembly (£)	Packaging (£)
Depreciation	Net book value of assets	80,000	32,000	8,000	24,000	16,000
Rent and rates	Square metres occupied	120,000	30,000	12,000	24,000	54,000
Indirect labour costs	Actual allocation	97,900	40,500	18,300	12,400	26,700
Direct assembly costs	Actual allocation	15,600	0	0	15,600	0
Totals		313,500	102,500	38,300	76,000	96,700

Task 1.5

Budgeted fixed overhead absorption rate: July

Total departmental overheads/Total budgeted machine hours

£400,000/10,000 = £40/machine hour

Task 1.6

a) i) **Cost per unit of product D: marginal costing**

	Per unit £
DIrect materials per unit	10.60
Direct labour per unit	16.40
Prime cost	27.00
Variable overheads per unit: £60,000/10,000	6.00
Marginal cost per unit	33.00

   ii) **Cost per unit of product D: full absorption costing**

	£
Marginal cost per unit	33.00
Fixed overheads per unit: £80,000/10,000	8.00
	41.00

b) Fixed overheads will be under-recovered if actual production of units in a period is less than was expected. This is because fixed overheads are absorbed at a fixed rate per unit, so if production falls short of the level at which the rate was calculated, they will not be fully recovered in the units actually produced.

In addition, fixed overheads will be under recovered even when actual production reaches budgeted levels if the actual level of fixed overheads exceeds the budgeted level.

SECTION 2

Task 2.1

a)

Units made	1,000,000	1,500,000	2,000,000
Costs:	£	£	£
Variable costs:			
▪ direct materials	5,000,000	7,500,000 (W)	10,000,000
▪ direct labour	4,600,000	6,900,000	9,200,000
▪ overheads	3,200,000	4,800,000	6,400,000
Fixed costs:			
▪ indirect labour	2,500,000	2,500,000	2,500,000
▪ overheads	6,300,000	6,300,000	6,300,000
Total cost	21,600,000	28,000,000	34,400,000
Cost per unit	21.60	18.67	17.20

b) Variable costs per unit remain steady at every level of production, but fixed costs per unit fall as output rises, since the same level of cost is spread across more and more units. As a result, total costs fall as output rises.

c) In the short term (ie less than say one year) it may be realistic to assume that variable costs will vary proportionately with the level of production, and the fixed costs will remain the same whatever happens. In the medium to long-term, however, this is not such a realistic assumption. Most costs have an element of both fixed and variable costs, for instance, direct labour may be a fixed cost up to the level of paying all permanent workers their basic wage; it is only for the units produced over and above that level that costs vary. Similarly, direct materials may vary exactly with the level of production until a certain point when bulk discounts for large purchases are earned; at this point direct costs per unit will fall.

In the case of fixed costs, these may be fixed up to a certain level of activity, and they suffer a 'step' increase. An example is rent. This may stay the same for 1 million or 1.5 million items being produced in the same premises. To produce 2 million items, additional premises may need to be rented, at a significant 'step' rise in rent.

Task 2.2

Product	B	C	Total (£)
Units selling price (£)	10.00	12.00	
Less: unit variable costs			
▪ direct materials (£)	(2.00)	(3.00)	
▪ direct labour (£)	(2.50)	(3.50)	
▪ variable overheads (£)	(3.00)	(2.00)	
Contribution per unit (£)	2.50	3.50	
Sales volume (units)	500,000	750,000	
Total contribution (£)	1,250,000	2,625,000	3,875,000
Less: fixed costs			(3,450,000)
Budgeted profit or loss			425,000

Task 2.3

a)

Product	B	C
Fixed costs (£)	1,000,000	2,450,000
Unit contribution (£)	2.50	3.50
Break-even sales (units)	400,000	700,000
Forecast sales (units)	480,000	910,000
Margin of safety (units)	80,000	210,000
Margin of safety (%)	16.67	23.08

b) The percentage margin of safety is a measure of how far forecast sales can fall before the break-even point is reached and the product ceases to make a profit. In the case of Product B, the sales forecast could be over-optimistic by 16.67% before this situation is reached; in the case of Product C there is even more room for error in the forecast, so that actual sales could be 23.08% less than forecast before the product reaches the point when it fails to break even.

The margin of safety is calculated as: $\dfrac{\text{Forecast sales} - \text{breakeven level of sales}}{\text{Forecast sales}}$

If we had actual sales data then the margin of safety could be calculated using this, to show by how much actual sales could fall before the product fails to make a profit.

431

Task 2.4

Product	B	C	Total
Contribution/unit (£)	2.50	3.50	
Machine hours/unit	2	5	
Contribution/machine hr. (£)	1.25	0.70	
Product ranking	1	2	
Machine hours available			3,500,000
Machine hours allocated to: Product B Product C	1,000,000	2,500,000	3,500,000
Total contribution earned (£)	1,250,000	1,750,000	3,000,000
Less: fixed costs (£)			3,450,000
Profit/loss made (£)			(450,000)

Task 2.5

a)   The net present value

	Year 0 £'000	Year 1 £'000	Year 2 £'000	Year 3 £'000
Capital expenditure	(1,500)	0	0	0
Sales income	0	700	800	1,000
Operating costs	0	(200)	(250)	(300)
Net cash flows	(1,500)	500	550	700
PV factors	1.0000	0.8929	0.7972	0.7118
Discounted cash flows	(1,500.00)	446.45	438.46	498.26
Net present value	(116.83)			

b)   The payback period

	Year 0 £'000	Year 1 £'000	Year 2 £'000	Year 3 £'000
Net cash flows as above	(1,500)	500	550	700
Cumulative net cash flows	(1,500)	(1,000)	(450)	250

The project pays best during year 3. To be precise, its payback is:
2 years + ((450/700) × 12 months) = 2 years and 7.7 months

Task 2.6

REPORT

To:	The Management Accountant	**Subject:**	Product E appraisal
From:	Accounting Technician	**Date:**	13 June 2007

a)   The net present value (NPV) of this investment is a negative amount, £116,830, but it does pay back the £1,500,000 capital investment within the very short product life of 3 years (in 2 years and just less than 7 months). Assuming the product life and the rather high cost of capital are estimates that we are happy with, the product should be rejected on the basis that its NPV is negative, and would result in a diminution of the company's overall value. We cannot accept the project on the basis of its payback period as we do not know what the acceptable period for payback is.

b)   The investment in Product E could also have been appraised using Internal Rate of Return (IRR) or Accounting Rate of Return (ARR), both of which could have been compared with the rates of return which the company uses for appraising investments.

c)   Commercial factors that could also be considered when finally deciding whether to reject this investment include:

- whether the cash flows could be improved at all

- whether Product E has a strategic importance for the company

- how Product E fits into the company's overall product portfolio

- whether the life of Product E could be extended

- how sales of Product E would affect other Delcom sales and the sales of competitor products

- the level of risk represented by the project

(Only TWO commercial factors required.)

PRACTICE EXAM 5
UNIT 6

CHINA LTD

ANSWERS

SECTION 1

Task 1.1

a) The FIFO method of valuing issues to production and stocks of materials has been used to prepare the stock card shown.

b) The FIFO method issues the oldest items of stock to production first.

   i) The issue to production of 45,000 kgs of clay on 9 November is calculated as follows.

	£
15,000 kgs at £0.50	7,500
30,000 kgs at £0.45	13,500
	21,000

   ii) The issue to production of 50,000 kgs of clay on 17 November is calculated as follows.

	£
30,000 kgs at £0.45	13,500
20,000 kgs at £0.55	11,000
	24,500

Task 1.2

Reorder level = buffer stock + (budgeted usage × maximum lead time)
              = 25,000 + (25,000 × 2)
              = 25,000 + 50,000
              = 75,000 kgs

Task 1.3

Code	Dr	Cr
	£	£
1000	33,000	
7000		7,400
7001		5,100*
9001		20,500

* £2,100 + £3,000 = £5,100

Task 1.4

Fixed overheads for November	Total £	Moulding £	Glazing £	Maintenance £	Canteen £
Indirect glazing materials (allocated)	1,140		1,140		
Rent and other property overheads (W1)	15,000	9,000	3,000	1,500	1,500
Power costs (allocated)	5,040	1,200	3,290	250	300
Indirect staff costs (allocated)	8,910	1,100	2,010	3,800	2,000
Machine depreciation (allocated)	8,310	1,710	6,600		
	38,400	13,010	16,040	5,550	3,800
Canteen (W2)		2,600	800	400	(3,800)
Maintenance (W3)		1,190	4,760	(5,950)	
	38,400	16,800	21,600		

Workings

1) **Rent and other property overheads**

Rent and other property overheads are apportioned on the basis of the floor space occupied by each centre.

Total floor space = (3,000 + 1,000 + 500 + 500) sq m
= 5,000 sq m

Apportioned to moulding centre $= \dfrac{3,000}{5,000} \times £15,000$

$= £9,000$

Apportioned to glazing centre $= \dfrac{1,000}{5,000} \times £15,000$

$= £3,000$

Apportioned to maintenance centre $= \dfrac{500}{5,000} \times £15,000$

$= £1,500$

Apportioned to canteen centre $= \dfrac{500}{5,000} \times £15,000$

$= £1,500$

2) **Reapportionment of canteen overheads**

Canteen overheads are reapportioned on the basis of the number of employees in each centre.

Total number of employees = 26 + 8 + 4 = 38

Total canteen overheads = £3,800

Reapportioned to the moulding centre = 26/38 × £3,800
= £2,600

Reapportioned to the glazing centre = 8/38 × £3,800
= £800

Reapportioned to the maintenance centre = 4/38 × £3,800
= £400

3) **Reapportionment of maintenance centre overheads**

Maintenance centre overheads are reapportioned to the moulding and glazing centres in the ratio 20:80.

Total maintenance centre overheads after adding the reapportioned canteen overheads = £5,950

Reapportioned to the moulding centre = 20% × £5,950
= £1,190

Reapportioned to the glazing centre = 80% × £5,950
= £4,760

Task 1.5

a) Budgeted overhead absorption rate $= \dfrac{\text{Budgeted overheads}}{\text{Budgeted hours}}$

i) The budgeted overhead absorption rate for the moulding centre will be based on budgeted labour hours.

Budgeted overhead absorption rate $= \dfrac{£16,800}{4,000 \text{ labour hours}}$

$= £4.20$ per labour hour

ii) The budgeted overhead absorption rate for the glazing centre will be based on budgeted machine hours.

Budgeted overhead absorption rate $= \dfrac{£21,000}{6,000 \text{ machine hours}}$

$= £3.60$ per machine hour

b) Under or over absorbed production overheads for November

i)   the moulding centre

(4,200 × £4.20) – £17,200 = £440 over absorbed

ii) the glazing centre

(5,600 × £3.60) – £20,850 = £690 under absorbed

Task 1.6

Overhead costs are charged to individual products through budgeted overhead absorption rates. The formula for calculating budgeted overhead absorption rates is as follows.

$$\text{Budgeted overhead absorption rate} = \frac{\text{Budgeted overheads}}{\text{Budgeted activity}}$$

Therefore, if the budgeted activity in the moulding and glazing centres were to increase, then the budgeted overhead absorption rate would fall. If the budgeted overhead absorption rate were to fall, then the overhead cost charged to individual products would be lower.

SECTION 2

Task 2.1

Product	Alpha £	Beta £	Gamma £	Total £
Sales revenue (W1)	50,000	24,000	40,000	114,000
Less: Variable costs				
Direct materials (W2)	10,000	4,800	8,000	22,800
Direct labour – moulding (W3)	10,000	4,000	7,500	21,500
Direct labour – glazing (W4)	3,000	4,800	3,000	10,800
Total contribution	27,000	10,400	21,500	58,900
Fixed overheads				52,000
Profit				6,900

Workings

1) Sales revenue – Alpha   = 1,000 × £50 = £50,000
    Sales revenue – Beta   = 200 × £120 = £24,000
    Sales revenue – Gamma   = 500 × £80 = £40,000

2) Direct materials – Alpha = 1,000 × £10 = £10,000
    Direct materials – Beta   = 200 × £24 = £4,800
    Direct materials – Gamma = 500 × £16 = £8,000

3) Direct labour moulding – Alpha =   2 hours × £5 per hour × 1,000 = £10,000
    Direct labour moulding – Beta   =   4 hours × £5 per hour × 200 = £4,000
    Direct labour moulding – Gamma =   3 hours × £5 per hour × 500 = £7,500

4) Direct labour glazing – Alpha = 0.5 hours × £6 per hour × 1,000 = £3,000
    Direct labour glazing – Beta   =   4 hours × £6 per hour × 200 = £4,800
    Direct labour glazing – Gamma = 1 hour × £6 per hour × 500 = £3,000

Task 2.2

$$\text{Forecast contribution per unit} = \frac{\text{Total contribution forecast per product}}{\text{Number of units of product produced}}$$

$$\text{Forecast contribution per unit – Alpha} = \frac{£27,000}{1,000 \text{ units}} = £27$$

$$\text{Forecast contribution per unit – Beta} = \frac{£10,400}{200 \text{ units}} = £52$$

$$\text{Forecast contribution per unit – Gamma} = \frac{£21,500}{500 \text{ units}} = £43$$

Task 2.3

| | Product | | |
	Alpha	Beta	Gamma
Contribution per unit (W1)	£27	£52	£43
Glazing centre labour hours required per unit	0.5	4	1
Contribution per glazing centre labour hour	£54	£13	£43
Ranking	1st	3rd	2nd

Workings

| | Alpha | Beta | Gamma |
	£ per unit	£ per unit	£ per unit
Selling price per unit	50	120	80
Direct materials	10	24	16
Direct labour cost – moulding centre	10 (2 × £5)	20 (4 × £5)	15 (3 × £5)
Direct labour cost – glazing centre	3 (0.5 × £6)	24 (4 × £6)	6 (1 × £6)
Total variable cost per unit	23	68	37
Contribution per unit *	27	52	43

* Contribution per unit = selling price per unit – total variable cost per unit.

China Ltd should make and sell 1,000 units of Alpha first as this product earns the highest contribution per unit of limiting factor.

1,000 units of Product Alpha require 1,000 × 0.5 glazing centre labour hours = 500 hours.

Product gamma should be made secondly as it earns the second highest contribution per unit of limiting factor. 500 units of Product Gamma will require 500 × 1.0 glazing centre labour hour = 500 hours.

	Hours
Total glazing centre labour hours available	1,400
Glazing centre hours – Product Alpha	(500)
Glazing centre hours – Product Gamma	(500)
Glazing centre hours available for production of Beta	400

Each unit of Product Beta requires 4 glazing centre hours, therefore 400 glazing centre hours will be sufficient to make and sell 400/4 = 100 units of Beta.

Summary

In order to maximise profits, China Ltd should make and sell its products in the following quantities.

Product Alpha – 1,000 units
Product Beta – 100 units
Product Gamma – 500 units

Task 2.4

a)   Breakeven point $= \dfrac{\text{Fixed costs}}{\text{Contribution per unit of Beta}}$

$= \dfrac{\pounds52,000}{\pounds52^*}$

$=$ 1,000 units

* See answer to Task 2.2

b)   **Reasons for not selling the high value Beta range only**

i)   If breakeven point = 1,000 units

1,000 units will require ($\times$ 4 glazing centre labour hours) = 4,000 hours. Since glazing centre labour hours are limited to 1,400 per month, it would be impossible to make and sell enough units of Product Beta to break even.

ii)   Forecast sales and production of Product Beta = 200 units, therefore it is highly unlikely that the breakeven level of sales is achievable in the current situation.

Task 2.5

MEMO

To:	Board of Directors	**Subject:**	Investment Appraisal
From:	Accounting Technician	**Date:**	29 November 2007

Payback

If a large amount of money is to be spent now on a project, such as the purchase of a major fixed asset, one decision criterion that the management of the business may apply is keeping the length of time over which the benefits from this asset **pay back** the original cost within acceptable limits. This is what is meant by the **payback period**.

The investment under consideration has a payback period of three years which means that the £50,000 investment in the new machinery will be paid back within a three year period.

Internal rate of return

The **internal rate of return** is the discount rate or interest rate that will result in a net present value of zero for a set of cash flows.

If the internal rate of return of a project is higher than the organisation's cost of capital or higher than its required return from investments the project should be accepted.

The investment under consideration has an internal rate of return of 12%. This rate should be compared with the organisation's cost of capital in order to decide whether to accept or reject the proposed machinery purchase.

Net present value

We can also use the net present value method in order to consider the investment in machinery for the glazing centre. This method works by finding the net present value of all the cash flows of the investment. Firstly, the present value of each individual cash flow is calculated and then they are totalled and then the net present value is calculated as follows.

Net present value = total of present value of inflows – outflows

The initial cost of the investment is a cash outflow.

If the net present value is a positive figure then the investment should be accepted as this means that even after having taken account of the time value of money the cash inflows from the project exceed the cash outflows. It, however, the net present value is a negative figure, then the investment should be rejected.

Recommendation

The Board of Directors should invest in the new machinery as it has a positive net present value of £4,800.

AAT

SAMPLE SIMULATION
UNIT 6

QUALITY CANDLES LTD

ANSWERS

Task 1

STORES RECORD CARD

Materials description: Candlewick thread, 200 metre rolls   Maximum quantity: 400
Code no: CW728   Minimum quantity: 140
                                                             Reorder level: 230
                                                             Reorder quantity: 80

Date	Receipts				Issues				Stock balance		
	Document number	Qty	Price per roll (£)	Total (£)	Document number	Qty	Price per roll (£)	Total (£)	Qty	Price per roll (£)	Total (£)
1 Oct									28	2.20	61.60
									26	2.30	59.80
									__54__		__121.40__
3 Oct					249	26	2.30	59.80			
						4	2.20	8.80			
						__30__		__68.60__	24	2.20	__52.80__
6 Oct	419	80	2.35	188.00					24	2.20	52.80
									80	2.35	188.00
									__104__		__240.80__
8 Oct					252	40	2.35	94.00	24	2.20	52.80
									40	2.35	94.00
									__64__		__146.80__
9 Oct	427	80	2.38	190.40					24	2.20	52.80
									40	2.35	94.00
									80	2.38	190.40
									__144__		__337.20__
10 Oct	75	3	2.35	7.05					24	2.20	52.80
									43	2.35	101.05
									80	2.38	190.40
									__147__		__344.25__

Task 2

MATERIALS REQUISITION

Department: Manufacturing

Document no: 252

Date: 08/10/2007

Code no	Description	Quantity	Cost office use only Value of issue (£)
CW728	Candlewick thread 200m rolls	40	94.00

Received by: .... **Signature:** ....

MATERIALS RETURNED

Department: Manufacturing

Document no: 75

Date: 10/10/2007

Code no	Description	Quantity	Cost office use only Value of issue (£)
CW728	Candlewick thread 200m rolls	3	7.05

Received by: .... **Signature:** ....

Task 3

MEMO

To: General Manager
From: Bobby Forster, Accounts Assistant
Subject: Stock levels of candlewick thread, week ending 10 October 2007
Date: 14 October 2007

The stock levels on this item have been a cause for concern during the last week.

The stock level began the week below the minimum quantity of 140 rolls and, although two deliveries brought the balance to 147 rolls by the end of the week, it is clear that the minimum level is soon to be reached once more.

This could lead to the company running out of stock before a new batch of candlewick is received from the supplier. Customer orders could be lost or it may be necessary to pay high prices to acquire urgent supplies.

I suggest that we should review the stock control levels and reorder quantity. Perhaps usage patterns have changed since the levels were set. If this is the case the levels and the reorder quantity should be recalculated, taking account of any changes in usage patterns and supply lead times.

I would be happy to discuss the problem with you at any time.

Task 4

QUALITY CANDLES LIMITED
PIECEWORK OPERATION CARD

Operative name   Mary Roberts   Department: Manufacturing

Clock number   R27

Week beginning   6 October 2007

Activity	Monday	Tuesday	Wednesday	Thursday	Friday
Batches produced	120	102	34	202	115
Batches rejected	5	7	4	11	5
Batches accepted	115	95	30	191	110
Rate per batch	£ 0.50	£ 0.50	£ 0.50	£ 0.50	£ 0.50
Piecework payment	£ 57.50	£ 47.50	£ 15.00	£ 95.50	£ 55.00
Bonus payable	£ 2.30	£ nil	£ nil	£ nil	£ 2.20
Total payable for day*	£ 59.80	£ 50.00	£ 50.00	£ 95.50	£ 57.20

Total wages payable for week:

	£
Direct wages	308.00
Indirect wages	4.50
Total wages	312.50

* Guaranteed daily wage of £50 is payable if piecework payment plus bonus amounts
  less than £50

Supervisor's signature: *A Peters*

Task 5

INTERNAL MEMO

To: Roy Hart, Manufacturing Department Supervisor
From: Bobby Forster, Accounts Assistant
Subject: Discrepancy on piecework operation card
Date: 10 October 2007

I have a query on a piecework operation card for the week beginning 6 October, a copy of which is attached. The employee concerned is Mary Roberts, clock number R27.

The output recorded for Wednesday is exceptionally low and correspondingly the output for Thursday is very high. It is possible that some of the output for Wednesday was recorded in error for Thursday. This distorts the wages payable because of the guaranteed daily rate.

Could you please look into this for me, to see whether there was in fact a genuine reason for the unusual pattern in output levels.

Thank you for your help.

Task 6

Production overhead analysis sheet for 2008

Production overhead item	Total £000	Manufacturing £000	Painting/ finishing £000	Packing £000	Stores £000	Maintenance £000
Indirect labour	98	22	14	11	35	16
Indirect materials	40	12	2	2	12	12
Rent and rates	105	45	15	24	12	9
Protective clothing	31	31				
Power	40	20	4	12	2	2
Insurance	24	11	4	6	2	1
Heat and Light	35	15	5	8	4	3
Depreciation	48	22	8	12	4	2
Other	15	5	5	5		
Total department overheads	436	183	57	80	71	45
Apportion maintenance total	–	21	12	9	3	(45)
Apportion stores total	–	36	20	18	(74)	
Total production dept overheads	436	240	89	107		

Task 7

Working paper

Calculation of production overhead absorption rates for 2008

Manufacturing department

Machine hour rate $= \dfrac{£240,000}{200,000}$

$= £1.20$ per machine hour

Painting and finishing department

Labour hour rate $= \dfrac{£89,000}{28,000}$

$= £3.18$ per labour hour

Packing department

Machine hour rate $= \dfrac{£107,000}{90,000}$

$= £1.19$ per machine hour

Task 8

Sample calculations: working paper

Reversing the order of service department re-apportionments

Production overhead item	Total £000	Manufacturing £000	Painting/ finishing £000	Packing £000	Stores £000	Maintenance £000
Total department overheads (from Task 6)	436	183	57	80	71	45
Apportion stores total	–	27	15	13	(71)	16
Apportion maintenance total	–	31	17	13	–	(61)
Total production dept overheads	436	241	89	106		

Task 9

INTERNAL MEMO

To: General Manager
From: Bobby Forster, Accounts Assistant
Subject: Re-apportionment of service department costs
Date: 5 November 2007

I have carried out the analysis you requested and the results are attached.

As you will see, the change in method does not result in a material difference in the total overhead for each production cost centre. Therefore I suggest that we should not change our apportionment methods since the value of the management information would not be materially affected by the change.

Task 10

Journal entry for production overheads

October 2007

Entries for overhead absorbed during the month

	Debit (£)	Credit (£)
Work in progress: manufacturing dept	18,500	
Work in progress: painting and finishing dept	7,400	
Work in progress: packing dept	8,300	
Production overhead control		34,200

Entries for overhead under-/over-absorbed during the month

	Debit (£)	Credit (£)
Overhead over-/under-absorbed (P+L)		18,400
Production overhead control	18,400	

INTERNAL MEMO

To: Production Manager
From: Bobby Forster, Accounts Assistant
Subject: Overhead absorption for October 2007
Date: 9 November 2007

A significant over absorption arose during the month. The total amount over absorbed was £18,400 compared with total actual expenditure of £15,800.

Could you please check the data for me to ensure that no recording errors have occurred?

The actual production overhead figure may be too low, perhaps because of miscoding of invoices. Alternatively, the activity data for the production departments may have been recorded incorrectly.

Thank you for your help.

Task 11

Workings for determination of revenue and cost behaviour patterns

Sales revenue

Selling price per case = £28,000/7,000 = £4

Check: 6,200 x £4 = £24,800; 5,900 x £4 = £23,600

Candles cost

Candle cost per case = £9,100/7,000 = £1.30

Check: 6,200 x £1.30 = £8,060; 5,900 x £1.30 = £7,670

Packing materials cost

Packing materials cost per case = £5,250/7,000 = £0.75

Check: 6,200 x £0.75 = £4,650; 5,900 x £0.75 = £4,425

Packing labour cost

Packing labour cost per case = £2,100/7,000 = £0.30

Check: 6,200 x £0.30 = £1,860; 5,900 x £0.30 = £1,770

Packing overhead cost

	Cases	£
High	7,000	5,400
Low	5,900	5,180
Difference	1,100	220

Variable cost per case = £220/1,100 = £0.20. Fixed cost = £5,400 – (7,000 x £0.20) = £4,000

Check: for 6,200 cases cost is £4,000 + (6,200 x £0.20) = £5,240

Other overhead cost

Fixed cost = £2,500 per month

Quality Candles Limited: mail order division
Planned results for December 2007

	December
Number of cases to be sold	6,800
	£
Candles cost (@ £1.30)	8,840
Packing materials cost (@ £0.75)	5,100
Packing labour cost (@ £0.30)	2,040
Packing overhead cost	5,360
Other overhead cost	2,500
Total costs	23,840
Sales revenue (@ £4)	27,200
Profit	3,360

Packing overhead cost

	£
Fixed	4,000
Variable (6,800 x £0.20)	1,360
	5,360

Task 12 (i)

Quality Candles Limited: mail order division
Planned results for December 2007: increased activity

	December
Number of cases to be sold	7,600
	£
Candles cost (@ £1.30)	9,880
Packing materials cost (@ £0.60)	4,560
Packing labour cost (@ £0.30)	2,280
Packing overhead cost	5,520
Other overhead cost	2,500
Total costs	24,740
Sales revenue (@ £4)	30,400
Profit	5,660

Packing overhead cost

	£
Fixed	4,000
Variable (7,600 x £0.20)	1,520
	5,520

Task 12 (ii)

Quality Candles Limited: mail order division

Planned results for December 2007: increased activity

Calculation of breakeven point and margin of safety: working paper

	£	£
Contribution per case:		
Selling price		4.00
Less variable costs:		
Candles	1.30	
Packing materials	0.60	
Packing labour	0.30	
Packing overhead	0.20	
		2.40
Contribution per case		1.60
Fixed overhead:		
Packing overhead		4,000
Other overhead		2,500
		6,500

Breakeven point

Number of cases to break even $= \dfrac{£6,500}{£1.60}$

$= 4,063$ cases

Margin of safety $= 7,600 - 4,063$ cases

$= 3,537$ cases

$= 47\%$ of planned activity

Task 12 (iii)

INTERNAL MEMO

To: General Manager
From: Bobby Forster, Accounts Assistant
Subject: Mail order division: bulk discounts for December 2007
Date: 11 November 2007

I have evaluated the proposal to increase sales and take advantage of a bulk discount for packing materials.

The planned profit will increase considerably to £5,660 for the month compared with £3,360 without the increased activity. The breakeven point will be 4,063 cases which results in a margin of safety of 47% of planned activity.

Since the company is looking for opportunities to increase profit, the high profit and the wide margin of safety mean that this represents a very attractive proposal.

However the following assumptions affect the validity of the projections.

- The increased sales volume can be achieved at the current selling price. It is possible that the selling price would have to be reduced in order to sell the greater output.

- All other unit variable costs and fixed costs will not be altered by the increase in activity. Since the volume projection is outside the range for which data is available this may not be a valid assumption. For example it may be necessary to pay overtime rates to labour in order to achieve the increased output.

- The increased volume can be achieved with the existing packing and delivery capacity.

Please let me know if you require any further information.

Task 13 (i)

Working paper for the financial appraisal of purchase of delivery vehicles

Year	Cashflow £	Discount factor @ 12%	Present value £
2007	–90,000	1.000	–90,000
2008	34,800	0.893	31,076
2009	34,800	0.797	27,736
2010	34,800	0.712	24,778
2011	39,800	0.636	25,313
Net present value			18,903

Working space for calculation of payback period

	Cumulative cashflow (£)
2007	–90,000
2008	–55,200
2009	–20,400
2010	14,400

Payback period = 2 years + (20,400/34,800) = 2.6 years

Task 13 (ii)

INTERNAL MEMO

To: General Manager
From: Bobby Forster, Accounts Assistant
Subject: Purchase of delivery vehicles for mail order division
Date: 14 November 2007

The proposal to purchase delivery vehicles is acceptable from a financial viewpoint because it returns a positive net present value of £18,903 at a discount rate of 12%. This calculation assumes that all cashflows occur at the end of each year.

The payback period is between two and three years. If we assume even cashflows during the year the payback period can be calculated as 2.6 years. This is acceptable since it is shorter than the company requirement of three years, although there is not much room for error in the cashflow calculations.

Please let me know if I can help any further with the evaluation.

PRACTICE SIMULATION
UNIT 6

HIGH HEAT LTD

ANSWERS

Task 1

Oven 900 – contribution to fixed costs for October 2007

	£	£
Sales		78,530
Less: Cost of sales		
Opening stock	13,850	
Materials issued	32,135	
Direct labour	28,200	
Variable overheads	1,970	
Closing stock	(16,830)	
		(59,325)
Contribution to fixed costs		19,205

Task 2

STOCK RECORD (STOCK CARD)

Part description: Hi-grade filters
Code: FF783
Maximum purchase price: £17.00

Maximum quantity: 100
Minimum quantity: 20
Reorder level: 50
Reorder quantity: 75

Date	Receipts			Issues			Balance		
	Quantity	Price £	Total £	Quantity	Price £	Total £	Quantity	Price £	Total £
1 Oct							20	16.30	326.00
2 Oct	75	16.50	1,237.50				20	16.30	326.00
							75	16.50	1,237.50
							95		1,563.50
8 Oct				20	16.30	326.00	45	16.50	742.50
				30	16.50	495.00			
				50		821.00			
12 Oct	75	16.70	1,252.50				45	16.50	742.50
							75	16.70	1,252.50
							120		1,995.00
15 Oct				45	16.50	742.50	60	16.70	1,002.00
				15	16.70	250.50			
				60		993.00			
29 Oct	80	17.10	1,368.00				60	16.70	1,002.00
							80	17.10	1,368.00
							140		2,370.00
31 Oct				60	16.70	1,002.00	50	17.10	855.00
				30	17.10	513.00			
				90		1,515.00			

Task 3

MEMORANDUM

To: Production Director
From: Management Accounts Assistant
Subject: Stock of hi-grade filters, October 2007
Date: 5 November 2007

A number of problems have arisen during October concerning the application of our stock control and purchasing practices to the stock of hi-grade filters, code number FF783.

Stock levels above the maximum quantity

The maximum stock level is 100 units for this item, but the level rose to 120 units on 12 October, and 140 on 29 October. It looks as though this was done in anticipation of the unusually large requisition for 90 units on 31 October.

Stock ordered before the level reached the reorder level

The order on 27 October was placed when the stock level was 60 units, whereas the reorder level is 50 units.

Order placed for an amount greater than the reorder quantity

The order of 27 October was for more than the reorder quantity of 75 units.

Order placed at too high a price and not checked by a person in authority

The order of 27 October had a number of errors which may have been picked up if it had been authorised: it was placed when the reorder level had not yet been reached, it was for more than the reorder quantity, and it was at a price that exceeded the maximum stated on the Stock Record.

Conclusion

These breaches of good practice, especially the lack of authorisation and the errors on the order on 27 October, should be thoroughly investigated. Holding too much stock is expensive, can lead to obsolescence and pilfering, and shows a lack of good control.

However, if it transpires that the levels for this part have not been updated for the apparent increase in activity then this should also be looked at as part of production planning.

Task 4

MEMORANDUM

To: Management Accounts Assistant
From: Ismay Ratliff, Production Director
Subject: Stock valuation October 2007
Date: 3 November 2007

Raw materials stock valuation

Please find attached a stock record for hi-grade filters as requested, prepared on the alternative AVCO basis.

Part-finished goods valuation

Oven 678s at 31 December 2007 (estimate)

	£
Materials: 100% x 565	565.00
Labour: 60% x £890	534.00
Variable overheads: 100% x 200	200.00
	1,299.00
Value in year-end accounts: £1,299 x 40	£51,960.00

Finished goods valuation

Absorbing fixed production overheads into the valuation of finished goods will lead to a higher value for finished goods at the year-end. This will increase profits, as expenses that would otherwise have been written off to the profit and loss account in 2007 will instead be carried forward into 2008 as stock.

Task 4 (continued)

STOCK RECORD									

Part description: Hi-grade filters
Code: FF783
Valuation basis: AVCO

Date	Receipts			Issues			Balance		
	Quantity	Price £	Total £	Quantity	Price £	Total £	Quantity	Price £	Total £
1 Oct							20	16.30	326.00
2 Oct	75	16.50	1,237.50				20	16.30	326.00
							75	16.50	1,237.50
							95	16.46	1,563.50
8 Oct				50	16.46	823.00	45	16.46	740.70
12 Oct	75	16.70	1,252.00				45	16.46	740.70
							75	16.70	1,252.50
							120	16.61	1,993.20
15 Oct				60	16.61	996.00	60	16.61	996.60
29 Oct	80	17.10	1,368.00				60	16.61	996.60
							80	17.10	1,368.00
							140	16.89	2,364.60
31 Oct				90	16.89	1,520.10	50	16.89	844.50

Task 5

TIME SHEET						
Week ending 31/10/07						
Name Sanjeev Patel						
Area Machine shop			**Employee number**		M042	
Grade B						
Activity	**MON**	**TUES**	**WED**	**THURS**	**FRI**	**TOTAL**
Oven 900 machining	9		9			18
Oven 778 machining		9		3		12
Sick				4.5		4.5
Training					7.5	7.5
Hours attendance	9.0	9.0	9.0	7.5	7.5	42
Bonus hours	0.5	0.5	0.5			1.5
Employee's signature Sanjeev Patel						
Manager's signature Malcolm Harrison						
ANALYSIS OF HOURS						
Basic rate hours	7.5	7.5	7.5	7.5	7.5	37.5
Overtime hours	1.5	1.5	1.5	0	0	4.5
Bonus hours	0.5	0.5	0.5	0	0	1.5

ANALYSIS OF GROSS PAY

	Hours	Rate £	£	£	
Direct hours (25.5 + 4.5)	30	8.50		255.00	
Indirect hours					
Sick	4.5	8.50	38.25		
Training	7.5	8.50	63.75		
Overtime hours at premium	4.5	4.25	19.13		
Bonus hours	1.5	17.00	25.50		
Total indirect				146.63	
Gross pay				401.63	

Task 5 (continued)

TIME SHEET						
Week ending 31/10/07						
Name Jacob Ellis						
Area Machine shop			**Employee number**		M042	
Grade C						
Activity	**MON**	**TUES**	**WED**	**THURS**	**FRI**	**TOTAL**
Oven 900 machining	8	7.5	8	9	9	43.5
Hours attendance	8	7.5	8	9	9	43.5
Bonus hours	1		1	1	1	4
Employee's signature **Jacob Ellis**						
Manager's signature						
ANALYSIS OF HOURS						
Basic rate hours	8	7.5	8	9	9	41.5
Overtime hours						
Bonus hours						

ANALYSIS OF GROSS PAY

	Hours	**Rate £**	**£**	**£**	
Direct hours	41.5	7.00		290.50	
Indirect hours					
Sick					
Training					
Overtime hours at premium					
Bonus hours					
Total indirect					
Gross pay				290.50	

Task 6

MEMORANDUM

To: Malcolm Harrison, Machine Shop Manager
From: Management Accounts Assistant
Subject: Discrepancy on Time Sheet for Jacob Ellis
Date: 2 November 2007

I have some queries on the Time Sheet for Jacob Ellis for the week ending 31 October 2007. I attach a copy of the Time Sheet.

The Time Sheet relates only to direct hours on Oven 900 machining but the hours have been added incorrectly to 43.5 hours, when the correct total is 41.5 hours. Because of this discrepancy, in line with the Payroll Guide I have calculated these 41.5 hours at his basic rate only.

In addition, the Time Sheet has not been signed by you, although Jacob has signed it. I have therefore not included the 4 hours bonus hours indicated on the Time Sheet in my calculations. These appear to have been filled in by Jacob himself.

Until the Time Sheet is signed by you I cannot proceed with any payment to Jacob. Could you please look into this as a matter of urgency therefore?

Task 7

Calculation of under/over absorption of production overheads

October 2007

Total number of machine hours worked	4,590.00
Pre-determined overhead absorption rate per machine hour, 2007	£13.00
Total production overhead absorbed, October 2007	£59,670.00
Actual production overhead incurred	£68,750.00
Production overhead ~~over~~/(under) absorbed, October 2007	(£9,080.00)

The amount of £9,080 has been ~~over~~/under* absorbed and will be debited/~~credited~~* to the profit and loss account.

(*Delete as applicable.)

Task 8

MEMORANDUM

To: Production Director
From: Management Accounts Assistant
Subject: Production overhead absorption rates for 2008
Date: 14 November 2007

Calculation of single machine hour rate

If we continue to use the current overhead absorption basis of a single, factory-wide machine hour rate in 2008, we can calculate the absorption rate as follows.

$$\text{Machine hour rate} = \frac{\text{total budgeted production overheads}}{\text{total budgeted machine hours}}$$

$$= \frac{£855,000}{52,600}$$

$$= £16.25 \text{ per machine hour}$$

Problems with the single rate

The Assembly Shop Manager has indeed highlighted a problem with the use of a single factory-wide absorption rate: it does not reflect the different activities in the two production cost centres and therefore the different ways in which they incur overhead costs. In the Assembly Shop, there are more labour hours and fewer machine hours, as it is a labour-intensive rather than a machinery intensive operation.

If we use different rates for each area, we would begin by allocating certain production overheads directly to the cost centres that incur them, then apportioning or sharing other types of cost on an agreed basis to the cost centres so as to reflect the use of the resources. Our aim is to determine as fairly as possible the total cost of operating both the Machine Shop and the Assembly Shop, including a share for each of the Testing Centre and Staff Amenity Centre costs.

The activity data shows us that the Assembly Shop is more labour-intensive and uses fewer machine hours, so it would seem fair to absorb the overheads for this department according to labour activity, using a direct labour hour rate. The Machine Shop makes far more use of machinery, so a machine hour rate should be calculated for it.

The two separate absorption rates would then be applied to each cost unit depending on the amount of time (on machines, or on labour) spent in each area. The final absorbed overhead cost should be a more accurate reflection of the resources consumed by each cost unit.

Task 9

Overhead Analysis Sheet: Budget 2008

Rate using step down method of apportionment.

Overhead expense item	Basis of allocation/ apportionment	Total £	Machine Shop £	Assembly Shop £	Testing Centre £	Staff Amenity Centre £
Primary allocations and apportionments						
Indirect labour	Indirect employees 1:1	406,600	203,300	203,300		
Manager salaries.	Allocation	82,000	41,000	41,000		
Testing Centre costs	Allocation	124,800			124,800	
Staff Amenity Centre costs	Allocation	70,500				70,500
Depreciation	Net book value	25,200	17,080	3,900	3,000	1,220
Rent, rates, etc.	Floor area	101,300	30,390	50,650	14,182	6,078
Other o'heads	Equal app'ment	44,600	22,300	22,300		
Total primary allocation		**855,000**	**314,070**	**321,150**	**141,982**	**77,798**
Reapportion Staff Amenity Centre	No employeed 26:41:6		27,709	43,695	6,394	(77,798)
Re-apportion Testing Centre	25:75		37,094	111,282	(148,376)	
Total production cost centre overhead allocation			**378,873**	**476,127**		

ABSORPTION RATES
FOR EACH PRODUCTION DEPARTMENT USING STEP DOWN METHOD:

Machine Shop $= \dfrac{£378,873}{41,500} = £9.13$ per machine hour

Assembly Shop $= \dfrac{£476,127}{85,900} = £5.54$ per direct labour hour

Task 9 (continued)

Alternative rates using direct method of apportionment

Overhead expense item	Basis of allocation/ apportionment	Total £	Machine Shop £	Assembly Shop £	Testing Centre £	Staff Amenity Centre £
Total primary allocation		855,000	314,070	321,150	141,982	77,798
Apportion Test Centre costs	25:75		19,449	58,349		(77,798)
Apportion Staff Amendity Centre costs	No employees 26:41		55,097	86,885	(141,982)	
Total production cost centre overhead allocation			388,616	466,384		

CALCULATION OF ABSORPTION RATES
FOR EACH PRODUCTION DEPARTMENT USING DIRECT APPORTIONMENT:

Machine Shop $= \dfrac{£388,616}{41,500} = £9.36$ per machine hour

Assembly Shop $= \dfrac{£466,384}{85,900} = £5.43$ per direct labour hour

Task 10

Working paper for calculation of payback period and net present value

Payback period

Year	Cash flow £	Cumulative cash flow £
0	(1,000,000)	(1,000,000)
1	250,000	(750,000)
2	350,000	(400,000)
3	500,000	100,000
4	650,000	750,000

Payback period   = 2 years + (400,000/500,000 × 1 year)
                    = 2.8 years

Net present value

Year	Cash flow £	Discount factor at 6%	Cumulative cash flow £
0	(1,000,000)	1.0000	(1,000,000)
1	250,000	0.9434	235,850
2	350,000	0.8900	311,500
3	500,000	0.8396	419,800
4	650,000	0.7920	514,800
Net present value			481,950

Task 10 (continued)

MEMORANDUM

To: Production Director
From: Management Accounts Assistant
Subject: Production overhead absorption rates for 2007
Date: 14 November 2007

HIGHLY CONFIDENTIAL

I have calculated the payback period and the net present value, as requested, for the planned expansion to three sites and the development of new product ranges.

Payback period	2.8 years
Net present value (NPV) at company's cost of capital, 6%	£481,950

The results of the evaluation on this basis are that it should be accepted, since it returns a positive NPV when discounted at the company's cost of capital. It also achieves a payback period of less than the three year maximum set by the company. Whether the amount by which the net present value is positive is acceptable to the company is a question of considering the relative risk. It may be worthwhile calculating the internal rate of return (IRR) of the move.

Assumptions underlying the above results include the following.

■   For the calculation of the payback period of 2.8 years it is assumed that cash flows occur evenly during the fourth year. If the cash flows occurred instead later on in the third year then the payback period would be even closer to the company's cut-off point of three years

■   For the NPV calculation, all cash flows are assumed to occur at the end of each year

Task 11

Working paper to determine sales volume, cost behaviour patterns and projected costs and revenues

Projected sales volume

Projected sales volume = 150 dishwashers + (300/75 x 5) machines = 170 machines

Analysis of cost behaviour

Direct material cost

Variable materials cost = £880 per machine

Projected total variable materials cost = 170 x £880 = £149,600

Direct labour cost

Variable cost = £412 per machine

Projected total variable labour cost = 170 x £412 = £70,040

Production overheads cost

Machines		Total cost
		£
160	(× £355)	56,800
150	(× £364)	54,600
10		2,200

Variable production overhead cost per additional machine = £2,200/10 = £220

Fixed production overhead cost = £56,800 – (£220 x 160) = £21,600

Projected total overhead cost:

		£
Fixed overhead		21,600
Variable overhead	(170 × £220)	37,400
		59,000

Other (non-production) overhead cost

Total cost for 150 machines = 150 x £50.00 = £7,500

Total cost for 160 machines = 160 x £46.88 = £7,500

This is a fixed overhead cost.

Sales revenue

Projected sales revenue = 170 machines x £2,000 = £340,000

Task 11 (continued)

Projected costs and revenues for new product range next year

	£	£
Output volume (machines)		170
Sales revenue		340,000
Projected costs		
Direct material	149,600	
Direct labour	70,040	
Variable production overhead	37,400	
Fixed production overhead	21,600	
Other (non-production) overhead	7,500	
Total projected cost		(286,140)
Projected annual profit		53,860

Task 12

Working paper to calculate margin of safety, P/V ratio and maximum possible change in fixed production overheads

Margin of safety

Contribution per machine = £2,000 - £(880 + 412 + 220) = £488

Breakeven sales $\quad = \dfrac{\text{Fixed costs}}{\text{Contribution per machine}}$

$\qquad\qquad = \dfrac{£21,600 + 7,500}{488}$

$\qquad\qquad$ = 60 machines (rounded up to nearest whole number)

Margin of safety = forecast sales – breakeven sales $\qquad$ = 170 – 60 machines
$\qquad\qquad\qquad\qquad\qquad\qquad\qquad\qquad\qquad\qquad\qquad$ = 110 machines

As a percentage of projected sales volume $\qquad\qquad$ = 110/170 x 100
$\qquad\qquad\qquad\qquad\qquad\qquad\qquad\qquad\qquad\qquad\qquad$ = 65%

Profit/volume (P/V) ratio

Profit/volume ratio $\quad$ = (Contribution per unit/Sales revenue per unit) x 100
$\qquad\qquad\qquad\qquad$ = (£488/£2,000) × 100
$\qquad\qquad\qquad\qquad$ = 24.4%

Possible change in fixed production overheads

Forecast profit from new product range $\qquad$ = £53,860

Forecast production overhead cost $\qquad\qquad$ = £59,000

Possible change required to negate profit $\quad$ = (53,860/59,000) x 100
$\qquad\qquad\qquad\qquad\qquad\qquad\qquad\qquad\quad$ = 91%

Task 12 Continued

MEMORANDUM

To: Production Director
From: Management Accounts Assistant
Subject: New large size dishwashers
Date: 30 November 2007

HIGHLY CONFIDENTIAL

I attach the calculations that I have made in response to your memo of today's date.

Analysis of dishwasher product

The projected annual profit for a selling price of £2,000 is £53,860. The margin of safety is 65 per cent of projected sales volume, which amply meets the company's criterion of a 30 per cent safety margin.

The proposal therefore would seem attractive because it achieves the company's goals of increasing profit without unacceptable risk, and it also exceeds the minimum PV ratio of 20%.

My calculations show that the forecast of fixed production overhead could increase by 91% before the new product line fails to earn a profit. Therefore there is some room for error in this difficult forecast.

Please note that I have made the following assumptions in preparing these calculations.

■   The cost behaviour patterns observed for 150 machines and 160 machines will continue to apply for a volume of 170 machines. The projected volume is outside the range of data supplied, therefore this assumption might not be valid. In particular, there may be a step increase in fixed costs necessary to meet this level of production (see below).

■   Variable costs behave in a linear fashion. It is possible that the unit costs may alter for higher output volumes, particularly if we obtain bulk discounts for materials and if the workforce becomes more skilled and therefore spends fewer hours per machine.

■   There will be no unexpected steps in the fixed costs. Storage or financing costs may increase if the output increases, and this will affect the calculations.

Task 13

MEMORANDUM

To: Production Director
From: Management Accounts Assistant
Subject: New products at the new site
Date: 30 November 2007

Contracts required by Welsh consultancy

As far as the Welsh consultancy business is concerned, the calculations are as follows:

	£
Projected fixed costs	50,000
Target profit	80,000
Total contribution required	130,000
Contribution per contract	2,000
Number of contracts required	£130,000/2,000 = 65

Limiting factor on production of large electric woks in Scotland

| Machine hours | 2,000/14 = 142 woks can be produced |
| Labour hours | 4,500/20 = 225 woks can be produced |

Therefore machine hours are the limiting factor, meaning that only 142 woks can be produced.

AAT SAMPLE SIMULATION
UNIT 7

HOMER LTD

ANSWERS

Task 1

Sales to external customers
Manufacturing and Sales divisions combined

	Monthly totals £'000	Cumulative total for the year £'000
2005/2006		
April	384	384
May	271	655
June	222	877
July	309	1,186
August	346	1,532
September	262	1,794
October	240	2,034
November	329	2,363
December	279	2,642
January	277	2,919
February	244	3,163
March	385	3,548
2006/2007		
April	381	381
May	242	623
June	237	860
July	339	1,199
August	330	1,529
September	299	1,828
October	231	2,059
November	372	2,431
December	355	2,786
January	310	3,096
February	272	3,368
March	291	3,659

Notes

1. In the first column, enter the monthly total of external sales achieved by the two divisions.
2. In the second column, enter the cumulative total of external sales in the accounting year.

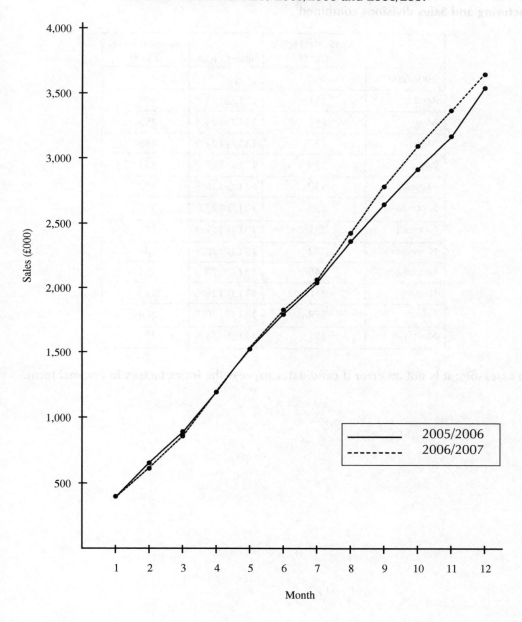

Cumulative external sales 2005/2006 and 2006/2007

Task 3

Indexed sales to external customers
Manufacturing and Sales divisions combined

	Unadjusted totals £'000	Index factor	Indexed totals £'000
2006/2007			
April	381	131.0/123.8	403
May	242	131.0/124.4	255
June	237	131.0/124.9	249
July	339	131.0/125.7	353
August	330	131.0/126.3	342
September	299	131.0/127.0	308
October	231	131.0/127.5	237
November	372	131.0/128.1	380
December	355	131.0/128.9	361
January	310	131.0/129.6	313
February	272	131.0/130.2	274
March	291	131.0/131.0	291

Note to assessors: it is not an error if candidates express the index factors in decimal form.

Task 4

LOAN APPLICATION (extract)

Name of applicant company		Homer Limited
Latest year for which accounting information is available		Year ended 31 March 2007
Total sales revenue		
In latest year for which accounts are available	£	3,659,000
In previous year	£	3,548,000
Percentage change (+/–)		+3.13%
Net profit after all expenses, before taxation		
In latest year for which accounts are available	£	310,000
In previous year	£	278,000
Percentage change (+/–)		+11.51%
Gross profit margin (%)		40.17%
Net profit margin (%)		8.47%
Return on capital employed (%)		4.70%

Notes

1. In the case of a company with a divisional structure, all figures should refer to the results of the company as a whole, not to individual divisions within the company.

2. Unless otherwise stated, all questions relate to the latest year for which accounting information is available.

3. Figures should be actual historical values, with no indexing for inflation.

4. Return on capital employed is defined as net profit for the year before taxation, divided by total capital employed.

MEMO

To: Sonia Liesl
From: Amir Pindhi
Subject: Loan application form
Date: 14 April 2007

I attach the completed loan application form for your approval before its submission to the bank.

If it is in order, I assume you will forward the form to the bank for processing. However, if you need further clarification please come back to me.

Task 5

MEMO

To: Sonia Liesl
From: Amir Pindhi
Subject: Ratios and performance indicators for the year ended 31 March 2007
Date: 14 April 2007

Here are the required ratios and performance indicators for the year ended 31 March 2007.

Gross profit percentage: 40.17%. This has fallen from 43.15% in the previous year, possibly because of higher production costs (see 'production cost per unit' below).

Net profit percentage: 8.47%. Despite the fall in GPP, this has risen from 7.84% in the previous year, possibly because of tighter control of overheads.

Production cost per unit: (£2,190,000/199,000=) £11.01. This has risen from £10.83 in the previous year, possibly because of higher materials costs.

Value of sales earned per employee: (£3,659,000/143=) £25,587.41. This has fallen from £26,018.13, possibly because increases in sales have not kept step with increases in the number of employees.

Task 6

Value Added Tax Return

For the period
01 01 07 to 31 03 07

For Official Use

Registration number	Period
625 7816 29	03 07

You could be liable to a financial penalty if your completed return and all the VAT payable are not received by the due date.

Due date: 30.04.07

For Official Use

HOMER LIMITED
SESTOS DRIVE
PANTILE TRADING ESTATE
CV32 1AW

If you have a general enquiry or need advice please call our National Advice Service on 0845 010 9000

ATTENTION

If this return and any tax due are not received by the due date you may be liable to a surcharge.

If you make supplies of goods to another EC Member State you are required to complete an EC Sales List (VAT 101).

Before you fill in this form please read the notes on the back and the VAT Leaflet "*Filling in your VAT return*" and "*Flat rate schemes for small businesses*", if you use the scheme. Fill in all boxes clearly in ink, and write 'none' where necessary. Don't put a dash or leave any box blank. If there are no pence write "00" in the pence column. Do not enter more than one amount in any box.

For official use			£	p
	VAT due in this period on sales and other outputs	1	139,618	95
	VAT due in this period on acquisitions from other EC Member States	2	NONE	
	Total VAT due (the sum of boxes 1 and 2)	3	139,618	95
	VAT reclaimed in this period on purchases and other inputs (including acquisitions from the EC)	4	91,197	54
	Net VAT to be paid to Customs or reclaimed by you (Difference between boxes 3 and 4)	5	48,421	41
	Total value of sales and all other outputs excluding any VAT. Include your box 8 figure	6	873,012	00
	Total value of purchases and all other inputs excluding any VAT. Include your box 9 figure	7	520,568	00
	Total value of all supplies of goods and related services, excluding any VAT, to other EC Member States	8	75,190	00
	Total value of all acquisitions of goods and related services, excluding any VAT, from other EC Member States	9	NONE	00

If you are enclosing a payment please tick this box. ☑

DECLARATION: You, or someone on your behalf, must sign below.

I, _SONIA LIESL_ declare that the
(Full name of signatory in BLOCK LETTERS)
information given above is true and complete.

Signature_____ Date _____ 20 _____

A false declaration can result in prosecution.

Task 7

HOMER LIMITED
Sestos Drive, Pantile Trading Estate CV32 1AW
Telephone: 02467 881235

14 April 2007

H M Revenue & Customs
Bell House
33 Lambert Road
Coventry
CV12 8TR

Dear Sir/Madam

This company is considering the idea of importing raw materials from a Far Eastern supplier. We are unsure of the VAT implications of doing this.

I would be grateful if you would send me a copy of any relevant publication dealing with VAT on imports.

Yours faithfully

Sonia Liesl
ACCOUNTANT

Registered office: Sestos Drive, Pantile Trading Estate CV32 1AW
Registered in England, number 2007814

Task 8

MEMO

To: Sonia Liesl
From: Amir Pindhi
Subject: VAT on imports
Date: 14 April 2007

I enclose a draft letter to the local VAT Office requesting copies of publications on this topic.

Briefly, the rule is that if we import goods from a non-EC country we have to pay VAT on import at the standard rate. It will normally be possible to reclaim this as recoverable VAT.

It may be possible to arrange the imports through an appropriate agent (one who is approved for duty deferment). If so, we can then defer the payment.

PRACTICE SIMULATION – UNIT 7

DONALD RATHERSON & CO

ANSWERS

Task 1

	Actual 2006		Factor	Restated 2006	
	£	£		£	£
Sales					
Mail Order		1,001,456	1.04		1,041,514
Showroom		924,763	1.08		998,744
		1,926,219			2,040,258
Cost of sales					
Raw materials	125,896		1.03	129,673	
Goods for resale					
Mail Order	281,546		1.02	287,177	
Showroom	216,875		1.02	221,213	
		(624,317)			(638,062)
Gross profit		1,301,902			1,402,196
Wages					
Manufacturing Unit	169,842		1.05	178,334	
Mail Order	155,246		1.05	163,008	
Showroom	139,000		1.07	148,730	
		(464,088)			(490,072)
Expenses					
Manufacturing Unit	15,746		1.04	16,376	
Mail Order	52,463		1.03	54,037	
Showroom	55,126		1.03	56,780	
		(123,335)			(127,193)
Costs of Ascot site, including					
accounting and admin		(89,750)	1.05		(94,238)
Net profit		624,729			690,694

Restatement using Institute of Decorators indices

	2006	Index factor	Adj 2006 figure
	£		£
Total revenue	1,926,219	1.02	1,957,825
Total gross profit	1,301,902	1.01	1,319,967

Note

The percentage price increases given in the memo from Ian Yates relate to price changes over the period from 1 October 2006 to 30 September 2007. The year 2006 is considered as the base, with an index of 100. Showoom and mail order price levels, for instance, can be expressed as 108 and 104 respectively. The factor in each case is 104/100 or 1.04 and 108/100 or 1.08 respectively.

We must ensure that the Institute of Decorators' indices relate to the increase for the same period, ie from 2006 to 2007. The relevant indices therefore are:

$$\frac{2007\,\text{Index}}{2006\,\text{index}} = \frac{111.5}{109.7} = 1.02 \text{ for revenue} \qquad \frac{2007\,\text{index}}{2006\,\text{index}} = \frac{109.6}{108.1} = 1.01 \text{ for gross profit}$$

Task 2

Donald Ratherson & Co
Consolidated statement of revenues and costs for the year ended 30 September 2007

	£	£	£
Sales			2,238,594
Cost of sales			
Raw materials			
Opening stock	14,016		
Purchases	134,352		
Closing stock	(20,736)		
		127,632	
Goods for resale (Working 1)			
Opening stock	61,750		
Purchases	518,485		
Closing stock	(63,099)		
		517,136	
			(644,768)
Gross profit			1,593,826
Wages (Working 2)			(488,413)
Expenses (Working 3)			(131,987)
Costs of Ascot site, including			
accounting and administration costs (Working 4)			(92,500)
Net profit			880,926

Workings

1	**Goods for resale**	Mail Order unit	Showroom	
	Opening stock	24,130	+ 37,620	= 61,750
	Purchases	289,645	+ 228,840	= 518,485
	Closing stock	21,717	+ 41,382	= 63,099

2	**Wages**	Manufacturing unit	Mail Order Unit	Showroom	
		178,685	+ 165,728	+ 144,000	= 488,413

3	**Expenses**	19,145	+ 55,242	+ 57,600	= 131,987

4	**Costs of Ascot site**	60,125	+ 18,500	+ 13,875	= 92,500

Task 3

MEMO

To: Ian Yates

From: Deputy Accountant

Subject: Report on results for year ended 30 September 2007

Date: 12 November 2007

In reply to your memo of yesterday, I attach the table with my calculations of the differences in monetary and percentage terms between this year's results and those for 2006, as adjusted for inflation.

You can see that:

- the gross profit margin has risen from 68.73% to 71.20%
- the net profit margin has risen from 33.85% to 39.35%
- return on capital employed has risen from 5.76% to 6.96%

I also attach the component bar chart and time series analysis graph you requested.

I hope this gives you what you need, but please get back to me if there is anything more I can do.

Donald Ratherson & Co
Report on comparison of revenues and costs
For the year end 31 October 2007 with inflation-adjusted figures for 2006

	2007 £	2007 £	Adjusted 2006 £	Adjusted 2006 £	Difference £	Difference %
Sales		1,146,354		1,041,514	104,840	10.07
Mail Order		1,092,240		998,744	93,496	9.36
Showroom		2,238,594		2,040,258	198,336	9.72
Cost of sales						
Raw materials	127,632		129,673		(2,041)	(1.57)
Goods for resale						
Mail Order	292,058		287,177		4,881	1.70
Showroom	225,078		221,213		3,866	1.75
		(644,768)		(638,062)	(6,706)	1.05
		1,593,826		1,402,196	191,630	13.67
Gross profit						
Wages						
Manufacturing Unit	178,685		178,334		351	0.20
Mail Order	165,728		163,008		2,720	1.67
Showroom	144,000		148,730		(4,730)	(3.18)
		(488,413)		(490,072)	1,660	(0.34)
Expenses						
Manufacturing Unit	19,145		16,376		2,769	16.91
Mail Order	55,242		54,037		1,205	2.23
Showroom	57,600		56,780		820	1.44
		(131,987)		(127,193)	(4,794)	3.77
Cost of Ascot site, inc. acc'ing & admin		(92,500)		(94,238)	1,738	1.84
Net profit		880,926		690,694	190,233	.27.54
Average capital employed		12,650,000		12,000,000		

Working

	%	%
Gross profit margin	71.20	68.73
Net profit margin	39.35	33.85
Return on capital employed	6.96	5.76

Time series 2001–08

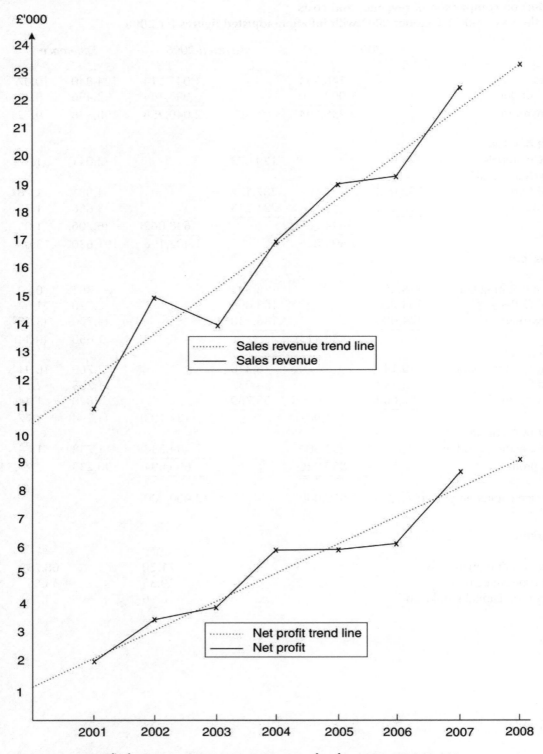

£'000

Forecast net profit for 2008: £920,000   Forecast sales for 2008: £2,340,000

Component bar chart

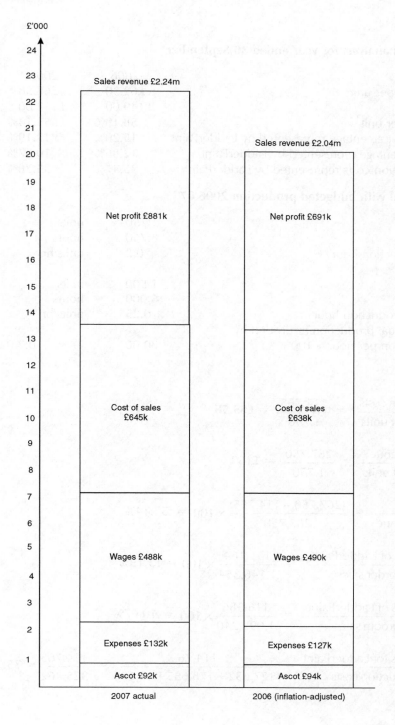

£'000

24
23 — Sales revenue £2.24m
22
21
20 — Sales revenue £2.04m
19
18
17 — Net profit £881k — Net profit £691k
16
15
14
13
12
11
10 — Cost of sales £645k — Cost of sales £638k
9
8
7
6
5
4 — Wages £488k — Wages £490k
3
2
1 — Expenses £132k — Expenses £127k
— Ascot £92k — Ascot £94k

2007 actual   2006 (inflation-adjusted)

Task 4

LadderPaint
Production and sales analysis for year ended 30 September

	2006	2007	Workings
Total production cost per unit	£62.30	£68.58	1
Sales value per unit	£149.00	£153.00	2
Gross profit margin per unit	58.19%	57.14%	3
Mail Order Unit sales percentage represented by LadderPaint	15.20%	13.19%	4
Showroom sales percentage represented by LadderPaint	12.85%	10.67%	5
Percentage of production costs represented by LadderPaint	35.47%	35.26%	6

Comparison of actual with budgeted production 2006/07

Actual production	1,750	units
Actual hours	8,750	hours
Actual units per production hour	0.2	units/hr
Budgeted production	1,500	units
Budgeted hours	6,000	hours
Budgeted units per production hour	0.25	units/hr
Productivity ratio: actual production/hr divided by budgeted production per hour ×100%	80.00	%	0.2/0.25×100%

Workings

1   $\dfrac{\text{Total production costs}}{\text{Total number of units}} = \dfrac{114,765}{1,750} = £65.58$

2   $\dfrac{\text{Total sales revenue}}{\text{Total number of units}} = \dfrac{267,750}{1,750} = £153$

3   $\dfrac{\text{Gross profit}}{\text{Total sales revenue}} = \dfrac{(267,750 - 114,765)}{267,750} \times 100 = 57.14\%$

4   $\dfrac{\text{Mail order sales of LadderPaint}}{\text{Total mail order sales}} = \dfrac{151,164}{1,146,354} \times 100 = 13,19\%$

5   $\dfrac{\text{Showroom sales of LadderPaint}}{\text{Total showroom sales}} = \dfrac{116,586}{1,092,240} \times 100 = 10.67\%$

6   $\dfrac{\text{Production costs for LadderPaint}}{\text{Total production costs}} = \dfrac{114,765}{127,632 + 178,685 + 19,145} = \dfrac{114,765}{325,462} = 35.26\%$

498

Task 5

Institute of Decorators – standard form of return 2007

Name of business: Donald Ratherson & Co

	Actual current year			Actual prior year		
Year ended	30 Sept 07			30 Sept 06		
Average no of employees	31		%	32		%
		Workings	of sales (1)		Workings	of sales (1)
	£			£		
Sales	2,238,594	(W1)	100	1,926,219	(W1)	
Sales per employee	72,213	(W2)		60,194	(W2)	
Gross profit	1,593,286	(W3)		1,301,902	(W3)	67.59
Net profit before taxation	880,926	(W4)		624,729	(W4)	32.43
Average capital employed	12,650,000			12,000,000		
	%			%		
Return on capital employed(2)	6.96	(W5)		5.21	(W5)	

	Inflation-adjusted prior year £	
Prior year sales revenue adjusted for inflation using Institute index	1,957,825	*
Prior year gross profit adjusted for inflation using Institute index	1,319,967	*

		Comparison	% of prior year
		£	actual figure
Current year actual sales exceed prior year actual sales by	Box 1 (W6)	312,375	16.22
Amount of increase accounted for by inflation (4)	Box 2 (W1)	(31,606)	
Amount of increase in real terms	Box 1–Box 2	280,769	14.58
Current year actual gross profits exceed prior year's actual gross profits by	Box 3	291,924	22.42
Amount of increase accounted for by inflation (4)	Box 4	(18,065)	
Amount of increase in real terms	Box 3–Box 4	273,859	21.04

Notes

1   All percentages are to be expressed to two places of decimals

2   Return on capital employed is the net profit, divided by the average capital employed for the year, expressed as a percentage to two decimal places

3   All entries are to be based on figures for the business as a whole, excluding any transactions between divisions or business units within the business

4   Deduct actual results from inflation-adjusted results based on Institute of Decorators' indices

* These figures are obtained from Task 1.

Workings

1   Year 2007:   Mail order unit sales + showroom sales = £1,146,354 + £1,092,240 = £2,238,594

    Year 2006:   As given in Task 1

                (£1,926,215 = £1,001,456 + £924,763)

2   Year 2007:   Sales per employee

                £2,238,594/31 = £72,212

    Year 2006:   Sales per employee

                £1,926,219/32 = £60,194

3   Year 2007:   £1,593,826 from Task 1

    Year 2006:   £1,301,902 from Task 1

4   Year 2007:   £880,926 from Task 1

    Year 2006:   £624,729 from Task 1

5   Year 2007:   £880,926/£12,650,000

    Year 2006:   £624,729/£12,000,000

6   £2,238,494 − £1,926,219 = £312,375

7   Increase due to inflation as measured by Decorators' Index

    £7,967,825 − £1,926,219

Task 6

MEMO

To: Ian Yates

From: Deputy Accountant

Subject: Institute of Decorators' return and report

Date: 11 November 2007

I enclose the completed return and report for your authorisation prior to despatch.

Task 7

Reconciliation of business units balances as at 31 October 2007

	£	£
Mail Order Unit balance brought forward		15,985
Add: transfer from Manufacturing		107
Closing Mail Order balance with Manufacturing		16,092
Showroom Unit balance brought forward	10,644	
Add: transfer from Manufacturing	386	
Closing Showroom balance with Manufacturing		11,030
Production cost of items transferred to Mail Order Unit and Showroom		27,122

Task 8

Donald Ratherson & Co

VAT Control Account

Administration/overheads

Date	Description	Debit £	Date	Description	Debit £
2007			2007		
31 Aug	Pay HMRC	49,654	1 Aug	B/d	49,654
31 Oct	Input tax – PDB	30,384	31 Oct	Output tax (SDB)	98,338
	Input tax – CB	44			
	Balance c/d	67,910			
		147,992			147,992

Value Added Tax Return

For the period
01 01 07 to 31 03 07

For Official Use

Registration number

482 912 5407

Period

01/07

You could be liable to a financial penalty if your completed return and all the VAT payable are not received by the due date.

Due date: **30 November 2007**

For Official Use

Donald Ratherson & Co
Park Drive Trading Estate
Sunninghill Road
Ascot Gu8 5ZD

Your VAT Office telephone number is 01682-386000

ATTENTION

If this return and any tax due are not received by the due date you may be liable to a surcharge.

If you make supplies of goods to another EC Member State you are required to complete an EC Sales List (VAT 101).

Before you fill in this form please read the notes on the back and the VAT Leaflet *"Filling in your VAT return"*. Fill in all boxes clearly in ink, and write 'none' where necessary. Don't put a dash or leave any box blank. If there are no pence write "00" in the pence column. Do not enter more than one amount in any box.

For official use			£	p
	VAT due in this period on sales and other outputs	1	98,338	00
	VAT due in this period on acquisitions from other EC Member States	2	NONE	
	Total VAT due (the sum of boxes 1 and 2)	3	98,338	00
	VAT reclaimed in this period on purchases and other inputs (including acquisitions from the EC)	4	30,428	00
	Net VAT to be paid to Customs or reclaimed by you (Difference between boxes 3 and 4)	5	67,910	00
	Total value of sales and all other outputs excluding any VAT. Include your box 8 figure	6	591,329	00
	Total value of purchases and all other inputs excluding any VAT. Include your box 9 figure	7	193,416	00
	Total value of all supplies of goods and related services, excluding any VAT, to other EC Member States	8	29,397	00
	Total value of all acquisitions of goods and related services, excluding any VAT, from other EC Member States	9	NONE	00

If you are enclosing a payment please tick this box. ✓

DECLARATION: You, or someone on your behalf, must sign below.

I,.. declare that the
(Full name of signatory in BLOCK LETTERS)
information given above is true and complete.

Signature.................................... Date .... 20 ....
A false declaration can result in prosecution.

F

0196929   IB (October 2000)

VAT 100 (Half)

Task 9

DONALD RATHERSON & CO

Park Drive Trading Estate, Sunninghill Road, Ascot, Berks GU8 5ZD
Telephone 01344 627896

VAT Office
Lyle House
Henry Road
Guildford
Surrey
GU8 5CM

12 November 2007

Dear Sirs

Registration number 482 912 5407

We have recently been informed that a net sale of £15,000 to GHA Stores plc in February on 30 days credit is now a bad debt. Please confirm that the steps set out below will enable us to claim bad debt relief for the VAT element of the debt (£2,625.00) in our next VAT return.

- write off the entire debt of £17,625.00 in our accounts before 31 January 2008

- retain a copy of the VAT invoice and the journal writing it off

- in our next VAT return, for the quarter ending 31 January 2008 (when the debt will be more than six months overdue), add £2,625.00 to Box 4 (input tax box).

I understand that we do not need to inform GHA Stores plc that we are taking this action.

I look forward to receiving your confirmation. Thank you for your help

Yours faithfully

Deputy Accountant

Task 10

Checklist re VAT

Prepared for: Donald Ratherson

By: A N Accountant

1   The three types of supply for VAT purposes are: **standard-rated**, **zero-rated** and **exempt** supplies.

2   A taxable person who makes only zero-rated outputs **can** reclaim input tax on their purchases.

3   In a month when the VAT registration limit is exceeded, a trader must notify HMRC within **30 days of the end of that month**.

4   The effects of registration for VAT are that the trader:

    1   **must charge VAT on sales**
    2   **may reclaim VAT on purchases**
    3   **must issue VAT invoices showing the VAT registration number**

5   A VAT invoice must show:

    information about the supplier: **name, address, registration number**
    information about the invoice: **date of issue, tax point, invoice number**
    information about the customer: **name, address**

6   A less detailed VAT invoice can be issued where the total including VAT is less than **£250.**

7   The basic tax point for a VAT invoice is **the date on which goods are removed or made available to the customer, or the date on which services are completed.**

8   An earlier tax point than the basic tax point applies if **a VAT invoice is issued or payment is received earlier than the basic tax point.**

9   To find out more detail about VAT without reference to the VAT Office one should refer to **the VAT Guide.**

10   If we import raw materials from outside the EU we **must** pay input VAT on them.

11   If we export goods to buyers outside the EU we must treat them as **zero rated**.

12   We would get automatic bad debt relief if we could be part of the **cash accounting** scheme, but our annual taxable turnover is too high.

13   We would only have to complete one VAT return per year if we were part of the **annual accounting** scheme, but our taxable turnover is too high.

14   In any dispute with the local VAT Office we would need to decide between:

    1   **asking the VAT Office to review its decisions, and**
    2   **formally appealing to a tribunal**

15   If we submit our VAT return late, HMRC will issue us with a surcharge liability notice.

You also asked me for some information on other matters:

16 The government body responsible for publishing government statistics is **the Office for National Statistics.**

17 An example of a regulatory body seeking a report or return is **the Financial Services Authority (FSA).**

18 Other types of outside organisation which may seek a report or return from us are: **grant-awarding bodies, lenders, trade unions, the Office for National Statistics.**